D1605994

Parchment, Paper, Pixels

PARCHMENT PAPER PIXELS

Law and the Technologies of Communication

PETER M. TIERSMA

The University of Chicago Press
Chicago and London

PETER M. TIERSMA is professor of law at Loyola Law School in California. He is the author of *Legal Language* and *Frisian Reference Grammar* and coauthor of *Speaking of Crime: The Language of Criminal Justice.*

The University of Chicago Press, Chicago 60637
The University of Chicago Press, Ltd., London

Printed in the United States of America

19 18 17 16 15 14 13 12 11 10 1 2 3 4 5

ISBN-13: 978-0-226-80306-7 (cloth)
ISBN-10: 0-226-80306-6 (cloth)

Library of Congress Cataloging-in-Publication Data

Tiersma, Peter Meijes.
Parchment, paper, pixels : law and the technologies of communication / Peter M. Tiersma.
p. cm.
Includes bibliographical references and index.
ISBN-13: 978-0-226-80306-7 (cloth: alk. paper)
ISBN-10: 0-226-80306-6 (cloth: alk. paper) 1. Technology and law. 2. Communication in law. 3. Communication—Technological innovations. 5. Law—Technological innovations. 6. Law—Information tehnology. 7. Legal documents. I. Title.
K487.T4T54 2010
343.09'9—dc22

2010002014

⊗ The paper used in this publication meets the minimum requirements of the American National Standard for Information Sciences—Permanence of Paper for Printed Library Materials, ANSI Z39.48-1992

For Matthea

Contents

Acknowledgments

Anyone who carefully peruses the endnotes of this book will be able to surmise that it has been in the making for over a decade. I owe a debt of gratitude to many people with whom I have discussed the issues raised in the book or who have read and commented on some or all of it. In particular, I wish to thank Peter Alldridge, Stephen Barnett, Bob Brain, Paul Callister, Richard Cappalli, Charles Collier, Sydney DeLong, Jan Engberg, Edward Finegan, Lidewij van Gils, Victor Gold, Robin Kar, Daniel Martin, Michael Sinclair, Larry Solan, Elizabeth Traugott, and participants at workshops or presentations at Chicago-Kent Law School, the City University of Hong Kong, Loyola Law School in Los Angeles, the Law and Society Association, the Deutsch-Amerikanische Juristenvereinigung, the International Association of Forensic Linguists, and the Linguistics Department at the University of California in Santa Barbara. Research assistance was provided by Loyola Law School graduates Dale Kim, Scott Bishop, Heidi Brooks, Irene Farinas, and Shiva Heydari (in chronological order). I also benefited from suggestions made by the reviewers and editors of the University of Chicago Press. Finally, the writing of this book was supported financially by the Joseph Scott Fellowship and later by the Honorable William Matthew Byrne Chair at Loyola Law School in Los Angeles.

A longer version of chapter 6 was published by the *Notre Dame Law Review* as "The Textualization of Precedent" (82 Notre Dame L. Rev. 1187 [2007]). Bits and pieces of this book may also be found in various articles that I have written over the years, but as with any authoritative legal text, this book is currently the definitive and complete expression of my thoughts on the matter and supersedes any positions I may have taken, whether orally or in writing, on any previous occasion.

As to my ruminations about what the future will bring, I will doubtless be proven right in some areas and wrong in others. If this book were published only in electronic format on a website, I could revise it as developments in the technology of communication occur. It would always be up-to-date, but never finished. Would that be better than fixing it in print, which provides stability and finality but also guarantees obsolescence? These are the sorts of issues I hope to address.

1
Introduction

Written texts are ubiquitous in our legal system. Lawyers and judges create such texts just about every day, and when they aren't drafting them, they are often struggling to interpret and apply them. Law is surely one of the most literate of all professions. Legal texts are also extremely important to the rest of society. Documents like statutes, judicial opinions, deeds, wills, and contracts literally govern much of our lives.

Currently, the nature of such texts is undergoing tremendous changes. Many of these changes result from developments in the technologies of storing and communicating information. For thousands of years, the primary technology for storing and communicating legal information has been writing. During the past millennium or two, writing has generally consisted of using ink to place marks on paper or parchment. The process could be done by hand or by a mechanical device like a printing press.

Today many people do most of their writing by typing on a computer keyboard. The texts that they produce may reside only on a hard disk or other electronic storage medium. What appears on the screen is not really letters of the alphabet but rather tiny dots, called pixels, which create the impression of writing but which can also represent images. Not only are legal texts stored on computers, but the Internet has made it increasingly possible to communicate those texts electronically.

Because law is such a textual enterprise, one would expect that the technologies of storing and communicating legal texts would have been the topic of much discussion by the profession. Lawyers do indeed concern themselves with these issues, but they almost always do so within the context of a specific area of the law, such as requirements that contracts or wills be in writing. Surprisingly, even legal academics have paid relatively little attention on a more general level to the nature of legal texts, the literary conventions that produced them, and the technologies used to store and disseminate them. This book aims to start remedying that deficiency.

Writing, Civilization, and Law

During the past few decades, scholars of literature, psychology, education, history, anthropology, linguistics, and related fields have begun to investigate the evolution of writing and its impact on our culture and its institutions. David Olson has suggested that the development of alphabetic writing systems gave Western civilization many of its defining features.[1] According to an influential article by Jack Goody and Ian Watt, writing made it possible to begin distinguishing myth from history.[2] It is therefore "not accidental that major steps in the development of what we now call 'science' followed the introduction of major changes in the channels of communication in Babylonia (writing), in Ancient Greece (the alphabet), and in Western Europe (printing)."[3]

Some scholars suggest that the development of writing, especially the phonetically based alphabet that arose in ancient Greece, has not merely influenced our civilization and culture in dramatic ways, but has fundamentally altered how people think. According to Eric Havelock, "Greek literacy changed not only the means of communication, but also the shape of the Greek consciousness." In a similar vein, Walter Ong argued that the development of literacy fostered abstract thinking, categorization, and logical deduction.[4]

Although no one doubts that the rise of literacy has had a profound influence on human civilization, the extent of its impact is controversial. Even more so is the issue of whether and how literacy influences cognition.[5] Nonetheless, a literate society is quite different from one that is purely oral. The debate is not about *whether* writing has had an impact on our civilization, but rather about *how* and *how much*.

The spread of literacy is also held to have had important ramifications for our legal systems. Goody has posited that writing effectively distinguishes custom from law.[6] And the ability of the population to read and write is claimed to have promoted important political and legal institutions, democracy in particular.[7]

One of the central aims of this book is to investigate these issues as they relate to the law. What impact does the adoption of writing have on the law? What is the role of writing in our legal system today? What is the nature of legal texts? And how are written wills, contracts, or statutes different from those that are retained solely in the minds and memories of those subject to them?

The Technologies of Writing and Communication

A closely related issue is the technologies of communication. Despite the undeniable effect that developing literacy had on ancient civilizations, the process of writing changed very little over the ensuing millennia. Essentially, it involved an individual placing meaning-bearing marks of some kind on a medium (parchment, paper, stone, wax, etc.) that was capable of displaying those marks. We still do this today when we write with pencil or ink.

Only in the fifteenth century did the next major revolution in communication technology occur. Before this time, scribes had to laboriously write and copy texts one at a time. As a result, written materials were expensive and scarce. The invention of the printing press made relatively cheap and identical copies of a text widely accessible. Like writing, printing has been associated with monumental societal movements, such the Renaissance, Protestantism, and the scientific revolution.[8]

As we will see, the printing press also had implications for several areas of the law. It now became possible to create and distribute very large numbers of copies of important legal documents, especially statutes and judicial opinions. For example, when the English parliament first started to enact statutes, lawyers and judges would have been unlikely to rely very much on the exact words of the law. At best, they would have had a handwritten copy of an original document contained in a government archive. But once they had a printed copy that was certified to be an exact reproduction of the text that Parliament had debated and adopted, the words in that text began to assume much greater significance.

Interestingly, there are other major developments in the technologies of communication, such as radio, telephones, and television, that have had a huge impact on our lives and culture. Yet they have had little influence on the law. True, it is almost impossible these days to imagine the practice of law without telephones. And television depicts one trial after the other, both real and fictional. Still, the nature of the law and our legal system (as opposed to the daily practice of the profession) have scarcely been affected by these technologies.

Why is it that the development of writing and printing have had much greater influence on the law than have radio, telephones, and television? All of them are important technologies of communication. The difference, I believe, is that law has traditionally been a predominantly textual enterprise. Radio, telephones, and television transmit sound and images. Law, on the other hand, relies very heavily on the written word.

More recently, the technology of writing and the nature of the texts that it produces are undergoing epochal changes caused by the development of computers, mass storage devices, and the Internet. Now that cases and statutes are easily and cheaply accessed online, the shelves of books that traditionally line the walls of law firms have largely disappeared or become decoration. Lawyers are increasingly filing documents such as motions and briefs electronically, rather than sending a courier to court with a bundle of papers. Almost all legal research is conducted via computers and the Internet. Electronic contracting has become routine.

Some scholars take the view that computers and the Internet will have as great an impact on our civilization as the development of writing and printing did. Jeff Gomez, in a printed book bearing the title *Print Is Dead*, points out that reading on a computer screen is a vastly different enterprise than reading out of a book: "What's going to be transformed [is] the ability to read a passage from practically any book that exists, at any time you want to, as well as the ability to click on hyperlinks, experience multimedia, and add notes and share passages with others. All this will add up to a paradigm shift not seen in hundreds of years."[9]

A more sanguine view is taken by Nicolas Carr, who has written extensively about technology. He recently published an article with the title "Is Google Making Us Stupid?"[10] The basic point is that people read less than they used to, or read differently. Carr quotes people who were once voracious readers but who have stopped buying books altogether, or who claim to have lost the ability "to read a longish article on the web or in print."[11] A survey published by the National Endowment for the Arts in 2004 found a "dramatic decline" in the percentage of the population that reads literature (defined as novels, short stories, plays, and poetry).[12]

Similarly, research from University College London, sponsored in part by the British Library,[13] reports that people seeking digital information on the Internet do not usually read the content of websites from start to finish. Instead, they engage in a type of "skimming activity": "they view just one or two pages from an academic site and then 'bounce' out, perhaps never to return. The figures are instructive: around 60 per cent of e-journal users view no more than three pages and a majority (up to 65 per cent) never return."[14] According to the authors, people searching for information online do not engage in "reading" in the traditional sense; rather, they are browsing through titles, abstracts, and content pages looking for "quick wins."[15] Carr, who cites this study, concludes that Internet users today not only read differently, but they also think differently.[16] These claims, of course, mirror those made regarding the impact of writing, and like those claims they should be taken with a grain of salt.

Nonetheless, there can be no doubt that many aspects of our lives and culture are being radically transformed by modern technologies of communication. This is true also of the legal world.

Technology and Law

A scholar who predicts that computers and the Internet will result in dramatic changes in legal culture is Ethan Katsh. He observes that, as opposed to conventional writing or printing (that is, traditional text), electronic media distribute information much more broadly and quickly, that users interact differently with it, that images become relatively more prominent, and that information can be organized more flexibly.[17] Electronic media are less stable, less fixed, and less tangible than writing and printing.[18] And the boundaries between different types of media (such as text, graphics, and sound) are beginning to blur.[19] Katsh predicts that these developments will have significant consequences for the system of precedent and how lawyers research and access the law.

The process is well underway. The best example is contracts, which today are routinely transacted online, sometimes without a scrap of paper being exchanged or printed. In a similar vein, lawyers are more likely to read a case or statute online these days than in a book.

Yet while the media are changing, writing and text remain tremendously important to the law. A will or testament still invariably consists of ink on paper, without multimedia content or other modern embellishments. Statutes remain almost entirely written text, even though they are widely distributed by electronic means and could easily include sound, pictures, or video. Likewise, judicial opinions remain mostly text, although they occasionally contain graphics (usually in an appendix) and in one instance contained a reference to a video available on the court's website.[20] These exceptions prove the rule, however.

Past experience suggests that it is easy to overstate the potential impact of new technologies on the law. In 1992, two legal scholars, Ronald Collins and David Skover, published an article entitled "Paratext" in the *Stanford Law Review*.[21] They suggested that, although our legal consciousness is mediated by print, nontextual forms of storing and transmitting information, which they call "paratexts," will ultimately challenge the dominant role of traditional text and writing in the legal system. Collins and Skover predicted that paratexts, which can include any form of electronic communication, will come to supplement and eventually replace written evidence and documentation. The official record of trials, as well as wills and contracts, will become paratext. This will rapidly change the "Gutenberg mindset of the printed word."[22]

Collins and Skover were mainly concerned with audio and video recording, since they were writing before computers were common in courtrooms and law offices. It is true that some courts have replaced the stenographer with mechanical audio or video recording machines. Yet, for the most part, a videotaped record must be transcribed into written text and be printed on paper for purposes of appeal.[23] Moreover, video has not replaced written text in most other areas of law. Video can be a useful evidentiary tool, but when the law requires wills and contracts to be in writing, paratext has so far not proven to be an acceptable alternative.

We should also be cautious in drawing causal connections between technological changes and our culture in general or our legal system in particular, as Richard Ross has emphasized. The effect of social, economic, and political factors should not be ignored.[24] The invention of alphabetic writing in ancient Greece did not cause the rise of democracy in Athens, although it may have enabled or promoted its development. Nor can we predict with complete confidence the changes that modern technology will cause.

Overall, however, the trend is clear. The traditional supremacy of written text, in the sense of ink on paper, is being challenged. Whether it will be entirely supplanted is open to serious doubt, but it will almost certainly be demoted—or enriched—by modern technology.

Another aim of this book is therefore to assess the impact that changes in the technologies of communication have had or may in the future have on the law. It goes without saying that the daily practice of lawyers is being profoundly affected by computers and the Internet. In addition, the nature of the law and of legal transactions is also changing. Just as a written statute is different from an oral decree, a statute printed on paper and bound into a book is not the same as a statute that is typed into a computer and accessed on the Internet.

Speech, Writing, and Conventions of Literacy

To set the stage, we will begin in chapter 2 by examining the phenomenon of writing more closely, concentrating on how it differs from speech. In many respects, writing is nothing more than a means of representing speech in a more enduring form. Yet this simple observation has tremendous implications. For example, the relative permanence of written language makes it possible for a text to be transmitted over great distances and long stretches of time. Writing may not be essential to governing a large state or empire, but it certainly facilitates the process.

Moreover, as societies become more literate, a strong belief tends to arise that it is good for laws, as well as for many private legal transactions, to be reduced to written text. When that happens, there is a tendency for the text of those writings to become increasingly authoritative, a process to which I refer as *textualization*.

Historically speaking, the earliest legal texts were almost always records of spoken transactions. As such, they functioned merely as evidence of an underlying oral event. Over time, however, the written text often became regarded not just as evidence of a legal event, but as constituting the event itself. The text was no longer just a record of the law. Rather, it had become the law. Statutes therefore had become textualized.

Legal professionals textualize a contract or statute not just by writing down the essence of what they agreed to or decided. They carefully choose and edit the exact words that will function as a definitive statement of the terms of the will, contract, or statute. The essential transaction is no longer the act of reaching agreement or making a decision; it is the text that the authors created. It is therefore not surprising that those who need to interpret a contract or statute—often judges—tend to take the words in the text very seriously.

Textualization is just one of the literary practices of the legal profession. Of course, most of the textual conventions of lawyers and judges (such as rules relating to spelling) are the same as those in other realms of human endeavor. Yet some of the law's distinctive literary practices, in particular textualization, are unknown to the lay public. These conventions have the potential to create problems for those who engage in a legal transaction but are not familiar with the literary practices that govern the drafting and interpretation of the resulting text.

Having explored in general the nature of writing and the textual practices of the law, we will be in a better position to examine and understand specific categories of legal texts. Although we will spend a fair amount of time discussing the evolutionary development of wills, contracts, statutes, and judicial opinions, our concern is not in the first instance with what happened hundreds of years ago. The history is often interesting for its own sake, but the reason for exploring it here is primarily to illuminate our current situation. Thus, by comparing oral lawmaking in medieval England with the highly literate process that is used today, we can better understand the nature of modern statutory texts.

Wills

Testaments or wills were typically declared orally in the presence of witnesses in Anglo-Saxon England. After literate clerics came to England around AD 600, members of religious orders would sometimes write down the terms of a will. Such documents were merely evidentiary, and for a long time they were not considered very good evidence when compared with the memories of the witnesses who were present.

As the society became more literate, however, writing gained greater respect, so that the written will came to be viewed as the best evidence of what happened. Eventually, the concept of a will (a word that originally referred to a mental state) became coextensive with the document that bore this title. More recently, the text of a will has come to be regarded as the final and only expression of the testator's intentions. Wills have, in other words, become highly textualized.

The literary conventions of will making have often created difficulties for the testators on whose behalf the will is deemed to "speak." For instance, suppose that a testator makes informal changes to a will after it is executed, such as crossing out one amount of money and substituting a larger amount. Such changes are usually invalid and in some jurisdictions can have the perverse effect of invalidating the gift entirely, even if the testator meant to increase it. Also surprising to most people is that in many American states a will that is handwritten and signed by the testator is more likely to be carried out than one that is typed, signed by the testator, and notarized.

The legal system needs to become more aware of ordinary conventions and beliefs relating to texts, especially when they conflict with legal conventions regarding writing. These problems are likely to become even worse as people begin to type and store their testamentary desires on computers, which the law of wills does not currently recognize as being "writings" (and which are therefore invalid).

Contracts

Contracts are interesting from our perspective because they can still be entirely oral, as in early England, or they can be made orally with a written memorandum as evidence, or they can fully textualized. This is reflected in the fact that the word *contract* is ambiguous: it can refer either to an agreement (which is a mental state) or to the document containing the agreement.

Whereas writing and textualization are mandatory in wills law, parties to a contract can generally choose whether or not to textualize their agreement. The customary way of textualizing a contract is to add what is called an integration or merger clause, which usually says something to the effect that this writing is the final agreement between the parties and that it supersedes any prior oral or written terms. From a legal point of view, the agreement is no longer something contained in the parties' minds; instead, it consists of the text that they have created.

On the positive side, textualization adds a great deal of certainty to commercial transactions. Yet it can, once again, become problematic when ordinary consumers are involved. Most people are not familiar with the textual conventions associated with merger or integration clauses, which can bind them to the text of an agreement that is at variance with what may have been said or negotiated. And the clauses are often buried in small print or lurk behind an easily overlooked link on a web page.

Furthermore, rapidly evolving communication technology has dramatically transformed the nature of the contractual text. Unlike wills law, which continues to demand writing on paper and very strict execution requirements (typically, a signature by the testator in the presence of two witnesses), it has become extremely easy to enter into a contract on the Internet. The very loose requirements of electronic contract formation (best illustrated by "one-click shopping") promote quick and easy commercial transactions, a boon for both businesses and consumers. Yet modern contracts are often imposed with so little formality (by merely opening a box of software, for instance, or by clicking on a link of a website) that consumers may find themselves unwittingly bound by a text that contains highly one-sided terms, often reinforced by an integration clause whose effect they do not understand. Whereas the textual practices of wills law are sometimes too strict, those relating to contracts may be too lax.

Statutes

We will next discuss statutes. The earliest laws written in English were various Anglo-Saxon codes. These codes were almost entirely evidentiary or descriptive of current customs. But in the twelfth and thirteenth centuries, formal efforts at lawmaking become evident. These early statutes were written down by a clerk after a legislative proposal had been adopted. They were generally quite loosely interpreted by judges, who might not even have had a copy of the statute in their possession. It's hard to be a textualist if you don't have a text!

Eventually, a formalized procedure for enacting statutes developed, whereby Parliament, with royal assent, enacted written proposals into law. The words of a statute were no longer merely evidence of what Parliament and the king decided; rather, those words came to be viewed as constituting the statute. In other words, statutes had become highly textualized. Judges in consequence began to pay more attention to the text.

Printing was the next major development. Early printed versions of statutes were not always reliable. But by the eighteenth century, accurate printed copies that contained the exact words that Parliament had enacted became widely available. Courts began to scrutinize the text of statutes ever more closely. Although the practice has been moderated recently, a fairly literal method of interpreting statutes is still common in England.

In the United States, legislatures also routinely enact written text, and accurate copies of legislation have been widely accessible since the founding of the republic. Nonetheless, American courts have never adopted as literal an approach as those in England. This difference illustrates that while textualization may enable a more literal style of interpretation, it does not require it or inexorably lead to it. Yet once the elements are in place, the attractions of a textual mode of interpretation are strong, as the recent rise of textualism in the United States has illustrated.

Statutes will almost certainly remain written text for the foreseeable future. Their dissemination in an electronic format makes it possible to add multimedia content and to change them almost instantaneously when the need arises. But do we really want to be ruled by a paperless statutory regime that is maintained on a legislative website subject to continual updating? I may be hopelessly old-fashioned, but I greatly prefer to be governed by statutes that cannot be frequently changed in the way that an Internet site updates stock prices and its weather report.

Judicial Opinions and Precedent

The other major source of law in a common law system consists of judicial opinions (usually called *judgments* in Britain). In contrast to statutes, which have long been regarded as quintessentially *lex scripta* ('written law'), English lawyers and judges traditionally considered the common law, as revealed in their judgments, to be *lex non scripta* ('unwritten law'). These lawyers were aware, of course, that many judgments were written down and published in books of reports. But the writing was done by reporters sitting in the courtroom, not by the judges themselves. The reports were summaries of what the lawyers and judges said in court, followed by a brief description of the result. There were sometimes multiple and somewhat different reports of a single case, and some of them were not considered very accurate.

More recently, the reports of cases in England have become quite reliable. Nonetheless, English judgments have resisted the textualization that is so evident in other areas of the law. Consequently, the law that is contained in those judgments remains surprisingly oral in style. The main reason is that English judicial opinions were traditionally delivered by word of mouth, as they often still are today. Judges pronouncing an oral (extempore) judgment choose their words carefully, but because of the limitations of the medium, they simply cannot plan and fine-tune the wording of their decisions to the extent that a writer can.

It goes without saying that English lawyers pay close attention to what judges say in their judgments, but they do not dissect the language in the way that they would analyze the text of a statute. They are concerned with recovering the gist or essence of the judge's words, especially in how it reveals the reasoning that the judge used to determine the outcome. For these and similar reasons, it is fair to say that the common law of England, and in particular the notion of precedent, is relatively more conceptual and less textual than its American counterpart.

The orality and conceptual nature of English common law adjudication has largely disappeared in the United States. Early in the history of the republic, most jurisdictions began requiring appellate judges to issue opinions in writing. Courts also adopted the practice of having one judge draft an opinion that spoke, in a single voice, for the majority. Accurate copies of the texts of opinions, precisely as written by the judge, became widely available.

It would go too far to say that American courts have fully textualized their opinions, making them similar to statutes. Yet they have clearly embarked on a path in that direction. The advantages of clear text in certain sorts of cases suggests that it may sometimes be worth proceeding. At the same time, there are some very real benefits to traditional common law reasoning, which allows the law to evolve more naturally in the light of changing circumstances. Before heading further down the path of textualizing the common law, judges should sit back and contemplate the nature of the texts that they are creating, as well as the textual mode of interpretation that they are encouraging.

Ultimately, however, the future of the legal text is not entirely within our control. In particular, online databases have started to include more and more judicial opinions, including many that in the past would not have been published and would therefore be relegated to obscurity. This practice has resulted in a massive increase in the case law that is available to lawyers. The only effective way to search through these databases is by means of an electronic search engine. Unlike a human being with legal training, who can peruse a judicial opinion for concepts or principles, current search engines can only locate strings of text. As a consequence, the digitizing of judicial opinions has the potential to make the common law more textual and, concomitantly, less conceptual. It may lose the flexibility it once had to be interpreted and reinterpreted to fit new and unforeseen situations.

Like the Mesopotamian scribes who first began to write contracts, wills, and statutes on clay tablets, we cannot fully foresee the impacts of our technological innovations. What we do know, however, is that it matters whether we make law by oral decree, by chiseling edicts into stone, by enacting written text that is spread far and wide on parchment or printed copies, or by typing on a computer keyboard and posting the result on a website.

2

Speech, Writing, and Text

Although the word *text* is sometimes applied to spoken language, I will use it here to refer to written documents. Just about any writing can be considered a text, even if quite informal. A grocery list is a type of text, as is a tattoo that includes words, or a message written in the sky by an airplane. Each of these text types can be considered a distinct genre, with its own conventions relating to style, format, and content. We will be concentrating on legal texts, which tend to be quite formal and conventionalized compared with other genres.

In this chapter we will first consider the nature of writing, the first and by far the most important technology for storing and communicating information. In particular, we will examine the features of writing and how it differs from speech. We will see that many of the features associated with writing make it a natural choice for communicating legal norms and engaging in legal transactions. At the same time, given that oral communication is more natural and generally more convenient than writing, the really interesting questions are why and under what circumstances the legal system prefers or requires writing.

Also relevant is that the distinction between speech and writing is not as clear-cut as it once was. Modern technologies have made it possible to preserve speech for long periods of time as well as to transmit it over large distances. In addition, writing is no longer done exclusively by placing marks on paper, parchment, stone, or some other surface.

Although writing when it first originates is just a means of representing speech, it tends over time to take on a life of its own. After cultures become familiar with literacy, they develop textual practices (or literary conventions) regarding issues such as spelling, punctuation, and how texts ought to be structured. The legal profession, which has become a highly literate endeavor, has developed its own distinct textual practices. We will discuss them in a general manner in this chapter and then explore specific examples in the rest of the book

We will conclude by observing that writing is not an essential ingredient of lawmaking or other legal transactions. Although cultures that become literate tend to quickly apply writing to memorializing public law and private legal transactions, it is possible for a legal system to be entirely oral. Even today, it can sometimes be an advantage to rely on speech and memory. In fact, orality retains a great deal of vitality in our legal system. Consider the typical English or American trial.

At the same time, the law is an extremely textual enterprise. If there is indeed a resurgence of orality in today's culture, aided and abetted by technological advances that make it possible to store and transmit speech, as well as images and sound, what impact will these developments have on the highly textual practices of the profession? As we describe the role of writing and text in the legal system, that question will be lurking in the background.

The Nature and Consequences of Writing

One of the founders of the modern field of linguistics, Leonard Bloomfield, wrote in the 1930s that "writing is not language, but merely a way of recording language by means of visible marks."[1] Like Bloomfield, many early linguists had little interest in text. This was largely a reaction to the popular belief, which persists even today, that writing is somehow superior to speech or that it is a purer form of the language.

Battling this common misconception, early linguists endeavored to show that spoken language is very much worth studying, and that it is possible to describe a system of rules governing speech that might sometimes vary from the principles taught in grammar books but is nonetheless quite real.

Speech, of course, is a universal means of human communication. There are many societies that have survived remarkably well without writing, but speech exists in every culture. It is passed on effortlessly from one generation to the next. Even the most technologically primitive and illiterate societies have highly complex languages. Writing, on the other hand, is an artifact of culture. Consequently, linguists have traditionally devoted most of their research to spoken discourse.

In the past decade or two, however, linguists and other scholars of language have begun to examine writing with greater interest. It has become increasingly apparent that writing is far more than a system for transcribing speech. The mere fact that it is a different mode of communication, using relatively permanent marks on paper or parchment rather than evanescent sound waves, gives writing certain attributes that speech lacks. Moreover, as literate societies develop, writing begins to take on a life of its own and further distances itself from speech.[2]

We thus begin this chapter by exploring some of the attributes of speech and of writing, as well as some of the consequences of choosing one medium over another. One caveat: the following discussion is not meant to present a complete compendium of all the ways in which speaking and writing may differ. Rather, it concentrates on those features that are most relevant to understanding the nature of legal texts.[3] We will therefore not be discussing in any systematic way the growing literature on the impact that writing has had on cognition, education, or culture in general.[4]

A further caveat is that I do not wish to suggest that speaking and writing are fundamentally different. In fact, these differing modes of communication make use of the same, or very similar, vocabulary and grammar. There are few absolute distinctions between speech and writing, a point that Douglas Biber has convincingly made.[5] Nonetheless, there are some important differences, even if they are sometimes merely matters of degree.

Writing Is Durable

Speech disappears the moment it is uttered. Writing, in contrast, can endure, and in some cases has endured, for hundreds or even thousands of years. The permanence of writing was until recently a distinctive feature of this mode of communication. Of course, the degree of permanence can vary depending on the medium that is used. Writing in sand usually does not last long before it is wiped out by a gust of wind or an ocean wave. Stone, in contrast, can preserve writing for millennia. It is still possible to read inscriptions on ancient temples and other monuments, even though they were engraved thousands of years ago. Marks made with ink on paper or parchment are less durable, but even they can last for centuries if protected from the elements.

The durability of writing is probably the most important way in which it differs from speech. Walter Ong, whose work in this area has been highly influential, emphasized what he called the "evanescence" of orality, as opposed to the relative permanence of writing.[6]

Of course, modern technologies have made it possible to preserve speech for long periods of time. Sound has been recorded for at least a century on wax cylinders, vinyl records, and audiotape. Theoretically, an audio recording can preserve speech for a long time. In practice, however, changing technology can quickly render such recordings obsolete, as evidenced by the fact that analog audio recording is being replaced by digital capturing. Most people no longer have phonographs or tape recorders, rendering many record and tape collections obsolete a few decades after the technology was first introduced.

The same problem exists for written text that is stored electronically—it can be very difficult or impossible to access digital information that was encoded using software that is no longer available or that exists on a medium that has become obsolete. Some readers may remember word processing programs like Wordstar and technology like floppy disk drives. As James Billington, the head of the Library of Congress, once remarked, "the best-preserved data tends to be on stone steles and cuneiform tablets."[7] He observed that papyrus, vellum, and parchment also tend to hold up well.[8]

In any event, the legal profession has a strong bias in favor of traditional writing and—despite predictions to the contrary—has made limited use of modern technologies for recording speech.[9] Although the recording of audio and video has been possible for decades, the official record of court proceedings must almost always be written. Even though a growing number of courts record their proceedings on audio- or videotape, or the digital equivalent, when that record is needed for an appeal, it will normally have to be converted into written text.

This is not to say that lawyers and judges have rejected new technologies of communication. Many, in fact, are gadget freaks. Yet they continue to have a strong preference for producing written texts, which look remarkably similar to writings that were created one or two thousand years ago. A Roman senator or judge would easily be able to read a computer printout, at least if it were in Latin. In fact, he could probably read text on a computer screen without too much trouble. Despite all the technological changes over the centuries, most people in our current culture still seem to prefer reading from pieces of paper inscribed with the Roman alphabet or at least reading from an electronic display that mimics text on paper. In legal transactions, therefore, writing remains essential.

In contrast to the durability of writing, speech is transient. Whatever is said disappears immediately, except to the extent that it is preserved in the minds of those who hear it. This point is important because people seldom remember the exact words that were spoken. Instead, we usually remember the gist of what was said.[10] We occasionally recall a critical word or phrase that made a particular impression on us, but for the most part we focus on the meaning that a speaker attempted to convey.

Moreover, memory is fragile. We may remember important events for our entire lifespan, but most ordinary conversations are quickly forgotten. And our memories of what someone told us can change with the passing of time.[11] An oral epic will be somewhat different with every retelling.[12] The reason is not just that the teller may wish to exercise some poetic license, but also that it is virtually impossible for someone to memorize a long narrative and then recite it verbatim.

Consequently, someone who hears a spoken utterance tends to focus on the intentions of the speaker, while an interpreter of written language tends to concentrate more on the words of the text. In both cases, we examine the language of a speaker or writer to try to determine his communicative intent. But someone who hears speech has only momentary access to the speaker's words, which arrive in a continuous stream. She has to process those words quickly and place the speaker's presumptive meaning into long-term memory so that she can prepare a response or be ready for the next batch of speech.

A reader, on the other hand, can usually peruse the words as long as necessary, since the text is stable. She can read it over and over. As Jack Goody has observed, "when an utterance is put in writing it can be inspected in much greater detail, in its parts as well as in its whole, backwards as well as forwards, out of context as well as in its setting; in other words, it can be subjected to a quite different type of scrutiny and critique than is possible with purely verbal [that is, oral] communication."[13]

The durability of writing also enables a text to reach a wider audience. Once again, modern technology allows speech to be heard by millions of people via radio or television and increasingly via the Internet. But historically, the spoken word could reach only a limited number of people who were close enough to the speaker to hear what was said. It was possible, of course, to spread the word more broadly by means of messengers, but they usually conveyed only the essence of the speaker's message, not the exact words.

Incidentally, an interesting legal use of messengers was the practice of transmitting a record in medieval England. At the time, a record was still something that resided in the mind rather than on paper. Thus, when a record of one court was needed in another court, four knights were sent to recount it orally.[14] Why four knights? Presumably because the memory of a single knight could not be trusted to recall all the details of complex legal material. Together, they should be able to remember the essence of what needed to be conveyed.

Writing, on the other hand, makes it possible to reach a much broader audience and also to convey the actual words of the text. A proclamation can be written down and posted in a central place or be chiseled into stone in a public square, where all who pass by can read it. Copies can be made and distributed over a wide geographical area, especially after printing became common, spreading the word even further.

Finally, the greater permanence of writing allows the storage of vast amounts of information. In an oral society, just about the only way to store complex information is in human memory. Many ancient Greek cities had remembrancers whose job it was to memorize important information.[15] Even when memory is aided by pictures or other mnemonic devices, however, it is inherently limited. Written text, on the other hand, allows for virtually limitless storage capacity.

Writing Is Accessible

Related to the durability of writing is that it is more accessible than speech and other nontextual means of communication. Information that is conveyed orally must be stored in memory, where we may or may not be able to easily retrieve it. In any event, we no longer have access to the original words. Technologies like audio recording preserve the information contained in speech, of course, but audio recordings are a very inefficient way of accessing information. To find a particular word or phrase, you generally have to listen to the recordings in real time from start to finish. The same is currently true of audio recorded in digital format. Ironically, the best way to search for and access information in an audio or video recording is to convert it to text or to produce a written index.

A written text is more accessible than speech for a number of reasons. One is that it can easily be divided into units, such as chapters and sections. The Bible became infinitely more useful to believers when, roughly a thousand years ago, it was divided into chapter and verse. As a result, it became possible to make a subject index, as was done at the end of the twelfth century.[16] A more modern approach is to number the pages. The written nature of texts thus facilitates compiling tables of contents, indexes, and concordances, all of which make it vastly easier for readers to locate relevant information.

The accessibility of written texts is obviously of critical importance to the development of law. We will see in a later chapter that the notion of precedent was able to evolve not just because judicial decisions were written down on paper or parchment, but also because the reports of decisions began to be bound into books organized by year. If you knew when a case was decided, you might find a report of the decision in the yearbook bearing that date. The texts became even more accessible through the compilation of abridgments, or digests, which assembled citations to cases under subject headings like "murder" or "theft." Once you can find cases or statutes in a book and have a practical method of citing them, it becomes possible to use them as the basis for creating a systematic body of law.

It's worth observing at this point that computers and especially the Internet have made information of almost all kinds, including pictures, video, and sound, more readily available than ever before. Not long ago, online information was difficult to access, but indexing services and search engines have made it far easier to find what you seek. Yet even today, writing remains vastly easier to access on the Internet than information preserved by other media. Your success in finding a graphic or visual representation depends critically on how well the material is described (in words) on the website where it is located. No doubt search engines will improve, but it will take some time before it is as easy to locate sounds or images as it currently is to find text.

Writing Can Be Planned

We have observed that because writing is relatively permanent, the reader has more time to process written words, as opposed to a hearer of speech, who must process an utterance almost instantaneously. The corollary is that the writer likewise has more time to place those words on paper. This difference is a matter of degree, rather than an absolute principle. Clearly, speakers can and do plan utterances in advance. A formal lecture is a good example, and even statements that we make in informal conversation may be scripted to some extent. But our ability to do so is necessarily limited. Even when we plan a speech, it is difficult to fix the exact words that we are going to say, as opposed to preparing a more general outline of the content. If the precise language is important, a speaker will almost invariably write out and memorize the speech or simply read it aloud.

Linguist Wallace Chafe has investigated some of the distinctive features of writing, including the ability of writers to plan texts. In an interesting study, he and Jane Danielewicz examined the spoken and written language produced by a group of twenty people. They found that the written samples had a significantly richer vocabulary than the spoken ones.[17] Because speakers produce language on the fly, "they hardly have time to sift through all the possible choices they might have, and may typically settle on the first words that occur to them."[18] Writers, in contrast, have the luxury of choosing their words more carefully, resulting in a more diverse vocabulary.

The fact that writers have the time to select their words with care has implications for interpretation. In speech, we usually tolerate an infelicitous word choice. We tend to overlook glitches, maladroit expressions, inconsistent uses of a word, and other performance errors, as long as we can figure out what the speaker meant.

With writing, on the other hand, especially with formal writing that has been carefully planned in advance, the reader will be inclined to pay more attention to the writer's choice of words. This is particularly true of legislation. Statutes tend to be drafted with great care, so it is natural for judges to wonder why the legislature used *residence* in one section of an act, as opposed to *domicile* in another. They will presume that each word was intended to have a distinct meaning, something we would not necessarily think when interpreting near-synonyms in spoken language. Likewise, if a statute uses the term *residence* throughout, and someone comes to court and argues that the legislature really meant *domicile*, most judges would respond that the word *domicile* was readily available and that if the legislature had meant *domicile*, it would or should have said so. The same dynamic allows a reader to focus on things like the placement of a comma, which can occasionally influence the meaning of a sentence. Such careful examination of exact words is vastly more difficult and far less likely with speech.

In addition, the ability to plan allows writers to use sentences that are relatively long and syntactically complex. A speaker who tries to construct a lengthy, complicated sentence may find that she has lost her train of thought halfway through the utterance. A writer has time to add phrases and clauses in multiple layers of embedding. Similarly, and for the same reasons, writing tends to be substantially more dense than speech, communicating more content with fewer words.[19]

Length, complexity, and density are amply evident in legal texts. Consider a California statute that prohibits the insuring of lotteries:

> Every person who insures or receives any consideration for insuring for or against the drawing of any ticket in any lottery whatever, whether drawn or to be drawn within this state or not, or who receives any valuable consideration upon any agreement to repay any sum, or deliver the same, or any other property, if any lottery ticket or number of any ticket in any lottery shall prove fortunate or unfortunate, or shall be drawn or not be drawn, at any particular time or in any particular order, or who promises or agrees to pay any sum of money, or to deliver any goods, things in action, or property, or to forbear to do anything for the benefit of any person, with or without consideration, upon any event or contingency dependent on the drawing of any ticket in any lottery, or who publishes any notice or proposal of any of the purposes aforesaid, is guilty of a misdemeanor.[20]

You can actually process this verbose sentence if you spend some time carefully reading it (although you may have to diagram it on paper). But it is virtually impossible to imagine someone saying these words in an oral proclamation that has not been written down in advance, and it is equally hard to conceive of a hearer understanding and retaining all of the details.

Because writing can be planned, it also allows for the possibility of collective authorship. It is conceivable, of course, that a group of people could jointly decide something and then agree on exactly how their decision should be phrased in words, without the use of paper and pen. But it would be difficult from a practical standpoint. When a collective decision is made orally, it usually involves some or all of the members of the group expressing their opinions individually, or perhaps agreeing with a previous speaker. Laws agreed upon orally by a popular assembly will consist of a concept or idea in the minds of those who adopted it, not exact words. In fact, this method of decision making is similar to the practice of seriatim opinion delivery in England, where judges by definition do not collectively author an opinion. Instead, they produce multiple (and often oral) opinions one after the other. We will see in chapter 6 that such opinion delivery remains common in England. The result is that there is no single text that authoritatively states the opinion of the court as a whole.

Writing allows groups of people to discuss a decision and then to formulate their communicative intentions on paper. There will doubtless be negotiations on which words should be used, but the end result will generally be deemed to speak for the entire group. This, of course, is the practice of most modern legislatures. It also describes how majority opinions are written in most appellate courts in the United States. The result is that these words will be imbued with particular authority. Not only was the text drafted by the decision makers themselves, but all of them will be assumed to have agreed to the precise phrasing of the resulting text.

Writing Can Span Distance and Time

Speech is immediate. A speaker can usually see the person with whom he is communicating. One consequence is that communication by speech is not restricted to words. Gestures of various sorts not only accompany our speech but can sometimes replace it. If a criminal defendant holds out his index finger in the shape of a gun and points it at a witness, it will probably be interpreted as equivalent to a verbal threat.[21] Moreover, we routinely point at things to indicate reference, as in "that's the oldest house in this town."

Nonverbal communication is more difficult for writers. Pictures or graphics can, of course, be added to a text, but they are often poor substitutes for gestures.[22] Typically, information that can be conveyed nonverbally in a spoken conversation must be expressed by means of words in a written text. Court reporters are well aware of this, which is why they add notations in a transcript (such as "laughter" or "witness nods head" or "pointing to defendant").

When you hear speech you also have access to what linguists call prosodic and paralinguistic features (intonation, loudness, tone of voice). We have all heard the expression, "it's not just what you say, it's how you say it." Such features can have important consequences for meaning, especially when the words themselves are subject to multiple interpretations. Intonation and gestures can signal whether an utterance was meant seriously or sarcastically ("That was a brilliant idea!").

An important issue during the impeachment proceedings against President Clinton was whether he encouraged his secretary, Betty Currie, to lie to investigators about whether he was ever alone in the White House with Monica Lewinsky. A critical incident involved utterances he made to Currie, including "You were always there when she was there, right?" According to Special Prosecutor Kenneth Starr, Clinton was trying to coach Currie regarding what she should say if asked about Lewinsky's presence in the White House.[23] Currie testified that Clinton's utterances were more like statements than questions, based "on the way he made most of the statements and on his demeanor."[24] Clinton, in contrast, testified that they were real questions and that he asked them simply to confirm his own recollection.[25] It is impossible to determine his intonation and tone of voice from the written evidence. But if we had an audio recording, these features would probably have made his intentions clear.

Writers must make do with punctuation, which is a poor substitute for prosodic and paralinguistic features of speech.[26] Of course, sometimes intonation can be effectively conveyed by devices like question marks. Even though "Your name is Jones" seems like a statement, a question mark turns it into a request for information. Yet notice that punctuation would not clarify Clinton's utterance to Currie. We can normally hear the difference between genuine requests for information (as when a sales clerk asks, "Your name is Jones, isn't it?" with rising intonation) and coercive questions that consist of a statement followed by a request for confirmation of that statement ("You killed your wife, didn't you?" with a falling intonation contour). The latter, of course, are routine during cross-examination. Both types of utterance could be followed by a question mark, so on paper there may be no distinction between them.

An additional function of nonverbal cues like gesture and intonation is that they are often used to indicate that an utterance should not be taken literally. Consider again the sentence, "That's a brilliant idea!" Its laudatory message can be subverted by the proper intonation and, perhaps, a raising of the eyebrows. Sometimes a mere wink of the eye can suggest that a statement should not be taken seriously.

Such phenomena help explain why writing tends to be interpreted more literally than speech. We often begin the interpretive process by taking words at their face value, and then we adjust our interpretation as we receive indications (like a wink) that the speaker did not intend an utterance to be taken literally. Writers have fewer mechanisms for indicating that a statement should not be taken seriously, and they usually cannot monitor whether the audience has properly understood it. Authors of formal prose therefore tend to write in a relatively literal way, and readers tend to interpret their work accordingly. A speaker on tax law, even in a very formal lecture, can easily sneak in a joke or sarcastic comment, but such devices are almost nonexistent in a written treatise on the same subject.

Another feature of face-to-face contact is that it permits the speaker to situate the hearer in a particular context and to speak to her in a way that will make sense in that context. Deborah Tannen has observed that the oral tradition emphasizes shared knowledge and the interpersonal relationship between communicator and audience.[27] In such a situation, there is much information that is obvious to interlocutors and therefore need not be overtly stated. This is often called *shared background information* or *joint knowledge* or *common ground*.[28]

If I enter a bakery, I can point at a group of scones and say, "One, please." The baker's assistant will know, based on the circumstances in which we find ourselves and on her observation of my pointing, that I wish her to give me a raisin scone and that I am willing to pay the posted price for it. She can hand me the scone and say, "One twenty-five." I will understand these words as a request for me to give her one dollar and twenty-five cents.

Glanville Williams made a similar point over half a century ago in an early article on language and law. He examined a man's statement to the family maid that she should "fetch some soup meat" and discussed how shared background knowledge could fill in many of the details about the type of meat the maid should buy, where she should buy it, and so forth.[29]

A reader and writer, especially if separated by time and space, are likely to share less background information and knowledge of the circumstances. For this reason, such information must often be expressed in words and placed into the text. Of course, some general knowledge of how the world works can always be assumed. In the legal context, a writer can often take for granted that the reader has a certain amount of knowledge about the law. The writer of a statute, for instance, can assume that the reader has some legal education and that he therefore does not need to explain the legal context into which the statute fits, including what a statute is, how it operates in our legal system, or the meaning of commonly used technical terminology. On the other hand, the factual context or background that created a need for the statute (that is, its purpose) may not be apparent, especially to readers in the future or those in a remote location. This explains why statutes often contain a preamble that explains why the statute is being enacted. The purpose of an utterance, knowledge of which can be helpful in understanding it, may be obvious to people in face-to-face contact and may therefore need not be stated. But because a piece of legislation might still be in force far in the future, when the reason for enacting it may have been forgotten, such information must usually be made explicit in a written statute.

Another feature of face-to-face communication is that it is possible for the speaker to monitor whether the hearer understands the utterance.[30] You can do so by looking for the hearer to nod her head or to say "yeah" periodically; if she does not, you may ask her whether she is following what you are saying. Or the hearer may ask you for clarification. In either case, you can explain or retell something in a different way or with greater detail. Such interaction makes it possible to clarify many of the ambiguities that naturally arise in language. Returning to the bakery example: if the attendant hands me a maple scone in response to my pointing, I can clarify that I meant one containing raisins. Linguists sometimes say that people who are engaged in spoken conversation "negotiate" meaning by strategies such as these.[31]

With written text, clarification and correction can be vastly more difficult or even impossible. Modern communication has once again modified the situation somewhat in that interaction by text messages or e-mail resembles face-to-face contact in some respects, especially in the ability to ask for immediate clarification. But certainly with respect to most legal texts, the process of drafting is radically different from face-to-face communication. Legal drafting is usually a one-way process in which the writer sends a message to the reader, who is neither expected to nor able to reply. Consequently, the writer cannot very well monitor whether the reader comprehends his message, and the reader in turn is usually not in a position to ask for an explanation if she does not understand it. Because a writing can last a long time, its author may be dead by the time the text is read, making it completely impossible for the reader to ask for clarification. This, of course, is almost always the case with wills.

Most writers, and certainly the drafters of legal texts, understand these realities. Lawyers therefore endeavor to make the language of the texts they create as clear as possible. Because they usually cannot interact with the reader, they try to anticipate every possible future contingency. The almost fanatical efforts of legal drafters to write as precisely as possible will never entirely succeed, but the nature of writing in general and the characteristics of legal texts in particular strongly encourage them to try.

Writing Can Be Relatively Autonomous

Speech is inevitably very contextual. It is almost impossible to separate an utterance from what we know about the person who made it and the surrounding circumstances. The speaker and the context are usually directly in front of us.

Written texts, on the other hand, can be—and often must be—much more autonomous. This is particularly true with documents that are likely to travel great distances or last a long time. Because readers may have little information about the circumstances in which such texts were produced, they must be written autonomously, using language that can stand on its own. Of course, in order to interpret an utterance or a text, we always need at least some background information. At a very minimum, we need some knowledge of how the world operates. Thus, there is no such thing as a completely autonomous text. Context is always relevant. Nonetheless, because writing is often used to transmit messages across space and time, it tends to be more autonomous than speech.

Paul Kay has described autonomous language as being minimally dependent on information passed over nonlinguistic channels, such as paralinguistic cues and gestures, and also as not extensively relying on shared background information.[32] The autonomous speech style, as Kay called it, "conveys the speaker's intent without reliance on tone of voice, facial expression, gesture, or posture and makes minimal appeal to prior understandings between the addressor and addressee."[33] In addition, Kay notes that as the interpersonal distance between individuals involved in communication becomes greater, their language necessarily becomes more autonomous.[34]

Like most linguists, Kay seems more interested in speech than in writing, and in the article in question he is specifically concerned with the evolution of language. Nonetheless, he draws a connection between the existence of writing in a culture and the development of autonomous language.[35] Walter Ong drew the connection more explicitly: "To make yourself clear without gesture, without facial expression, without intonation, without a real hearer, you have to foresee circumspectly all possible meanings a statement may have for any possible reader in any possible situation, and you have to make your language work so as to come clear all by itself, with no existential context."[36]

The greater possible autonomy of writing is related to the fact that it is more durable than speech and that it does not usually involve face-to-face contact. Because a text can communicate a message to an audience that is removed not only in terms of physical distance but also in terms of time, readers may have very little knowledge of the writer's intentions beyond what is expressed in the text itself. Information that need not be communicated in speech, because the speaker and hearer are in face-to-face contact, must be explicitly added to an autonomous text. Hence, to create a relatively autonomous communication, you must endeavor to express your intentions in words and to place them into the text.

Not all written language is particularly autonomous, of course. E-mail between friends or notes passed from one student to another during class are examples of written language that is highly dependent on context and shared background knowledge; writing in these circumstances is very much like speaking. Conversely, some types of speech, such as an oral judgment by an English judge, closely resemble a formal written document. There is, in other words, a general tendency for written language to be more autonomous than speech, but it is hardly an absolute correlation.

As Martin Nystrand has pointed out, both speakers and writers need to balance what needs to be expressly articulated with what, in context, does not need to be said (because it is obvious or can be assumed or is communicated nonverbally).[37] Perhaps the best formulation is that written language is not invariably more autonomous than speech, but because of its greater permanence, the ability to plan it in advance, and the ability to transmit a message over space and time, a text is more likely to need relatively autonomous language. In any event, the nature of writing facilitates the use of autonomous modes of expression when they are needed.

Consider a person stranded on a remote sandbar in the ocean. If a ship sails past, he can wave his arms and shout "Help!" at the top of his voice. The message should be clear to anyone who sees him. He does not need to specify his location because the sailors can see where he is. And although the word *help* by itself is very vague, its meaning in this context is obvious.

Now suppose that there is no passing ship. The man, out of desperation, begins to insert messages into empty bottles that have washed ashore, casting them into the surf in the hope that they will reach civilization. "Help" will no longer suffice. His message must be much more autonomous (informative and self-contained) if he is to have any chance of being rescued. Perhaps he could write something like, "I was sailing solo from Truk to Palau and was on course, traveling at an average speed of five knots, when my boat sank five days after leaving Truk Harbor. I am stuck on a tiny island with limited food and water. Please rescue me!" In other words, information that is obvious in face-to-face spoken interaction (such as the man's predicament and the location of the island) must often be expressly inserted into an autonomous writing.

Autonomous language is extremely common in legal texts, especially as societies and legal systems develop. The reason, of course, is that the interpersonal distance between the legal drafter and his audience can be substantial. Someone may have to read and try to make sense of such a text while having little information about who wrote it and why. Wills are a good example, since they are usually implemented years or decades after they are written, and the maker of the will is almost always dead and cannot be consulted on its meaning.

Consider the simple pronoun *I*, which is often the first word of a will. If you use the word *I* in ordinary speech, people have no trouble determining that it refers to you. The same is true for a nonautonomous writing, as when you hand a note to a friend. *I* is perfectly sufficient.

But when you communicate in writing with a reader who is not physically present, you need to add your name. This is the primary purpose of the signature at the end of a letter. Information that is obvious in face-to-face contact must be explicitly added to the text. Wills tend to be written even more autonomously than letters, including not just the name of the testator ("I, Jane Sanchez") but also the address ("residing at 123 Sand Dune Lane in Sunset Beach, California"). The same is true of references to real property. In speech, "my house" may suffice, but lawyers drafting wills tend to include an exact address or a legal description.

Statutes likewise tend to be highly autonomous. A statute can be in force for dozens or hundreds of years and may have to be read and interpreted by people who have little or no knowledge about why it was adopted. A statute's purpose, of course, can be an important aid in interpreting its scope and in resolving ambiguities. It is for this reason that drafters of statutes began to add a preamble explaining the background of its enactment. In a very real sense, a statement of the legislature's intent and purpose is placed into the text itself, in the form of words, thus making the text that much more autonomous.

The autonomy of a text has implications for its interpretation. If a writer is aware that contextual and background information will probably not be available to the audience, and if he therefore places more information about his communicative intentions into a text, a reader will pay more attention to the words of the text than she might otherwise. The interpreter will closely scrutinize those words to determine what the writer meant.

Consider that when someone makes an ambiguous utterance in ordinary speech, it is natural to think, "I wonder what he meant by that." But if we encounter an ambiguous traffic sign along a roadway, we seldom think, "I wonder what those traffic engineers meant by that sign." It is much more natural to ask, "I wonder what that sign means." The same is true of statutes. Unless we are closely associated with a legislature, we are naturally more inclined to ask what a statute means than to ask what the legislature meant by a statute. Thus, when reading and interpreting highly autonomous language, we tend to view intentions as something embodied in the text, rather than as something contained in the mind of the writer.

Linguists generally distinguish between *speaker's meaning*—what the speaker intended to communicate—and *sentence meaning*—what the words of a sentence mean. Roughly speaking, sentence meaning refers to the "literal" meaning of a sentence.[38] Typically, we begin the interpretive process by analyzing the sentence meaning, but the ultimate aim of interpretation is to discover the speaker's meaning. This is true of both speech and writing.

At the same time, when we interpret an autonomous writing, one accompanied by little contextual and background information, we tend to focus more on the meaning of the words and sentences in the text, with the writer's meaning receding into the background somewhat. As Rita Watson and David Olson have written,

> The comprehension of expressions in oral discourse, where speaker and hearer share the same "real-world" context, is usually accomplished by appeal to context and to the shared expectancies established prior to and during the conversation by the participants. In contrast, the meaning of written expressions must be recoverable from the text: writer and reader must construct and reconstruct interpretations largely based on the words alone.[39]

Watson and Olson conclude that the speaker's meaning is more relevant to a listener, while the meaning of the word or sentence is more relevant to a reader. This conclusion is consistent with evidence that hearers tend to remember more of the gist of what they heard and not so much the exact words, while readers have a better memory for the words that they read.[40]

Of course, it is impossible to make a text fully autonomous, and work by scholars like Olson sometimes strikes me as being overly optimistic about our ability to do so. Autonomous drafting is particularly problematic if, as in the case of statutes, the text attempts to govern future behavior.[41] Moreover, even though there may be less of it available, context is critical to interpreting any written text, just as it is in understanding speech.[42]

Yet it is undeniable that lawyers strive to make documents, especially texts that embody legal transactions, as autonomous as possible. James Bradley Thayer, in his treatise on evidence law, recognized as much when he satirized the practice of lawyers who aspire to a paradise "where all words have a fixed, precisely ascertained meaning; where men may express their purposes, not only with accuracy, but with fulness; and where, if the writer has been careful, a lawyer, having a document referred to him, may sit in his chair, inspect the text, and answer all questions without raising his eyes."[43] Thayer was right, of course, in suggesting that such a paradise is unattainable. But it does not prevent lawyers from trying to enter it.

Summary of the Features of Writing

We are now in a position to summarize what, for our purposes, are some of the main features of writing, along with some of the consequences:

Writing is durable.

- Thus, an interpreter of written language can concentrate on the text, since it is available for examination and close scrutiny. Someone who hears a spoken utterance tends to focus on the intentions of the speaker, since the exact words are seldom remembered.
- The relative permanence of writing allows it to reach a broad audience removed from the drafter in space and time. Until quite recently, speech could reach only those who were present physically and temporally.
- The durability of written texts gives them a virtually unlimited capacity to store information.

Writing is accessible.

- Thus, written text can be organized into units, such as chapters, verses, or pages, making it easier to refer to specific parts of the text.
- Once text has been divided in this way, reference tools like indexes, concordances, and digests become possible, making it easier to find relevant information.

Writing can be planned.

- Thus, the author can pick his words with great care.
- If a writer is known to have carefully crafted a text, the reader will give relatively greater attention to the words within it.
- The ability to plan a writing also enables collective authorship.

Writing can span distance and time.

- Thus, whereas speakers can readily use nonlinguistic modes of communication, including shared context and background, writers must usually express such information by means of placing words in text.
- The words of writers are more likely to be taken at face value (that is, fairly literally). Speakers can more easily signal that an utterance is being used metaphorically, jokingly, ironically, or in some other figurative sense.

- Because writing is often a one-way communication, an author may not be in a position to monitor whether the reader understands him or to clarify ambiguities. The writer may have only one opportunity to get it right, motivating him to draft a text as precisely and comprehensively as possible.

Writing can be relatively autonomous.

- When writers need to convey a message to an audience that is distant in space and/or time, they will strive to write autonomously by placing all relevant information into the text itself, since they cannot assume that they and the reader will share context and background knowledge.
- Knowing that a text has been drafted autonomously, readers will tend to interpret it in a relatively acontextual way. They will focus more on the word and sentence meaning and less on the writer's intended meaning.

This list of some of the more important features of writing and their consequences should not be taken as suggesting that writing is superior to speaking or other means of communication. At least with respect to law, the oral and written modes of communication have their respective strengths and weaknesses, making speech better for some purposes and writing for others.

Some of the disadvantages of writing have already been mentioned. We saw that speech generally occurs in a situation with more contextual and nonlinguistic clues to the speaker's meaning. Writers may need more words to convey the same information. Speakers can negotiate meaning in a way that is difficult for writers, who must take affirmative steps to anticipate and avoid ambiguity or vagueness.

We will see later in this book that while the permanence of writing makes it a natural medium for the articulation of laws, it has a serious drawback. Permanence promotes stagnation and inflexibility. As Goody has noted, rules transmitted through the oral channel can be subtly adjusted over time, whereas written rules must be deliberately altered, or ignored.[44] Most people also speak much faster than they can write,[45] which means that speech is usually the most economical mode of communication. This simple difference explains why even today, when virtually everyone in our society is literate, so many legal transactions (such as routine contracts and sales) are still performed orally.

Despite such drawbacks, the characteristics of writing suggest that it can be a useful tool for legislating. Laws are usually meant to remain in force for lengthy periods of time, or even indefinitely. The durability of writing helps achieve this goal. Written law can also reach a broader population. The permanence of the text promotes stability and predictability, important goals of any rational legal system. The fact that it is easier to plan a written text also suits the process of lawmaking, which typically involves deliberation and negotiation by a group of people. The greater accessibility of a written text promotes its use as a reference tool. And the ability to draft statutes in relatively autonomous language makes it easier for a distant or future audience to understand what the law means.

Thus, orality and literacy both have their place in a modern legal system. One of the major issues that I will attempt to address in this book is not which mode of communicating and storing information is superior to the other, but rather why the law prefers or demands that certain transactions be performed in writing, and what the consequences are.

Conventions of Literacy and Textualization

When cultures begin to write, the texts they produce tend initially to be very speech-like, since that is the mode of communication with which people are most comfortable. But as they become familiar with writing, cultures invariably develop textual practices or conventions of literacy.

Examples of textual practices in our society include a customary system of spelling that has never been enacted into law, but which is almost universally observed. Rules relating to punctuation are somewhat more flexible, but the basic principles (you should end a sentence with a period) are generally followed. We also have developed conventions regarding the format of texts. Letters start with a greeting, optionally include the sender's address and a date, and generally end with a signature. Memoranda likewise have a fairly predictable format, as do newspaper articles, directions for using a product, and various other kinds of writing.

Literary Practices of the Legal Profession

Being such a textual enterprise, the legal profession has developed a large number of distinct literary conventions. Young lawyers learn these textual practices in law school or by imitating older lawyers. By *literary conventions* or *textual practices* of the profession, I mean customs related to how one ought to write and structure legal texts. Some of these customs are useful. Others may have had some function hundreds of years ago but are now endlessly repeated purely out of habit or superstition.

In medieval English legal texts (which were mostly in Latin), the convention arose that when a party was first mentioned, the scribe or clerk would give the person's full name and then usually state where the person resided, followed by the person's occupation or title. Thus, a deed might refer to a buyer of property as "John Smith of the city of Norwich, merchant." All subsequent references would be done by means of a shortened description, as in "the aforesaid John" or "the same John." In theory, the scribe could save a lot of parchment by not repeating the full description over and over. In practice, this convention is downright silly. If there is only one party named John, there is no need to add "aforesaid" each time. And if there is more than one, "the aforesaid John" is underdeterminate.[46]

A more useful textual practice is the modern convention of using shortened titles for lengthy names. If a judge wishes to refer in an opinion to a previous case entitled *Jones v. People United against Inhumane Treatment of Animals*, 123 P.R. 24 (2007), the judge can simply cite "the *Jones* case." If there are two cases by that name, as can happen when a case goes through two appeals, the judge might state that she will refer to the first case as "Jones I" and the second as "Jones II."

The structure or format of legal texts is also severely constrained by custom. A will, for instance, almost always bears the caption, "Last Will and Testament." This is true even if it is the first will that the testator has ever made, and even if it is possible that she will make additional wills later. All of them will proudly bear the title "last will." In addition, "testament" and "will" mean exactly the same thing today, so one or the other would suffice. A more useful textual convention would be to use a title such as "Will of Samantha Perkins, executed June 22, 2006."

The body of a will typically begins with an introductory paragraph like the following: "KNOW ALL MEN BY THESE PRESENTS, that I, HELEN HOVANESIAN, of the Town of New Britain, County of Hartford and State of Connecticut, do hereby make, publish and declare this as and for my Last Will and Testament, hereby revoking all wills and codicils thereto heretofore by me made."[47] Of course, it's a good idea to identify the testator, including the place of residence. And it is also excellent practice to revoke any previous wills. Yet it is astonishing that even today lawyers routinely use the phrase "heretofore by me made." Why not just say, "I revoke any wills and codicils that I have previously made"?

American wills then typically continue by inserting routine provisions regarding the payment of debts, appointing an executor, and (of course!) giving the testator's property to various heirs. The language of all these clauses tends to be highly archaic and redundant, as illustrated by this residuary clause:

> I give, devise and bequeath all of said rest, residue and remainder of my property which I may own at the time of my death, real, personal and mixed, of whatsoever kind and nature and wheresoever situate, including all property which I may acquire or to which I may become entitled after the execution of this will, in equal shares, absolutely and forever, to [list of recipients].[48]

Once again, this convoluted language is purely customary, and much of it makes little sense, at least in today's world. If you give the "rest" of your property to someone, there is no need to also give them the "residue" and "remainder." Nor does it seem necessary to specify that you are including all "real, personal and mixed" property (since you just said you are giving away "the rest . . . of my property"). Moreover, there is absolutely no reason—besides custom or convention—to append the words "of whatsoever kind and nature and wheresoever situate."

A will generally ends with something like the following: "IN WITNESS WHEREOF, I have hereunto set my hand and seal at Hartford, Connecticut, this 2nd day of July, 1986."[49] The testator signs the will below this statement. The ritualistic language impresses on the testator that this is no ordinary document, so it may serve some purpose. Yet there is absolutely no requirement that the testator seal the will. In fact, this practice has been obsolete for at least a century. It is astonishing how often testators solemnly sign this statement, when it is factually false. It goes to show how incredibly conservative the textual practices of the profession can be.

We will explore some other textual conventions in the later chapters of this book. At this point, we will focus on one of the more important literary practices of the common law system, which I refer to as *textualization*. Despite its significance, its pervasive influence on the workings of the law, especially on interpretation, is not widely appreciated.

Textualization

The term *textualization* can be applied either diachronically (with regard to its historical development) or synchronically (relating to how it is used currently). Diachronically or historically, it refers to the process by which certain types of legal texts become increasingly authoritative over time. Written wills were once purely evidence of an oral transaction, but the text has become vastly more important during the past few centuries. Synchronically, I will use the term to refer to the process by which lawyers, and sometimes ordinary citizens, make a text the authoritative expression of a legal act. We will examine textualization throughout this book from both perspectives, although our main concern is synchronic: how the legal profession currently deals with text.

From a diachronic perspective, we will see that there are usually three main stages in the transition from oral legal transaction to authoritative written text. At the first stage, legal transactions are purely oral. Because of the consequences involved and the limitations of memory, such transactions often require the presence of witnesses. Oral Anglo-Saxon wills were typically declared in front of several witnesses, for example. Also common is some kind of ritual or other indication that a significant and binding legal event is taking place. The handing over of a clod of dirt symbolizing the transfer of real property is a well-known illustration.[50]

At the second stage, the legal act remains essentially oral, but someone now makes a writing that records or evidences the act. As we will see in greater detail in chapter 5, when we discuss statutes, most early English codes of law were evidentiary. They were compilations or collections of existing custom, rather than legislation in the modern sense. Even after the Norman conquest, lawmaking initially did not involve a king or parliament drafting and then enacting a written text. Rather, the king or parliament decided what the law should be, and a scribe later made a record of their decision. The law was what was in the minds and memories of the king and his council, not what the scribe had written on parchment.

When they first become literate, societies tend to have an ambivalent attitude toward the written word. On the one hand, writing is considered powerful, almost magical. It's often the exclusive domain of a privileged class of scribes or priests, who jealously guard their monopoly. At the same time, there tends to be a great deal of skepticism about it (especially by the illiterate part of the population, one would imagine). M. T. Clanchy writes that in twelfth-century England, to "record" something meant to bear oral witness, not to produce a document (the Spanish word *recordar*, 'remember,' reflects this earlier meaning). Clanchy observes that "[t]he spoken word was the legally valid record and was superior to any document."[51]

As a more literate mentality takes hold, such attitudes begin to change. The written record may remain evidentiary, but it becomes increasingly important evidence of what happened. A growing number of transactions are accompanied by a writing. If the legal act is sufficiently important, people will start to expect or demand that there be documentation. In England, the Statute of Frauds required that certain types of wills and contracts be evidenced by a written document. Today, of course, just about anyone knows that if you want a legal act to be valid and enforceable, you need to "get it in writing." In reality, the modern situation is more complicated, as we will see throughout in this book, but there is clearly a widespread appreciation in our society regarding the value of written evidence of a legal transaction.

At the third stage, the writing has become the transaction. Enacting or executing an authoritative text has become essential. What the parties said or intended recedes into the background or may even become irrelevant except for some very limited purposes. Whereas at the second stage writing serves as an aid to memory, at the third stage writing effectively replaces it.

Most legal acts do not need to be textualized in this manner. But when textualization is required, or where parties to a transaction decide to set down its terms in the form of an authoritative text, it has important ramifications. Although most people are aware of ordinary conventions relating to writing and literacy, the peculiar conventions of the legal profession, in particular those relating to textualization, are only dimly understood.

Attributes of Textualization

It can sometimes be difficult to determine whether a particular legal text, especially one from the past, is evidentiary or authoritative (that is, textualized). Often we do not know enough about the nature of historical texts, like many early law codes, to know what their function was, and there may be much debate among scholars on this question.[52] Did the Code of Hammurabi or the codes of early English kings create new law? Did they merely record customary law? Or, perhaps, a bit of each?

There are a number of criteria to help determine whether a text is authoritative, or has been textualized, in the sense in which the term is being used here. Perhaps the most important is that the legal actor must be the author. In other words, the parties to the transaction must either actually be, or they must be legally deemed to be, the authors of the text in question. The text must be viewed as the product of the actors themselves, rather than as a mere record produced by someone else.

Of course, legal documents are often drafted by lawyers and other professionals, not by the person who engaged in the transaction. What matters is that it speaks in the voice of the actor. Frequently this is reflected in the use of the first person, as is common in wills ("I, Julia Jones, declare that this is my will . . ."). Another example is the United States Constitution ("We the people . . ."). Sometimes the text is in the third person but nonetheless effectively speaks on behalf of the actor. Statutes are normally enacted in the third person ("the legislature enacts as follows . . ." or "the people enact as follows . . ."), but those phrases really mean "*we* enact as follows . . ."

Authorship of the text, whether real or fictional, is not enough, however. The writing, even though drafted by or for the legal actor, might still be a record, intended to aid the memory of the parties or prevent disputes about what was agreed upon, rather than being viewed as constituting the legal act itself.

An additional requirement therefore relates to when the text is written. Recall that if a written record is made of a transaction, it is typically done after the fact. What sets the stage for textualization is that the writing down of the transaction is done *before* the legal act occurs or perhaps concurrently. To be more exact, the legal act must be performed by means of the writing and any accompanying rituals. Oral transactions, of course, take place via spoken words. The writing, if there is one, is almost an afterthought. In contrast, a textualized transaction is performed by the act of writing, or by the act of executing or putting into force a writing that was prepared beforehand (for example, by signing or sealing it).

A linguistic correlate of this distinction is that evidentiary texts typically contain verbs in the past tense, as in "the king and his counsel *ordained* as follows . . ." or "George Smith *declared* his will in the following terms . . ." Use of the past tense is only natural, because an evidentiary text functions as a record of a legal transaction that has already transpired. Authoritative texts, in contrast, are almost invariably in the present because the actor is engaging in a transaction by means of the text.

A note of explanation is necessary here, because anyone who has been exposed to legal documents is aware of the ubiquitous use of the auxiliary verb *shall*, normally used to indicate the future. Although the status of *shall* in legal texts is complicated and controversial,[53] it is important to bear in mind that the essential verb in any authoritative text, whether expressed or implied, must necessarily be in the present tense. In a will, the essential language consists of verb phrases like *I give, I appoint*, and *I revoke*. In contracts it is the phrase *I/we promise*. In a statute it is a phrase like *we enact* or *the people of the state enact as follows*. These phrases all indicate that the legal actor is speaking through the text in question.

Readers familiar with speech act theory will recognize that authoritative texts almost invariably contain—expressly or by implication—a performative speech act. The English philosopher J. L. Austin, in a classic book called *How to Do Things with Words*, formulated a basic distinction between speech acts that perform an action and those that merely talk about or discuss or describe an action or state of affairs.[54] The former category of speech acts are called *performatives*, because speakers can perform an action merely by saying something. The examples in the previous paragraph (*I give, I appoint, I revoke, we promise, we enact*) are all performative speech acts in that a speaker who has the authority to perform an act can accomplish it merely by saying those words. Austin pointed out—as evident in the above examples—that performative speech acts generally require a verb in the first person, present tense.

Most speech acts are not performatives in this sense. They merely assert or describe or report events or states of affairs. To say that a house is green is purely informational; it will not change its color. But if I promise to paint your house that color, using the phrase *I promise* or an equivalent expression, I have performed an act that places me under an obligation to do so. Notice that if I use a verb in the past tense ("I promised to paint the house"), I am not promising by means of the speech act. Rather, I am reporting or describing a promise I made previously. Likewise, statements in the third person ("Jane promises to paint the house") are not performatives, except in the unusual situation in which the utterance is made by an agent who has the right to make promises on behalf of Jane.

Austin pointed out that when you engage in a performative speech act, you are doing something rather than merely saying or reporting something. He elaborated, "When I say 'I name this ship the *Queen Elizabeth*' I do not describe the christening ceremony, I actually perform the christening; and when I say 'I do' (sc. take this woman to be my lawful wedded wife), I am not reporting on a marriage, I am indulging in it."[55]

The difference between nonperformative and performative speech acts mirrors the distinction that I am making here between written reports or records, on the one hand, and authoritative legal texts, on the other. A report or record describes a legal transaction but does not constitute or perform it. In contrast, when the parties intend to textualize a transaction, the writing down (or signing or sealing) of a legal act constitutes or performs the transaction in question. It is therefore no accident that authoritative legal texts are so closely linked with performative verbs.

Who wrote the text, and when, are important prerequisites for textualization, but they are not sufficient. Nor is it enough that someone performs a legal transaction by means of writing. The truly critical element is that the author must intend the written text to be the definitive or authoritative expression of his intentions with respect to the transaction in question. In the legal sphere, the intent to textualize is often a fiction, just as authorship of a legal document like a will may be fictional. The maker of a will, whether she is aware of it or not, is deemed to speak through the will and is also deemed to have intended the will to be the definitive expression of her intentions with respect to the disposition of her property after she dies. Another way of saying it is that one of the literary conventions of Anglo-American law is that a will (with a few limited exceptions) can only be made by creating and executing an authoritative text. Every will is deemed to be textualized, even if the testator on whose behalf it speaks has no idea that this is so or what the consequences are. The same is true of statutes. Legislation consists of the text that the lawmakers enacted. What they said on the floor of the legislature or wrote down in reports can be useful in resolving ambiguities, but oral statements and unenacted documents are not statutes.

In other situations—contracts are the best example—legal actors are usually free to decide for themselves whether to textualize their agreement. Many contracts can be entirely oral. Even when a writing is required, making a record of the transaction—as opposed to an authoritative text—is usually sufficient. Textualizing the contract is an option, as we will explore in chapter 4, but it is usually not essential.

There are many other legal transactions that do not require the execution of an authoritative text. A common example is the marriage ceremony, which even today is almost always conducted orally before witnesses. You do not get married by signing a piece of paper but by saying the proper words ("I will" or "I do" or something along those lines) before someone who is legally authorized to marry people. Most states require that a record be made after the ceremony (usually by having a few witnesses sign a certificate), but that is purely evidentiary. The wedding is accomplished by engaging in the oral performance, not by signing a document.

In addition, one of the most important types of legal text, judicial opinions, are traditionally viewed as not being authoritative text, in contrast to statutes, which are heavily textualized. We will see in chapter 6, however, that in the United States there is a recent tendency to begin textualizing opinions.

Given the significance of textualization and its potential consequences, it is not surprising that it is generally accomplished with a certain amount of pomp and ritual. Wills are executed by being signed by the testator and witnessed by two or three people who must typically be present at the same time. Statutes must be enacted in accordance with detailed procedural rules, usually set forth in the constitutions of the federal and state governments.

The reason for the ritual is clear: to impress upon the actors and those affected by a transaction that the text in question is not just an informal record of a legal event. Rather, the text constitutes the transaction. This has a number of important implications.

Consequences of Textualization

When the parties to a legal transaction create an authoritative text, it is viewed as the definitive expression of its makers, who are deemed to speak through it. As a result, the text is viewed as replacing or superseding any words that might have been spoken before or during the execution or enactment of the text. The written supplants the oral, in other words. Any words or writing outside an authoritative text are effectively irrelevant. In some areas of the law, this principle is known as the *parol evidence rule*, one of the more important legal conventions relating to writing, which will be explored in detail in chapters 3 and 4.

Another consequence of textualization is that judges interpreting an authoritative text tend to determine its meaning primarily on the basis of the words contained in it. Under what is called the *plain meaning rule*, judges are not supposed to look at any other evidence of what the authors might have intended, including debates in the legislature before passing a statute, negotiations between parties to a contract, or what a testator told her lawyer before executing a will. Unless there is an obvious ambiguity or other recognized exception, the intentions of the makers of an authoritative legal text must be determined solely from the text. This convention has been weakened during the past century, especially in the United States, but to some extent it is still honored in England, as well as by textualist judges in America. The principle is relevant to both contracts and wills, but it has had its widest application in the law relating to statutes, as we will see in chapter 5.

Also, as a result of textualization, an authoritative text can usually be changed only by prescribed procedures that are similar to the formalities by which it was originally enacted or executed. This principle flows fairly naturally from the notion that the text is the definitive expression of the intentions of the legal actor. As a result, anything the author says or does outside the text—such as attempting to change the text informally—is legally invalid. For instance, the traditional rule is that a will can only be amended or revoked by executing another will (called a *codicil*). Statutes must also be formally amended or repealed. Even if a statute is declared unconstitutional, it technically remains in effect until it is repealed through the ordinary legislative process.

Lawyers, at least those in common law jurisdictions, will find these consequences unremarkable, since they have been steeped in the textual practices of the profession from the day they entered law school. Yet legal conventions of this kind, especially those relating to textualization, can cause problems for ordinary people who are unfamiliar with these practices. As we will elaborate in the next chapter, someone who makes a valid will giving $10,000 to her favorite niece, and who later crosses out "$10,000" and writes "$20,000" above it, has in many American jurisdictions made no change at all to the will, even if she places her initials or signature in the margin. In other jurisdictions, her niece will be shocked to discover that her dearly departed aunt inadvertently revoked the entire gift to her.

Likewise, many people would be surprised to find out that they are legally deemed the author of a will drafted for them in legalese by a lawyer, or of a lengthy and impenetrable contract that they accepted by opening a box containing software or clicking on a link. In cases of dispute, courts will generally hold them to the language of the will or contract, even if it was drafted by someone else and even if they scarcely understand it. In chapters 3 and 4 we will explore additional examples of conflict between ordinary and legal conventions of literacy.

To the average person, textualization may seem a rather bizarre phenomenon, something that only lawyers can appreciate. But despite the problems it can create for ordinary citizens, it fulfills some important functions. In the law of wills, for instance, it helps determine what is part of a person's will and what is not. Many people make numerous and often conflicting statements about who will get their possessions after they die. Yet if an asserted gift is not in the text of dear old uncle's testament, it will not be given to the nephew, no matter how often his uncle may have told him he would receive it. In the realm of contracts, rules requiring that certain types of agreements be written down can help prevent fraudulent claims about what might or might not have been said during negotiations. And the textualization of statutes is an important component of the rule of law. Only what a legislature properly enacts into law can be enforced. Lawmakers cannot govern by oral edicts or unexpressed intentions.

Modern technologies of communication will surely have an impact on authoritative legal texts. This is especially true with respect to how the documents are drafted or created. Almost all such texts are currently produced on computers using word processing software rather than being typed or handwritten. To the extent that these documents remain in an electronic format, they can easily be amended and updated, just as websites on the Internet are constantly being changed. The dynamic nature of the Internet is one of its most useful features.

In contrast, a traditional authoritative text is static and fixed, much like a printed book. Does this mean that textualization, along with the authoritative documents that it produces, is bound to become obsolete? Time will tell, but it seems to me that the benefits of being able to express your intentions in a relatively fixed and authoritative form are great enough that the process, in some form or other, is almost certain to endure for many years into the future.

Games and God

Obviously, legal texts are very different from more common documents like letters, grocery lists, novels, magazine articles, reports, memos, and the other types of writing with which most people are familiar. As a result, the discussion may so far have seemed quite esoteric and far removed from ordinary concerns. There are areas of life, however, that have textual practices similar to those of the law. One of them is games. Another is religion.

The Rules of the Game

Virtually all games have rules. Usually those rules develop organically, from the bottom up, rather than being imposed top down by a monarch or legislature. Suppose that a new game develops among a group of teenagers. As the need arises, they informally agree on rules that are considered binding on the players. When someone violates a rule, the other players object. The game spreads, and the rules spread along with it via word of mouth.

Now suppose that a graduate student in search of a dissertation topic discovers the game and begins to study it. She observes the teenagers playing it and is able to figure out what many of the rules seem to be. She also interviews the players to clarify some uncertainties. When the graduate student finishes her dissertation on the development of this new game, she includes a list of the rules in an appendix.

Obviously, the mere fact that someone has written down rules on paper does not change their essentially oral nature. The rules of the game are still whatever is in the memory of the players. The appendix to the dissertation is a record of the rules and might function as evidence of what they are, but the writing has no authority over the players. If the players acquire a copy of the dissertation, it is conceivable that one of them might refer to it in the event of a dispute about the rules. But the players will not feel themselves bound by what the researcher wrote in the appendix. Their memory and understanding of the rules is what matters.

Now suppose that as the number of players increases, they start to have more frequent disputes about what the rules require exactly. Sometimes there seems to be no rule when one is needed. So the players have a meeting during a large tournament and select five of their most experienced members to convene and write down the rules of the game. They all agree to abide by those rules. The five players hash out what the existing rules are and clarify some uncertainties. They then type them up and have copies distributed to all the team captains and referees.

This written list of rules is very different from the graduate student's appendix, even if the content is identical. It was created by the players themselves, who agreed to follow them. It is authoritative in a way that the graduate student's list of rules can never be. Like the graduate student's appendix, the text written by the players is evidence of what the rules are. But it is more. In a very real way, the players' text constitutes the rules of the game.

There is, of course, another way in which the players can create an authoritative written statement of their rules. They might have a copy of the graduate student's appendix and might find that she did such a good job that they consult it more and more frequently. With the passage of time, the players might agree—implicitly or expressly—that what is written in the appendix constitutes the rules of their game. Once they start quibbling over the choice of one word over another or the placement of a comma, we will know for certain that the rules have become authoritative text. The rules are no longer what is in the minds of the players. They now consist of the words on paper.

Religious Texts

Like the law, the major religions of the world all have their authoritative, or sacred, texts. Christians have the Bible, Jews the Torah, Muslims the Koran, and so on. I will discuss the Protestant tradition, which is most familiar to me, but all textual religions confront similar issues.

In the traditional view, the Bible is not just a historical record of God's involvement with the earth and the people who dwell there. Although the books of the Bible were obviously written by human beings, many Protestants believe that God himself is speaking through the text (via a process called *divine inspiration*). They base this view on texts like 2 Timothy 3:16, which states that "[a]ll scripture is given by inspiration of God."[56]

Of course, saying that scripture is divinely inspired does not necessarily mean that God dictated every word. But this is essentially how many Protestants view it. One of the fathers of the Reformation, John Calvin, wrote that through the Bible, God "opens his own sacred mouth."[57] Although the scriptures came to us "by the instrumentality of men," they actually emanated "from the very mouth of God."[58] To recognize the full authority of the scriptures, Calvin added, the faithful must believe them "to have come from heaven, as directly as if God had been heard giving utterance to them."[59] Although written by mortals, the scriptures were "dictated by the Holy Spirit."[60]

Although his views are not shared by all Christians, or even all Protestants, Calvin's approach to the sacred text of Christianity is remarkably similar to how the common law regards its own sacred texts. Just as God is deemed the author of the Bible, though the actual writing was done by mere mortals, a legislature is viewed as the author of statutes, even though most of the actual drafting is done by lawyers or bureaucrats. Legislators are held to speak through the texts they enact, just as God speaks through the Bible. Moreover, statutes are viewed not merely as containing the law, nor are they merely evidence of what the law is. They are the law. In the same way, many Christians reject the view that the Bible is just evidence or a record of God's word. Rather, it is the word of God. In fact, the Bible ends with a curse on anyone who adds to, or takes away from, the words of the book.[61]

This view of scripture does not inevitably require literal interpretation. But it does enable a textualist approach, just as the increasing authoritativeness of legislative texts over the centuries promoted the development of a very literal approach to the interpretation of statutes (a process discussed in chapter 5). Many Protestants have a similar view regarding interpretation of the Bible. Martin Luther declared that scripture interprets itself: *Scriptura sui ipsius interpres*.[62] If there are doubts or uncertainties regarding a particular passage, they should be resolved by looking at other parts of the text, not by seeking guidance from evidence outside of it.[63] God had essentially textualized his message in the Bible, according to Luther:

> [The Holy Spirit's] words cannot have more than one, and that the very simplest sense, which we call the literal, ordinary, natural sense. . . . We are not

> to say that the Scriptures or the Word of God have more than one meaning . . . We are not to introduce any . . . metaphorical, figurative sayings into any text of Scripture, unless the particulars of the words compel us to do so . . .[64]

Despite reverence for their sacred text, traditional Protestants never developed an extreme form of literalism. This was left to the Fundamentalist movement in the United States, which held sway particularly in the American South (the "Bible belt") during the first part of the twentieth century. The name of the movement comes from a series of tracts, called *The Fundamentals*, published by biblical scholars at Princeton Seminary. The Fundamentalists are probably best known for their opposition to the teaching of evolution in schools, but their basic premise was the inerrancy of scripture, which they believed required a strictly literal interpretation. Thus, because the Bible said that God created the world in six days and rested on the seventh, scientific claims relating to evolution must be false. *Six days* means six days, not millions of years.

It's interesting to observe that a strict textual interpretation can be completely consistent with the aim of trying to determine the meaning of the speaker. The standard view of legal commentators is that textualism and intentionalism are diametrically opposed approaches to interpretation and completely incompatible. Yet fundamentalists are clearly trying to figure out what God intended to communicate in the Bible. Their literalism derives from the great respect that they have for the text, which they believe came directly from the mouth of God and which is therefore God's definitive and complete expression of his intentions. It would border on heresy to suggest that God did not speak in the plainest of words. Textualist judges seem to have a similar attitude regarding the sacred texts of the law.[65]

In light of these similarities between law and religion, it is tempting to consider how notions of text and interpretation in these two realms may have influenced each other. Fundamentalism was a homegrown American movement, and the teachings of Calvin were the basis for Puritan theology in New England. Some scholars have suggested that Calvinism had an impact on the law that developed there, particularly in its attraction to written law and literal interpretation.[66] And Harold Berman has argued that Calvinism substantially influenced the development of the common law in seventeenth-century England.[67]

Cross-fertilization of ideas is certainly possible. Yet despite some thought-provoking similarities, we should probably not draw too close an analogy between legal and religious texts. It is worth observing that the common law system, which reached its fruition in a mainly Protestant society, is in many ways more Catholic than Protestant. Catholic theology is based not just on the Bible, but also on many traditions that have developed within the church over the centuries. Many important doctrines, like those relating to papal infallibility and the celibacy of the priesthood, have no clear textual basis in the Bible but are grounded primarily in tradition, both written and unwritten, and in the authority of the pope to authoritatively interpret the Bible in the same way that common law judges can interpret statutes.[68] Catholic tradition is therefore analogous to the common law in that both rely on a nontextual source of authority: tradition in the case of religion and precedent in the case of the law. At the same time, both recognize that tradition or precedent cannot contradict written law, be it scripture or legislation.

Yet even if there is no clear relationship between legal and religious theories of meaning, it is remarkable that these two spheres of life developed such similar hermeneutic traditions (including fierce debates about the proper method of interpreting their sacred texts). What we can learn by comparing religion and law is that any valid approach to interpretation must be informed by a theory regarding the nature of the text that it purports to interpret. Those who believe that the Bible was dictated by God are going to understand it differently from those who regard it as a historical record created by fallible human beings.

Analogously, a will that is made orally and whose terms are later recorded by a scribe will be interpreted differently from one that is written and signed by the testator herself. The same is true of laws made orally by the king and his council, as opposed to laws made by the king enacting written text. Likewise, how we understand a judicial opinion or judgment, which is at the core of our notion of precedent, depends a great deal on whether it was the judge or a reporter who wrote down the words, whether they were uttered orally or in writing, whether the judgment consists of multiple opinions or a single opinion written on behalf of the court as a whole. It also matters whether documents of this sort are handwritten on paper or parchment, are printed and widely distributed, or are available on the Internet for all the world to read.

In the rest of this book we will consider the impact that writing and other technologies for storing and communicating information have had on our legal system. We will concentrate on the common law that arose in England and spread to many of its former colonies, in particular, the United States. The common law distinguishes itself from most other legal systems in that the decisions or opinions of its judges are sources of law (collectively known as *case law* or *precedent*). Of course, statutes (laws enacted by Parliament, Congress, or some other legislature) are also sources of law in common law jurisdictions. We will see later in this book that the textual conventions relating to these two sources of law are quite distinct, in large part because statutes are quintessentially written, whereas judicial opinions have a long tradition of orality.

Contracts, wills, and other types of private legal texts made in common law systems are also quite distinct, especially when compared with those in civil law countries. The civil law, which holds sway in most of Europe and Latin America as well as in parts of Asia and Africa, derives to a large extent from Roman law and has very different textual conventions. Many legal documents are not drafted by the parties to the transaction (or their lawyers) but rather by a legal official known as a *notary*. Although a comparative study would be quite interesting, we will generally limit ourselves to the common law tradition that prevails in most English-speaking countries.

We begin with the law of wills, which are highly textualized, and then move on in the next chapter to contracts, where there is much variation in this regard. Moreover, the law of wills has stoutly resisted modern technologies of communication, whereas contracts law has embraced them. Juxtaposing these two text types may therefore allow us to better understand their similarities and differences, as well as to seek explanations for why they have taken such divergent paths.

3
Wills

The oldest known written wills come from the Middle East. There are some surviving wills from ancient Mesopotamia, for instance, although they are relatively scarce. For the most part, the rules of inheritance or succession were fixed and could not be changed by will.[1] Written wills also appear to have been used in ancient Egypt. The document had to be recorded in the vizier's office to be valid. It was also possible to make an oral declaration in court, which if witnessed and transcribed became a valid will.[2] Likewise, the ancient Athenians recognized wills, although for the most part they could only be used by testators who did not have male heirs.[3]

It was in Rome that written wills became common. The earliest Roman testaments appear to have been oral declarations before a popular assembly. During the classical period, the *testamentum per aes et libram* arose. It required a ceremony to be performed before several witnesses. The participants were the testator (the person making the will) and the *familiae emptor*, who represented the heirs and appears to have functioned something like a modern trustee or executor. Each of them uttered ritualistic words. The *familiae emptor* struck a weigh scale (*libra*) with a piece of copper (*aes*) and gave the copper to the testator. Although the ceremony seems to have normally involved a written will, it appears that initially the performance of the ritual was the critical element. Over time, however, the writing came to be regarded as essential, and the ceremony receded into the background.[4] Later Roman law developed some other varieties of wills, including one in which a blind man could dictate his will to a scribe before seven witnesses, as well as a *holographic* will (one written entirely in the handwriting of the testator, which therefore did not require witnesses).[5]

The Roman empire, which made extensive use of writing for legal purposes, came to an end around the fifth century, and in western Europe most of the Roman law was forgotten or superseded by tribal or customary law during the following centuries.

The eastern Roman empire, however, continued for several centuries in the form of the Byzantine empire, whose capital was Constantinople (now Istanbul). Roman law survived in Byzantium largely because of the emperor Justinian, who in the sixth century had scholars write down the law in a work called the *Corpus Juris Civilis*. It had largely been forgotten in the West. Some five hundred years afterward, in the latter part of the eleventh century, legal scholars in Bologna, Italy, acquired copies of the *Corpus Juris* and reintroduced Roman law to western Europe. Their work ultimately led to the development of the civil law, which is the name given to the legal systems of almost all of western Europe, Latin America, and many other countries around the world.[6] But that's another story. Our main concern in this book is the law of wills that originated in England.

A Brief History of English Wills

Although the Romans occupied England for several centuries, their language and law largely disappeared when the Roman legions left the British Isles. Of course, the Celtic inhabitants of England may well have preserved some Roman legal practices and customs even after the Romans departed. All this changed when various Germanic tribes from the continent, including Angles and Saxons, invaded the island. The Celtic people in England were killed, fled, or were assimilated into the Anglo-Saxon population.

The Anglo-Saxon Period

When they first came to England, the Anglo-Saxons were mostly illiterate, although some of them were familiar with a system of writing called the runic alphabet. The runes are variously thought to have been modeled on

Greek, Latin, or perhaps even Etruscan writing systems. Most of the runic texts, if we can call them that, are extremely short. Usually they consist of inscriptions on gravestones or on personal possessions declaring the name of the owner or maker. A famous inscription on the Golden Horn of Gallehus can be translated as "I, Hlegest of Holt, made the horn."[7] As far as we can tell, runes were not used for legal purposes.

During the early Anglo-Saxon period, therefore, legal transactions would have been entirely oral. This situation began to change with the conversion of the Anglo-Saxons to Christianity, beginning around the year 600. Along with the missionaries came the Latin language, the Roman alphabet, and a priestly class that had a tradition of reading and writing.[8] To be more exact, the Latin language and literacy returned to England after an absence of around two centuries. Before long, written compilations of laws began to appear. Not too much later we begin to see charters, wills, writs, and other legal documents. Although some of these texts were in Latin, many were composed in the Anglo-Saxon language, which is also known as Old English.

Our concern in this chapter is wills. A few dozen Anglo-Saxon wills have been preserved, and in some ways they seem surprisingly modern, reflecting many of the same concerns that people have today. Like current testators, Anglo-Saxons tended to give land to their spouses and children. Sometimes a man would give a life estate to his wife, with the remainder to go to their children. And testators often gave personal possessions, like jewelry or weapons, to friends or relatives.

Yet despite some superficial similarities, Anglo-Saxon wills are markedly different from their modern counterparts. For example, many of them contain a curse at the end, invoking eternal damnation on anyone who refuses to obey the instructions in the document. There are also requests to a king or other overlord to allow the will to carried out:

> *. . . god aelmihtig hine awende of eallum godes dreame. and of ealra cristenra gemanan. se ðe þis awende. butan hit min án cynehlaford sy. and ic hópyge to him swa gódan. and swa míldheortan [þat] he hit nylle sylf dón. ne eac nanum oþrum menn geþafian.*
>
> [. . . and whoever perverts this, may God Almighty remove him from all God's joy and from the communion of all Christians, unless it be my royal lord alone, and I believe him to be so good and so gracious that he will not himself do it, nor permit any other man to do so.][9]

The use of curses and appeals to the beneficence of the king suggest a legal regime in which the likelihood of having one's desires carried out after death was uncertain. The word *will* suggests as much, since if a person said "I will" in Old English (*ich wille*), it would have meant 'I desire,' rather than referring to what "will" happen in the future. Testamentary documents of this period also reflect a more religious era, as evidenced by the almost universal gifts to churches and monasteries, usually to finance masses and prayers for one's soul.

From our perspective, there is a more significant way in which the documents called Anglo-Saxon wills differ from their modern equivalents. Most or all of these legal texts were not what lawyers today would call *dispositive* or *operative* or what linguists might call a *performative* document. Rather, they are written records of spoken legal transactions. While in some respects they have the look and feel of a modern will, they actually perform a radically different function.

There are a number of indications that Anglo-Saxon wills were merely records of oral transactions. One piece of evidence is that the Old English word for a will, *cwide* or *cwiðe*, derives from the verb *cweðan*, whose primary meaning is "to speak." An archaic remnant of the verb is *quoth*, as in Edgar Allen Poe's famous line "quoth the raven 'nevermore'." It is also related to the verb *bequeath*.

Further evidence that Anglo-Saxon wills were not operative or performative documents is that they generally have no signature or seal or other type of authentication. This suggests that what really mattered was the words that came from the testator's mouth, not what was written on parchment afterward. The names of witnesses were typically included in the document, but they likewise did not normally sign or place a seal on the document. Their function was to remember the contents of the testator's will, on the basis of what the testator said. In contrast, modern witnesses testify mainly to the fact that the document is authentic. The contents of the testator's will are determined by examining the written text. As a matter of fact, in many or most cases modern witnesses have no idea what the will provides, since the testator is not required to explain the will's contents to them or to let them read it.

There is also linguistic evidence that Anglo-Saxon wills were primarily oral. Many begin with phrasing such as the following: "*HER is geswutelod an ðis gewrite hu Ælfheah ealdorman his cwidæ gecwæðan hæfð. . .*" [Here in this document it is declared how the ealdorman Ælfheah has declared his will . . .].[10] This language strongly suggests that the document is simply reporting or declaring (*geswutelod*) what the testator has already said (*gecwæðan*). A better translation might be, "This document reports how Ælfheah the ealdorman spoke his will . . ."

Additionally, grammatical evidence supports the notion that the texts called Anglo-Saxon wills are in fact records of oral acts that had already taken place. The philosopher J. L. Austin pointed out that certain types of utterances, which he called *performatives*, allow a speaker to do an act simply by saying something.[11] As we briefly discussed in chapter 2, performative statements usually have a verb in the first person and are in the present tense. Thus, the phrases *I appoint* or *we appoint* can be used to perform the act of appointing. In contrast, saying *I appointed* (past tense) or *Bob appoints* (third person) does not normally constitute the act of appointing; instead, it merely describes that act.[12] Austin also observed that performative utterances allow for the insertion of *hereby* into the sentence, while descriptive utterances generally do not. *I hereby appoint* sounds fine, while *I hereby appointed* is ungrammatical.[13]

Austin was aware of the legal implications of his observations. He noted that *I give and bequeath my watch to my brother* is a performative utterance, one that in the proper circumstances can be used to perform the act of giving or bequeathing.[14] Notice that *hereby* can easily be inserted in the above example. On the other hand, the sentence *I gave and bequeathed my watch to my brother* is not a performative utterance; it is merely a report or description of an act of bequeathing that has already occurred.

Applying these insights to early English wills, if the written texts that we have inherited were meant to perform the act of transferring property at death, we would expect to encounter mostly performative utterances, just as we do in a modern will (*I declare, I give, I appoint*, etc.). On the other hand, if the wills of that period were records of a primarily oral event, we might expect a more mixed picture. In that case, the essential performative utterances would be made orally by the testator, in the first person, present tense. The written record, made by a cleric, would either report those words directly, using verbatim quotation (*I give*), or indirectly as reported speech (*Peter gave*).

This mixed picture is precisely what we encounter. Some of the Anglo-Saxon written wills contain performative utterances that resemble language in modern wills. An example is the will of Bishop Theodred: "*Ic þeodred Lundeneware Biscop wille biquethen mine quiden mines erfes* . . ." [I, Theodred, Bishop of the people of London, wish to announce my will concerning my property . . .].[15] Initially, it might seem that Theodred—who as a priest would have known how to write—was speaking through a written text that he had drafted himself (or that was drafted for him in his voice).

After all, the words quoted above are in the first person and present tense, as is most of the rest of the will. Yet tellingly, the writer of the text at one point slipped into the third person, using *he* and *his*, and then later in the same sentence switched back to the first person (*ic*):

> *þat is þan erst þat he an his louerd his heregete. þat is þanne tua hund marcas arede goldes and tua cuppes siluerene. and four hors so ic best habbe. and to suerde so ic best habbe . . .*
>
> [First, he grants to his lord his heriot, namely, two hundred marks of red gold, and two silver cups and four horses, the best that I have, and two swords the best that I have . . .].[16]

It thus appears that when Anglo-Saxon wills use the first person, they are likely to be directly quoting an underlying oral event. When they switch to the third person, they also are reporting speech, but doing so indirectly. Both ways of reporting someone else's speech are quite common. We can say either, "John said 'I am going to the store,'" or "John said that he was going to the store." In contrast, it is highly unusual for people to refer to themselves in the third person (using *he* and *his*).

Anglo-Saxon scribes also tended to mix the present and past tense of verbs. An example is the will of Ælfhelm, which begins in the third person, past tense: "Herein is the declaration of how Ælfhelm has disposed of his property . . . " It continues in the third person, present tense: "And for his soul he grants to St Etheldreda's the estate at Wratting . . . " In the very next sentence, however, it states, "And I grant the estate at Brickendon to St Peter's at Westminster . . . "[17] It thus vacillates between first and third person, present and past tense. In other words, the scribe switches between direct and indirect reporting of an oral event. If the testator were speaking through the written text, one would expect to find the first person, present tense, consistently used throughout the will.

These observations have been made before. Cambridge law professor Harold Dexter Hazeltine, in his general preface to Dorothy Whitelock's compilation of Anglo-Saxon wills, argued quite compellingly that written Old English wills reflect underlying oral events.[18] Linguists Brenda Danet and Bryna Bogoch have also discussed the text of wills during the Anglo-Saxon period.[19] In contrast to Hazeltine, they argue that written wills from this time were not purely evidentiary and that there was at least an incipient attempt "to invest the document with performative power."[20]

It is certainly possible that the Anglo-Saxons were beginning to view writing as an important aspect of will making. Nonetheless, there is no doubt that, for the most part, to make a will in Anglo-Saxon England required engaging in an oral act before witnesses. The writing of the terms was either not required or was of secondary importance.

After the Norman Conquest

The essentially oral nature of English will making seems to have persisted after the Norman Conquest in 1066. As Michael Sheehan pointed out in his study of medieval English wills, "[a]ll evidence leads to the conclusion that the written wills were intended merely as evidentiary documents, that they were made when the legally effective act was complete and occasionally much later, and that, in some cases, their information was but a partial report of the provisions of the act."[21]

Not only were the written documents frequently incomplete, but they were also not authoritative text in the modern sense. If there was a question later about the testator's intentions, the document would probably have been consulted, but a court might give equal or greater weight to the testimony of witnesses.

Yet as people grew increasingly comfortable with literacy, the written text became more than just the recollections of a witness who wrote down a summary of what he had heard. Many of these changes become perceptible in documents from the thirteenth century, a time when—as historian M. T. Clanchy has shown—written records started to proliferate in England.[22] Sheehan observed that documents gradually ceased to be regarded as just another type of evidence of what had happened at an oral event. They were coming to be preferred to the testimony of witnesses. By the end of the century, wills were being read in court. And the function of witnesses was also evolving; they were increasingly being questioned about the authenticity of the seal.[23] Even though the oral act was probably still primary, writing was coming to be regarded as the best evidence of what the testator had said. Witnesses were being demoted to guarantors of the authenticity of the document.

There are distinct advantages to requiring written evidence of a person's will. Witnesses might not be able to remember all of a testator's bequests, or they might have died. Writing can preserve information, including precise details, over long periods of time. The evidentiary value of writing down the provisions of a will does not, however, mean that the will is a written text. Making a will can still be an oral act, even if there is a requirement that someone write down the terms.

Wills Become Text

This is not the end of the matter, however. Although the historical details are complex, the English law of wills came to require that the performative or dispositive act, which in the past consisted of the speaking of certain words, should now consist of writing those words. The text was no longer just a record of an oral will. It was now the will itself.

One indication of this change in attitude is that starting in the thirteenth century the tense of the dispositive verbs slowly shifted from the past to the present.[24] As we noted previously, use of the present tense in a legal text is an important indicator that the actor is performing the act in question by means of those words. Furthermore, the testator's bequests were often reduced to writing immediately, rather than some time after the fact.[25] And there is language in the wills themselves to suggest that the essential legal act is the writing of the document, including phrases like *virtute istius testamenti* ('by virtue of this testament') or *per hoc scriptum* ('by means of this writing'). Although testators did not yet normally sign their wills, they started affixing a seal. Sheehan concluded that there was developing, at least in some circles, the notion that the execution and sealing of a written will was essential to its validity.[26]

Writing was therefore no longer just an adjunct to the making of a will; it became the act itself. This principle was gradually codified by three important English statutes, which underlie not just the English law of wills but have also been extremely influential in the United States. One was the Statute of Wills of 1540, which allowed a person to dispose of certain types of land after death, but only (in modern English spelling) "by his last will and testament in writing."[27] Next came the Statute of Frauds, enacted in 1677, under which bequests or devises of land "shall be in writing and signed by the party . . . or by some other person in his presence and by his express directions and shall be attested and subscribed in the presence of the said devisor by three or four credible witnesses."[28] At the same time, the statute allowed for the continued use of oral (or nuncupative) wills for bequests of personal property, if made at the home of the deceased during his last sickness and in the presence of three witnesses.[29]

The Wills Act of 1837 finally required that all wills—not just those involving land—be in writing. It specified that they had to be signed by the testator at the end or foot thereof, that the testator had to sign the will, or to acknowledge his signature, before two witnesses who were present at the same time, and that the witnesses must attest and sign the will in the presence of the testator.[30] Although enacted in England, it was imitated in many American states.

The supremacy of writing was now complete. Not only must there be a writing, but the legal actor must sign it. Whether he writes the document himself or has someone draft it for him, by signing the will the testator adopts the words contained in it as his own. The testator's intentions are no longer reflected by what he said. Instead, his intentions are expressed by a document that he signed, a writing that was in most cases drafted by someone else using language and concepts that the testator himself might scarcely understand. Nonetheless, those written words are generally regarded as the definitive expression of his intentions. To apply the terminology introduced in chapter 2, the effect of these statutes is to require that all wills must be textualized. A person's will is no longer what is in his mind or in the memories of witnesses, but a text that has been formally executed by being signed, acknowledged, and witnessed.

A final critical development was the *parol evidence rule*. With some limited exceptions, the rule forbids judges from considering any evidence outside of the will itself. Thus, the text is not just supreme, but also exclusive.[31] All of the testator's intentions must be contained in the text of the will. Whatever else the testator might say or write becomes almost entirely irrelevant. At this stage, therefore, wills are fully textualized. Although there is somewhat of a backlash against it, this situation still largely holds true today.

The Execution of Wills

As a result of these developments, wills are among the most highly textual of all legal documents. The process of executing a will (that is to say, bringing it into effect or making it legally valid) also has some of the most rigid and strictly enforced requirements found in any area of the law. This is not just happenstance. The formalities of execution and the process of textualization are closely linked.

The Formalities of Execution

Although the details vary by jurisdiction, one of the requirements for executing a modern will is that it be in writing. The act of writing, in other words, is not just evidence but is essential to the process of making a valid will. Oral wills (sometimes called *nuncupative wills*) have become completely impossible in just about all common law jurisdictions.

Equally important is acknowledging and signing the will, which the testator must do in the presence of at least two witnesses. In the alternative, a modern testator can usually sign the will and then show the signature to the witnesses and declare to them that it is hers. Unlike the situation in Anglo-Saxon times, the witnesses do not need to know the contents, but they must be aware that this is the testator's will.

There are also strict rules regarding the witnessing of the will. To "witness" a will does not just mean seeing the testator sign (or acknowledge) the will and being prepared to testify to that effect in court. It requires that the witnesses also sign the document. Moreover, the traditional rule—still enforced in some jurisdictions—is that the witnesses must be present at the same time when witnessing and signing the will.[32] Thus, if the testator acknowledges a will before one witness, who signs it without another witness being present, and then does the same before a second witness, who also signs it, the will is invalid.[33]

Careful lawyers take additional precautions to ensure a will's validity. They attach all the pages to one another and number each page as "1 of 6," "2 of 6," and so on. They may also have the testator initial every page. They hold the signing ceremony in a room where no unnecessary persons are present and sometimes go so far as to lock the door while it is taking place. They may ask the testator, in the presence of the witnesses, whether she has read the will and understands it.[34]

Witnesses are not always essential. In a number of American jurisdictions it is possible to make *holographic* wills, just as in Roman law. Most commonly, they are found in southern and western states, which in days past were on the frontier, where lawyers were few and far between. Typically, the entire will, or at least all "material provisions," as well as the signature must be in the handwriting of the testator. Holographic wills are exceptional, however, and seem to be tolerated by those jurisdictions that allow them, rather than being encouraged.

Functions of the Formalities

The traditional reasons for requiring the rather burdensome formalities of execution were nicely summarized in a classic article by Ashbel Gulliver and Catherine Tilson.[35] One purpose of the formalities is what Gulliver and Tilson called the *ritual function*. People are often careless in conversation and informal writings. A court needs to be sure that the statements of the testator were meant to be legally effective, not just casual comments about who might inherit what. Therefore, some ceremony or ritual is usually required, since ritual puts people on notice that they are doing something important, in this case, disposing of their possessions after they die.[36]

Legal formalities may also increase the reliability of evidence presented in court. Gulliver and Tilson observed that oral testimony is often inaccurate because of lapses of memory, misinterpretation of the statements of others, and conscious or unconscious coloring of recollection in light of the personal interest of a witness. They referred to the importance of supplying satisfactory proof as the *evidentiary function*.[37]

Finally, Gulliver and Tilson identified what they called the *protective function*. Legal formalities may have the prophylactic purpose of safeguarding the actor against threats, undue influence, or other forms of imposition. While courts seem to place great emphasis on this function, Gulliver and Tilson themselves were less convinced of its importance, doubting both the value of this objective and the extent to which existing formalities accomplish it.[38]

These functions go far in explaining the often rigid attitude that courts have, even today, in insisting on compliance with the formalities associated with the execution of wills. The highly formulaic language of most wills and the ceremonials surrounding the signing and attestation help fulfill the ritual function. The requirements that a will be in writing and that it be signed by the testator provide excellent evidence of what the testator's intentions are. And the witnesses, who are usually present when the testator signs the will, provide some minimal protection against coercion or undue influence.

It's interesting to note that the Anglo-Saxon procedure for making an oral will likewise fulfilled these functions. There was typically a great deal of ritual. Although the act was oral, it was performed as a public ceremony, sometimes before the royal council.[39] Moreover, there was plenty of evidence. In contrast to the modern practice of having two or maybe three witnesses, old English will ceremonials could be formally witnessed by as many as ten or even fifteen people.[40] The highly public nature of the ceremony and the large number of witnesses would also provide some protection against coercion or undue influence.

Overall, however, it seems to me that the modern formalities do a better job promoting the functions identified by Gulliver and Tilson, especially in terms of evidence. Given what we know about the frailty of memory, having a written record of a testator's intentions is normally more reliable than testimony by witnesses many years after the fact. Of course, use of documents opens up the possibility of forgery and fraud. In fact, it is probably easier to forge a single document than to induce several witnesses to lie. Nonetheless, the current procedure of having the testator sign the will in the presence of witnesses, or acknowledge her signature, does provide a certain level of protection against forgery. In addition, when courts are trying to carry out the terms of a will, being able to refer to a written document is far more convenient than tracking down two or three witnesses to discover what the testator's intentions were.

The Textualizing Function

Gulliver and Tilson's analysis is enlightening as far as it goes, but I believe that it omits another highly significant function of wills formalities. This is what I will call the *textualizing function*. The formalities of execution take ordinary words and transform them into authoritative text. That text, as we have seen, will be deemed to be the definitive and complete expression of the testator's intentions regarding the disposition of her estate after her death.

As mentioned, a textualized document is regarded as authoritative or definitive in the sense that it is held to encapsulate the final intentions of the legal actor. In contrast, a mere record or memorandum does not have such pretensions. You can always argue that a record is incorrect, especially if it was made by someone other than the legal actor. A memorandum can function as a powerful witness to what the testator said but is often not the only indication of the testator's intent. An obvious advantage of textualizing the legal actor's intentions is that the writing is not just another piece of evidence of an underlying oral event, nor is it merely the best evidence, but it becomes the event itself. Absent special circumstances, any other indications of the testator's intentions become irrelevant. In theory, at least, textualization greatly simplifies the process of determining what a legal actor intended to accomplish. This benefits not just the legal system but also the testator, who is given a high degree of assurance that the intentions that she has written into a will or other legal document will be carried out. In other words, textualization empowers a person to authoritatively or definitively set forth her intentions in a way that would not otherwise be possible.

Textualization is also extremely useful in clarifying what is included in the will and what is not. A testator might leave behind an array of indications regarding her testamentary intentions, running the gamut from informal statements, to personal letters, to lists containing gifts of personal possessions, to documents that might or might not be considered wills. Given that they often contradict each other, which of these expressions of testamentary intent should be given effect?

Although the formalities of execution are strict, it turns out that the concept of a will is in certain respects very flexible and abstract. The text of a will includes not just the physical document bearing the title "Last Will and Testament." Rather, it extends to all writings that are executed with the proper formalities, along with those that become part of the text by ancillary doctrines like incorporation by reference or republication by codicil. A better term for a will in this more abstract sense is *testamentary text*.

Thus, if someone properly executes a will in the year 2000, it is clearly part of the testamentary text, assuming the formalities were observed. Suppose that the will states that it incorporates by reference a letter by the testator to her niece that is located in the testator's safe deposit box. As long as that letter was in existence when the will was executed, it becomes part of the testamentary text. Now imagine that in 2005 the testator executes a codicil, which is essentially an amendment to a will that must be executed with the same formalities. That codicil also becomes part of the testamentary text, and it effectively republishes it as well, so that all of the text is deemed to have been executed on the date of the codicil.[41]

When deciding what happens to the testator's estate after her death, the entire testamentary text—and only the testamentary text—must be considered. It must be interpreted as a single document, with more recent provisions superseding any inconsistent earlier provisions. On the other hand, any other documents or letters or utterances by the testator purporting to transfer property at her death are not part of it and will not be carried out. Textualization thus helps determine what is in and what is out, or—to be more exact—what is part of the testamentary text and what it not.

The text of wills is abstract in another sense. Despite the emphasis on writing, a will can often be probated even if the physical text has been lost. Of course, it will be necessary to prove its contents with sufficient evidence, such as the testimony of the lawyer who drafted it or the secretary who typed it. Thus, what is critical for the validity of a modern will is not the physical existence of a text, but the fact that the testator (often by means of a lawyer) expressed her intentions by the act of writing them down and complying with the requirements of execution. It is the process of textualization, not the resulting physical text, that is essential.

Finally, textualization also guarantees that the text is the complete expression of the legal actor's intent. To a some degree this overlaps with the points made previously, but it bears emphasizing. When you create an authoritative testamentary text, you can have a high degree of confidence that the intentions in that text will be carried out, and none other. There should be no unexpected surprises. You should not have to fear that an ill-considered offhand comment you made to a niece after a couple of beers or an e-mail you once sent her will allow her to claim part of your estate.

Conflicting Textual Conventions

Although the distinct literary practices of the legal profession perform several useful functions, they can severely frustrate the uninitiated. One reason is that our culture—despite high levels of literacy—remains surprisingly oral. Linguist Naomi Baron, in discussing the history of literacy in the English-speaking world, points out that throughout the Middle Ages, writing served mainly to transcribe or record speech. As we have seen, this is reflected in the oral character of early English wills, including those that were recorded in writing. Yet by the seventeenth century, according to Baron, the written word was developing its own autonomous identity.

More recently, however, that process has to some extent been reversed. Especially since World War II, writing is once again beginning to reflect speech more closely, narrowing the gap between spoken and written English.[42] Orality is on the rise.

Two or three hundred years ago, just about the only way to communicate a message over distance or time was by means of writing on paper or parchment. Modern modes of communication initially did little beyond transmitting the written word. But more recent technological developments, such as telephones and television, are almost entirely oral media. Even that most modern means of communication—e-mail—which in some respects has revived the written word, in many ways more closely resembles a spoken conversation than formal written text.

Writing has also become more like speech in that it has become less permanent. In the Middle Ages writing materials were costly and documents were expensive to produce, but the result (especially if written on parchment) tended to endure. Changing a text or producing a new one was not easy. Today, of course, creating or modifying a text is an almost trivial endeavor. Paper is cheap and ink is plentiful. Text on a computer is even easier to manipulate. Moreover, much modern writing—like speech—is not expected to endure.

Consequently, we live in a society that is relatively oral. Even though we still produce a great deal of written text, including e-mail and text messages, much of the writing we currently do is similar to speech in that it tends to be informal, contextual, and often quite transient. As David Crystal has observed, the characteristics attributed to speech and writing, which we discussed in the previous chapter, do not apply all that well to language on the Internet. Certain types of online writing are "much closer to the kind of interaction more typical of speech."[43]

Have these changes in the nature of literacy been reflected in the law? To a large extent, it seems to me, the legal system—especially but certainly not exclusively the law of wills—remains at a relatively high point of literacy, where writing is regarded as authoritative and permanent. Not surprisingly, this has led to a clash between the highly literate culture of the law and the substantially more oral culture of everyday life.

Oral and Holographic Wills

One of the most important textual requirements of wills is that they must be in writing. As we saw above, there is a long tradition of allowing oral wills, especially in situations in which people are likely to die soon, as is the case with soldiers on the battlefield or people on their deathbeds. Today, however, oral wills are completely invalid in almost all American jurisdictions. The same is true of attempted oral changes to a written will. You could declare your will under oath before the Supreme Court of the United States or proclaim it on television before millions of viewers, but legally it would be a nullity.

Of course, the average person in our society knows that when engaging in legal transactions, it is best to "get it in writing." He would also realize the importance of a signature, both to authenticate the writing and also to give it legal force. It seems that people are to some degree cognizant of the ritual and evidentiary functions associated with writing and signing a document.

Yet a substantial number of people would be surprised to discover that—ostensibly for their own protection—a document entitled "Last Will and Testament" and signed by the testator, but lacking the signature of two witnesses, is not usually a valid will. You can engage in just about any legal transaction by buying the proper form and signing it, unless it happens to be a will. This is true even if there is absolutely no question that you personally bought the document, filled it in, and placed your signature on it.

One exception is holographic wills, briefly mentioned above. Generally, the important provisions of the will and the signature must be in the testator's handwriting. If so, it is valid in many American states, even without witnesses. But here again the testator may be in for a surprise. Most literate people would think that an official legal document should be typed or printed rather than handwritten. Just about all important legal documents are printed or typed. Those who follow this quite logical assumption, carefully typing their last wishes into a computer, printing the document, signing it, and storing it with their important papers, will have their intentions frustrated.

An illustration is a case from Colorado, where a man invited two friends to a birthday party for his long-term partner. He presented the partner with a birthday card containing a typewritten letter, which expressed his wishes that if anything happened to him, the partner should inherit all his possessions. Not long thereafter, he died, and a relative contested this will. The courts held that the document was not a formal will, nor was it a holographic will, because the deceased had typed it rather than writing it out by hand.[44] If you type your will and sign it, it is not valid because you also need the signatures of two witnesses.

In contrast, those who handwrite their wills on the bottom of a chest of drawers or on a bedroom wall or on a stepladder or on the fender of a tractor stand a good chance of having their intentions carried out, assuming they had the good sense to include a signature or their initials, simply because they used handwriting rather than typing or printing.[45] No witnesses are required for a holographic will. In the law of wills, scrawling on a wall is good but typing on paper is bad. Who but lawyers could dream up such a system?

Legal scholar Adam Hirsch, in an article entitled "Inheritance and Inconsistency," refers to such competing doctrines as "jarringly, carelessly, almost randomly out of harmony with one another."[46] He notes, among many other examples, that the use of holographic wills has created a schizophrenic situation in those states that allow them. A will must either strictly comply with the required formalities or it must be completely informal (in the testator's handwriting and signed by her). He observes that this is the rule despite the fact that typing and printing typically indicate greater formality than handwriting.[47] A will must be completely formal or completely informal—anything in between is likely to be held invalid.

Printed (fill-in-the-blank) wills, sold in many stationary stores, create similar problems. People commonly buy them, fill in the blanks, sign them, and eventually die. Often this is the only testamentary instrument that they leave behind, but courts traditionally declare them invalid. They are not valid formal wills unless the testator properly executed them and had them signed by two witnesses. And they often do not qualify as holographic wills because too much of the will is printed (holographic wills must be entirely, or largely, in the handwriting of the testator).[48] Notice that those who download a form will from the Internet or who use will-making software will fare even worse if they simply fill in the blanks on their computer, print the form, and sign it. It would obviously not constitute a valid formal will, and even a sympathetic judge could not enforce it as a holographic will because none of it is in the testator's handwriting.

In addition to handwriting, holographic wills require a signature. That may seem natural enough, but this requirement can also lead to unjust results. Consider a recent case in which I had some personal involvement. A man in Los Angeles was in the hospital and apparently sensed that the end was nigh. He found a piece of paper and captioned it his "will." On it he wrote that he wanted all his money, which turned out to be a substantial sum, to go to a specified nonprofit organization that provides housing for people of modest means. He handed it to a doctor who came to check on him. The doctor added a note on the back of the paper indicating that the man seemed lucid and that he had told the doctor that the paper contained his will. The doctor initialed and dated the note. Soon thereafter the man's condition worsened and he died.

Was his will valid? In just about every state, the answer would be no. As a result, the man's money would go by operation of law to relatives with whom he had had no contact for decades.[49] The problem was that although the evidence of his testamentary intentions was extremely strong, he did not personally sign the note. You could argue that the doctor signed it on his behalf and also functioned as a witness, but one witness is not enough for a formal will. You could also argue that it was a holographic will, which would not require any witnesses, but such wills must be signed by the testator himself. Fortunately, the man's relatives were decent folk who agreed to let the foundation have the money, but if it had come to litigation, the will would almost certainly have been declared invalid.

Consider also the case of a lawyer from Oklahoma. His will, discovered after his demise, consisted of a single sheet of paper with three typewritten paragraphs. It looked very much like a routine will (the lawyer had successfully drafted quite a few during his career). Although it lacked the traditional "Last Will and Testament" title, the language, content, and structure were completely in accordance with legal textual practices. But it turned out to have a couple of major flaws. One was that he had not signed it. The other was that it was not witnessed. A small but significant further detail is that the lawyer had added a handwritten paragraph at the bottom of the sheet of paper giving ten dollars to his brother. Below this final paragraph was the date and his signature.

Obviously, the three typed paragraphs were completely ineffective. It was clearly not a valid formal will (which would have required the signature of two witnesses). You could argue that the entire document was a holographic will (they are recognized in Oklahoma), but because so much of it was not in the testator's handwriting, that effort would be doomed to fail. Only the handwritten part giving ten dollars to his brother would be part of the will—the typewritten paragraphs would be invalid.

Nonetheless, the Oklahoma Supreme Court found an ingenious way to carry out the lawyer's presumed intentions. It conceptually divided the document into two parts, severing the three typed paragraphs from the handwritten portion. It conceded that the typed part was an invalid will. The handwritten part, however, being signed and in the handwriting of the testator and viewed independently of the typewriting, was a valid holographic will. Thus, the brother got his ten dollars (obviously a slap in the face). More remarkably, the court held that the holographic will was a codicil (an addition or amendment) to the will. As a result, the holograph essentially incorporated (and validated) the three typed paragraphs into the testamentary text.[50]

It's a cunning textual trick. The question I always ask myself when teaching this case is, Was this lawyer afraid to contemplate his demise and therefore incompetent to draft his own will? Or was he fiendishly clever, anticipating that the state's supreme court would rule as it did?

Most people are not so lucky. The books of reports of judicial opinions are replete with examples of wills that were struck down because the testator violated one or more of the textual practices of the legal profession.

Lists of Gifts of Personal Property

While many problems are caused by people making their own wills, even those who are wealthy and wise enough to hire an attorney to draft their wills may encounter some very unpleasant surprises. A testator who has a valid will but wishes to make some additional bequests after its execution by attaching to it a list of gifts of personal possessions is almost certain to have her wishes stymied. As we have seen, a properly executed will is deemed to be the definitive and complete expression of the testator's intentions. This means that such a list, even if the testator keeps it with the will in her safe deposit box, is normally not part of the testamentary text and will not be given effect.

The result would be different if the will incorporates the list by reference, making it part of the text. Thus, if the will contains a clause stating, "I incorporate by reference a list of gifts of personal property contained in my safe deposit box," the list will be deemed part of the testamentary text. Yet incorporation is only possible if the list was in existence when the will was executed. And even if it was in existence, additions or modifications made to the list after the date of the will's execution are generally void. This rule is apparently aimed at protecting the testator from fraud and perhaps her own indiscretion. The results make perfect sense if you understand the textual practices of the legal profession, but they are likely to befuddle anyone else.

Revocation

Revocation of wills is an especially thorny issue because most people would think that you could undo a will's effectiveness by throwing it into a burning fireplace, tearing it to pieces, or destroying it in some other manner. However, a will can be carried out, or probated, even if the text itself has been lost or destroyed. If the literary conventions of wills law are strictly applied, properly revoking a textualized document should require executing (with all the formalities) another text that expressly revokes the first. For this reason, just about every will contains a revocation clause to deal with any previous wills that might still be in effect.

Because ordinary textual conventions suggest that burning or throwing away a document makes it ineffective, almost all common law jurisdictions have come to recognize what is called *revocation by physical act*. If the testator burns, tears, cancels, obliterates, or destroys her will, with the intent to revoke it, the will is in fact revoked.[51] This seems a perfectly reasonable concession to ordinary textual practices, assuming there is sufficient evidence of the intent to revoke. Yet it can produce some incongruous outcomes that are hard to justify.

Suppose that someone has a validly executed will that is kept in her lawyer's safe. She later meets her lawyer and tells him that she has changed her mind and under no circumstances is her written will to be carried out. Such an oral revocation would be entirely ineffective.

Now imagine that instead of meeting her lawyer, she calls him on the telephone and tells him she wants to revoke her will. The lawyer tears up the will or burns it in the fireplace. The will has not been revoked because the rule regarding revocation by physical act demands that the testator personally destroy the will or direct someone else to do so in her presence.

In fact, even a written revocation is invalid unless it complies with wills formalities. Consider the case of a woman from Illinois. After she died, her will was discovered inside an envelope. On the envelope she had written, "August 1st 1938 The enclosed will not to be executed Kate Bennet." The courts of Illinois held the attempted revocation on the outside of the envelope invalid because the text had not been executed with the proper formalities (there were no witnesses). Against her clearly evident wishes, the will was probated.[52]

In states allowing holographic wills, the outcome might have been more satisfying. Recall that in such jurisdictions, a holograph must be signed by the testator and either the entire will must be in the testator's handwriting or, in some jurisdictions, the material provisions must have been handwritten by the testator. Thus, the statement that the will in the envelope must not be executed (that is, must not be probated) could be considered a codicil or amendment to the will contained in the envelope, and being in the testator's handwriting and signed by her, would probably have revoked the will. But if she had typed the statement and then signed and dated it, it would not have been an effective revocation.[53]

Deletions and Revisions

Suppose that you have a properly executed will and would like to make a few small changes to the beneficiaries or the amounts they should receive. It does not seem worth the effort or money to go to a lawyer to have a new will drawn up. So you make some minor deletions or revisions to the text. Are these changes effective?

Let's begin with deletions. It's quite common for people to make some changes to a text by crossing out a word or sentence, whiting it out, or sometimes even physically cutting it out. Under ordinary textual practices, if you cut out or otherwise destroy a portion of text, what you deleted is no longer part of it.

Legally speaking, however, you have tried to revoke part of your will by a physical act. We have seen that you can revoke an entire will by physical act. But in many jurisdictions, partial revocation by physical act is not valid under any circumstances, apparently because of concerns that it would be too easy for someone else to selectively delete certain provisions. Thus, trying to revoke only part of a will (by burning, destroying, or crossing it out) would not be effective. Cousin Manny gets the $10,000 you gave him by will, even though you crossed out the gift and placed your initials in the margin.

An illustration is *Matter of Collins' Will*, where the decedent's will was found after his death in a safe deposit box. It had a number of markings, interlineations, and handwritten notations, some of which were dated and signed and some of which were initialed by him. For instance, the decedent, who was having marital difficulties, changed the recipient of the bulk of his estate from his wife to his children. Unfortunately for the children, the case took place in New York, which does not recognize partial revocation by physical act. Thus, the court ruled that the testator's attempted revocation of this gift was invalid. The will was admitted to probate in its original form, as though the deletions and changes had never been made.[54]

Other jurisdictions permit partial revocation by physical act. Just as the law somewhat incongruously allows informal revocation of an entire will by acts like tearing or burning the text, these jurisdictions allow the testator to revoke individual parts of the will by crossing them out or placing an X through them.[55] Although this undermines the sanctity of the text, the result is consistent with the expectations of ordinary people, who are used to making changes to documents in exactly this way.

Partial revocation by physical act may seem an enlightened doctrine, and generally it helps carry out the testator's intentions. But once again, it can produce unintended consequences, especially when combined with an attempt to make a substitute disposition for the part of the text that was revoked. Most people would simply call this a change or alteration to the text. More formally, it would be called an interlineation. As with deletions, it is a completely normal textual practice to make a change to a text by crossing out a word or sentence and writing a replacement above it or in the margin.

In contrast, legal textual conventions regard such changes with suspicion. The law of wills views interlineations as consisting of two distinct acts: an attempt to revoke part of the text, followed by an attempt to add to it.

Suppose that someone has a will stating, "I give $1000 to Alice." In a state that does not allow partial revocation by physical act, a testator who crosses out "Alice" and writes above it the name "Jane" will not have revoked the gift to Alice. Moreover, the attempt to add a gift to Jane is ineffective because it was not properly textualized. Contrary to the testator's intent, Alice receives the bequest.

In contrast, if the jurisdiction allows partial revocation by physical act, the gift to Alice is revoked by crossing it out. The attempted substitution of Jane fails, however. Once again, the attempted addition was not done with proper formalities, so it is not part of the testamentary text. Neither Alice nor Jane gets anything, once again frustrating the testator's intent.[56]

An example is a California case, *Estate of Martens*.[57] A man with a valid witnessed will asked his son-in-law to draw a line with a typewriter through the name of the executor and to insert the names of his daughter and son. The son-in-law did so and wrote a notation at the bottom of the will stating, "Article No. 5 above was changed by myself on this ten day of May, 1933." The testator placed his signature on the notation, witnessed by his son-in-law. Because the state recognizes partial revocation by physical act, the California Supreme Court held that the testator had revoked the appointment of the original executor. However, the attempted substitution of the daughter and son was invalid because it had not been executed with the required formalities (although the testator signed the notation, there were not two witnesses). Thus, the man died without naming an executor, completely contrary to his intentions, and no doubt contrary to what an ordinary literate person would expect.

Of course, making handwritten additions and corrections to typed documents is a completely normal textual practice in ordinary life. The same is true of cutting and pasting. Before computers, we had to physically cut the text and then paste it somewhere else with glue or tape. Nowadays we do it electronically, but most word processing programs still refer to it as "cutting and pasting." It seems absurd to say that when someone cuts and pastes some text, we should ignore the new text and stick with the old. But that is precisely what courts do when interpreting textualized documents. As one court noted, "The vice of this technique is that it creates a new dispositive sentence by the functional equivalent of cut and paste. The same policy which rejects an undated, unsigned, and unwitnessed interlineation must also reject any attempt to create new dispositive language by any process of editing the existing language."[58]

Mistakes

Another major aspect of textualization is that the resulting document is deemed to be the definitive expression of the author's intentions. The words in the will not only reflect the testator's intentions, but in a very real sense they embody them. A modern will is a physical document, not what is contained in the testator's mind. This aspect of textualization has some very important implications, especially when the text contains a mistake, and therefore does not reflect the actual will or desires of its maker.

Because the text is deemed to express the intentions of its maker, the basic rule is that courts will not correct a claimed mistake in a will. To be more exact, they generally refuse to consider any evidence to prove that there is an error in the text. This is completely contrary to ordinary textual practices, which dictate that if we find a mistake, we should fix it.

Quite appropriately, the law has created a number of exceptions to this draconian rule. One is that if a will contains an ambiguous description of a person or property, a judge may look outside the will to determine what or whom the language was meant to refer to. Courts justify the admission of extrinsic evidence in this case because it does not change the text but merely clarifies it.

But what if the text is obviously mistaken? Judges would like to do the right thing, of course, but they are extremely nervous about violating the sanctity of the text. So in many jurisdictions they have developed the rather odd doctrine that they can correct mistakes by deleting "false" language, but they cannot insert as much as a single word.[59]

Consider *Donnellan's Estate*. The testator left property "to my niece Mary, a resident of New York, said Mary being the daughter of my deceased sister." It seems that her sister had two daughters, one named Mary, who did not live in New York, and another named Annie, who did. The evidence suggested she had intended to refer to Annie, who was sometimes called Mary. The judge refused to correct the mistake by substituting "Annie" for "Mary." Conveniently, however, the court was able to fix the error by simply striking the name "Mary" in the will, leaving the language, "to my niece, a resident of New York." Annie was the only person meeting this description.[60] In another case, however, a will referred to a lot of land by the wrong legal description. Deleting the incorrect language would not have solved the problem, so the gift was held void.[61]

A few judges have boldly gone where no jurist has been before and have actually corrected mistakes in drafting (legally called "scrivener's errors"). Yet these decisions have generally come from relatively small states.[62] Most courts remain extremely reluctant to reform mistakes in a will.

Interpretation

When we interpret ordinary texts, such as letters or grocery lists, we normally approach them in much the way that we would a spoken utterance, trying to determine what the speaker or writer meant by the words. We use any evidence at our disposal to figure out what the speaker meant, including nonverbal cues, context, and background information.

Yet when judges interpret wills, they have traditionally ignored such information (called *extrinsic evidence*) regarding the speaker's or writer's intentions. Instead, they have concentrated on the plain meaning of the text. This is sometimes called the *plain meaning rule* or the *four corners rule*, in that the meaning must be determined from the language contained within the four corners of the document.[63] Judges make an exception when the language is ambiguous, but in practice such exceptions have been relatively rare.

Throughout the nineteenth and twentieth centuries, English judges applied this principle with great vigor. In 1915 the House of Lords decided *National Society for the Prevention of Cruelty to Children vs. Scottish National Society for the Prevention of Cruelty to Children*.[64] The name of the case probably says it all. A Scotsman left a legacy to the "National Society for the Prevention of Cruelty to Children." An organization by that name, headquartered in London, claimed the money. There was convincing evidence, however, that he intended to refer to the Scottish National Society for the Prevention of Cruelty to Children, with which he was familiar. He was, after all, a Scot. The Lords, sitting in London, held that the meaning of the will's language was plain and awarded the money to the English organization.

American courts have likewise tended to interpret the language of wills relatively literally, although their attitude has softened somewhat over the past decades. In a Massachusetts case the testator left her estate to her "heirs at law." Technically, an heir at law is someone who takes by intestate succession, and it turns out that this would have been her aunt. The testator's lawyer, however, was prepared to testify that she told him that she wanted the money to go to her cousins. The court held that the meaning of *heir at law* is plain, that the attorney's testimony was therefore inadmissible, and that her aunt would receive the estate.[65] The court explained that "[a] will duly executed and allowed by the court must . . . be accepted as the final expression of the intent of the person executing it," even if not consistent with what the testator told her lawyer.[66] Or as a California court once wrote, "While judges may pan the stream for golden nuggets of intent, they are required to stay within the banks of the testator's actual expression."[67]

Yet while the process of textualization, by which people can encode their intentions in a very precise and formal way, tends to encourage a textual decoding (that is, a literal interpretation), it does not require it. As we will explore in chapter 5, the same is true of statutes, which judges have also from time to time subjected to a relatively literal mode of interpretation, sometimes called *textualism*.

I am not necessarily an advocate of textualism in statutory interpretation, but the arguments in favor of adhering to the plain meaning of statutes have some appeal. They typically invoke democratic values and the rule of law. A legislature should govern by the words that it enacts into law, which are available for all citizens to consult, not by the unexpressed intentions of legislators. Courts should give those words a predictable meaning, based on ordinary usage, rather than digging through musty archives to find indications of what the legislature might have meant. Moreover, each of the legislators who voted to enact the statute may have had a slightly different intention, making it hard for courts to determine which intention should be given effect in cases of conflict. What they agreed on was the text. And if courts adhere to a statute's plain meaning, refusing to fill gaps and correct mistakes, the legislature may learn to express itself more clearly in the future. Finally, especially in the context of criminal law, how reasonable people interpret a statute should arguably be given as much weight, and perhaps more, than what the legislature might have meant by it.

But while these values might justify a textual approach to statutes (especially penal statutes), it is hard to see what application they have to wills. The rule of law has little relevance to the interpretation of wills. After all, a testator is free to amend a will at any time, which means that potential recipients cannot rely on the text of the will (if they even have access to it). Nor can I think of any good reason to take into consideration the interpretation of the recipients of the estate or of a reasonable person. What should matter is how the testator intended the text to be understood, not what some abstract reasonable person might have meant by it. There is, in addition, only a single intent—that of the testator—that needs to be discovered, unlike the multiple possible intentions of a legislature. Finally, teaching a testator to express himself more clearly is a pointless exercise, since he is almost certainly dead when the will is probated. Perhaps rigid enforcement of the plain meaning rule would force attorneys, who actually draft most wills, to pay more attention to the text, but it seems highly unfair to punish clients or their heirs for the poor drafting skills of their lawyers.

Moreover, when interpreting wills drafted by testators themselves, the plain meaning approach is downright silly. Wills written by nonlawyers should be interpreted as ordinary language, as some courts have begun to recognize.[68] It makes no sense to decode the language of a will using the textual conventions of the legal profession if the document was written by someone unfamiliar with them.

If we believe that people have a right to dispose of their property as they wish, then what a testator meant by dispositive language is far more important than the plain meaning of the text. Of course, people express their intentions by means of their words, but where there is a conflict between their words and their intentions, something has to give way. In the law of wills, it seems to me, the plain meaning of the text should submit to evidence of what the testator actually meant. Whatever appeal a textual approach might have in other areas of the law, it has no place in the interpretation of wills.

Taming the Testamentary Text

Those familiar with the law of wills know that a variety of solutions have been proposed to remedy some of the problems caused by the conflict between ordinary and legal textual conventions. The legal system has stubbornly resisted wholesale revision of the traditional requirements. But it also has come to recognize that injustice can result when the technicalities of the law frustrate the obvious intentions of testators.

We have already seen illustrations of how the law has to some extent accommodated ordinary textual practices. For instance, many American states allow holographic wills, and almost all jurisdictions recognize the doctrine of revocation by physical act. A substantial number also permit partial revocation by physical act. These doctrines allow people to make or modify wills without strictly complying with the traditional formalities (albeit at the risk of incurring unintended consequences).

More recently, many states have also adopted a more general doctrine called *substantial compliance*, which forgives minor errors made in the execution of a will. A somewhat more powerful proposal is the *dispensing power*, also called the doctrine of *harmless error*. As codified in the *Uniform Probate Code*, this doctrine would give courts the power to dispense with the formalities of execution if there is clear and convincing evidence that the testator intended a document to be his will or to be a revocation or modification of his will.[69] Thus, if an executor finds a validly attested will after the testator's death, with some changes later made to it by hand, the harmless error doctrine might allow the document to be probated as amended, assuming there was sufficiently strong evidence that the testator intended the handwritten changes to serve as a modification of the will.

The dispensing power is a potentially powerful tool that may be able to negate some of the more egregious consequences of the conflict between legal and ordinary textual practices. To date, however, it has been adopted only by some Australian jurisdictions and a few American states.[70]

In addition, the dispensing power is intended to address deficiencies in the execution of wills, not the problems posed more broadly by legal textual conventions. In its present form, at least, it may not suffice to deal with technological changes that may create an even wider gap between legal and ordinary textual practices. The dispensing power currently applies only to "a document or writing added upon a document."[71] It clearly presupposes the existence of written text. In other words, it would not be able to dispense with the requirement that the will be in writing.

Even in the few progressive jurisdictions that have adopted it, the dispensing power may therefore not be able to validate wills that are stored in some kind of audio, video, or electronic format. And that brings us to the final issue we will consider in this chapter: the impact of modern technology.

Text, Tape, and Pixels

As people become increasingly accustomed to new technologies for communicating and storing information, the pressure to allow wills to be made in novel ways is likely to intensify. Even if the profession defends its textual practices and the primacy of the written word, it may have to give way if torrents of video wills or e-wills start to appear in court. If they have not yet done so, people will almost certainly try to create wills in the form of a multimedia presentation, with graphic images of the items they wish to bequeath, links to their bank accounts or to property descriptions in the county recorder's office, and video clips of the testator explaining who should get what. Can the law continue to insist that a valid will must be a written text of some sort, preferably made by placing ink on paper?

Audio and Video Wills

People have already started to experiment with audio and video wills. A lawsuit from Wyoming involved a tape-recorded (audio) will that was contained in a sealed envelope on which was handwritten "Robert Reed To be played in the event of my death only! [signed] Robert G. Reed." The proponent argued that it could be viewed as a valid "holophonic" will, akin to a holographic will. In Wyoming, a holographic will must not just be signed, but it must also be entirely in the handwriting of the testator. The will's proponent suggested "that in this age of advanced electronics and circuitry the tape recorder should be a method of 'writing' which conforms with the holographic will statute."[72]

The court acknowledged that in evidence law, a tape recording might well be considered a "writing." Yet the rules of evidence did not change the substantive requirement of a writing in wills law. Hence the tape recording was not a legally effective will.[73] To date, no American case has held that an audio recording can be a valid will.[74]

Recently, it is not uncommon to make a video that shows the testator executing the will. A video recording can constitute valuable evidence of whether there was undue influence or whether the testator had capacity. But can a person's oral statements, if recorded on videotape, take the place of a will written on paper? Despite predictions about how videotape and other "paratextual" communication technologies will revolutionize the law,[75] virtually no jurisdiction, if any, considers a video recording to be a writing that satisfies the requirements of wills law.[76]

It seems likely that there have been or will be additional cases on the validity of audio and video wills. Nonetheless, they have clearly been a rare species, and in my opinion audio and video are likely to remain adjuncts to will making, mostly as a means of presenting evidence regarding whether the testator still had his wits about him.

E-Wills

What about wills stored on a computer? A computer can easily deal with sound and graphics these days, making it possible for a testator to orally state her will and have it captured in a digitized form that is preserved on a hard drive or other storage medium. Despite the more modern technology, it remains an audio recording that is not all that different from an old-fashioned recording on tape. The same is true of video, which can also be either recorded on tape or captured by a computer in digital form. None of these recording technologies produces a writing, so they are likely to remain marginal in the culture of will making.

Electronic wills, on the other hand, can consist entirely of written text. Although letters of the alphabet are presented on a computer display as tiny dots, or pixels, and are printed in a similar fashion, the overall impression they create is one very similar to traditional writing with ink on a sheet of paper.

Given that in many American jurisdictions a handwritten and signed letter, or a scribbled note with a signature, can constitute a valid holographic will, it may seem strange that the status of an e-mailed will or one contained in a file on a computer's hard disk is currently very uncertain. If you print it and properly execute it (with two witnesses, etc.), there is no problem, of course. On the other hand, if you print it and sign it, without witnesses and the other formal requirements, it will almost certainly be invalid under the current law of most states.

What if the will is not printed out but resides solely on a computer or in cyberspace somewhere? To date, the only state to allow true e-wills is Nevada, which has enacted legislation on the issue. Such a will must be created and stored in such a manner that

1. Only one authoritative copy exists;
2. The authoritative copy is maintained and controlled by the testator or a custodian designated by the testator in the electronic will;
3. Any attempted alteration of the authoritative copy is readily identifiable; and
4. Each copy of the authoritative copy is readily identifiable as a copy that is not the authoritative copy.

Moreover, it must contain the date and the electronic signature of the testator and include at least one authentication characteristic (such as a retinal scan or fingerprint) of the testator.[77] It's hard to imagine that many Nevada residents have taken advantage of this innovative statute. I would think that if your computer is attached to a printer, it is less risky and more efficient to press the print button and to sign the will in the presence of two witnesses. Admittedly, the law might be useful for technologically savvy hermits or astronauts in space, especially if they do not have access to a printer or cannot locate two witnesses.

As far as I can tell, there has not yet been a case testing the validity of an e-will (one that has not been printed) in American states.[78] There is, however, a case from Quebec, *Rioux v. Coulombe*, involving a will on a computer diskette. After being printed on paper, it was admitted to probate.[79] Quebec is a civil law jurisdiction, however, whose law is more similar to that of France than to the common law of England or the United States.

There is a case from Tennessee in which a man composed a will on his computer and, in the presence of two witnesses, attached a digital signature (apparently a scanned version of his normal signature). The witnesses then signed the will. The facts are not entirely clear, but it seems that it was printed before the witnesses signed it. The court held it valid, in large part because Tennessee defines a signature as including any mark intended to authenticate a writing.[80] The fact is that courts tend to be fairly relaxed regarding the signature requirement; a mark or very informal signature often suffices. But they have been quite strict in enforcing the rule that a will must be written, and because in this case the will seems to have been printed and then signed by witnesses, it does not deviate much from current practice.

Whether e-wills are ever going to supersede wills on paper is impossible to say, but it seems probable that Nevada will not be the only state to legitimize them. Of course, there are still technical issues to overcome. Because computers and software become obsolete so quickly, a will composed on a computer twenty years ago might not be decipherable today. And digital storage media still do not last as long as paper.[81]

Yet unlike audio and video recordings, which immortalize sound waves and graphic images, computers can store and transmit information that can be made to look like traditional text or writing. Moreover, it is technically feasible to create digital signatures that are at least as secure as those that are written by hand. In addition, the process of writing (or typing) on a computer allows for careful planning of the text, just like traditional writing. Such planning is more difficult with audio and video recordings. Finally, the problem of obsolescence of computers and software will almost certainly be solved at some point. If a computer can produce a written text that is accompanied by a secure digital signature of the testator and two witnesses or some other reliable method of authentication, there seems to be little reason to deny validity to the will. Of course, the judge would probably insist on a printed copy!

The Future of the Testamentary Text

Written Text Will Endure

Even in a world that in decades to come will offer communication technology that we cannot imagine, I believe that the significance of written text, as well as many of the textual conventions of the legal profession, will persist. One of the reasons is that language is a defining characteristic of human beings. Various nonverbal means of communication, such as gesturing, touching, or making graphic images, can also transmit a person's intentions, but usually only in limited contexts that do not require a precise message to be conveyed. Typically, gestures and pictures help us understand language; they do not replace it. It is hard to imagine that the supremacy of language as the primary means of human communication will be seriously challenged by technical innovations, certainly not during the lifetime of anyone alive today.

Second, writing is an extremely efficient way of representing human language in a durable form. It is true that new technologies have made it possible to preserve speech as speech and to transmit it over long distances, leading to a revival of orality in modern times. But when it comes to important legal transactions, writing has the advantage that it can be carefully planned and edited in a way that is much more difficult to accomplish orally. If you wish to specify exactly what should happen to your possessions when you die and hope to have your wishes carried out, creating a written document is surely your best option. Moreover, executing a written text is very useful in signifying to testators that they are engaging in an important legal transaction, something that sending an e-mail to your lawyer, or posting your intentions on a website or blog, does not do.

Writing on paper or some other durable medium will continue to be practiced for a long time to come, especially to memorialize solemn or important events. A hundred years from now, I imagine, colleges and universities will still be issuing paper diplomas to graduates in live ceremonies rather than just e-mailing them electronic degrees. The president will still be signing legislation printed on paper rather than clicking on a link ("I approve" or "I veto") in an e-mail sent to her by Congress. The perceived solemnity and significance of these acts will only increase as the use of paper becomes increasingly rare in ordinary life. That will enhance the value of writing wills on paper, since the testamentary act is one of the more solemn and significant transactions that a person can undertake.

Not only is the continued vitality of written wills likely, but so is the process of textualization. It may not endure in its present form, but it can be very helpful to have a formal procedure for authoritatively fixing the text of a will, guaranteeing that it represents the intentions of the testator and authenticating his identity as its author. This is especially valuable when fraud, undue influence, or declining mental capacity are realistic possibilities.

Of course, not all testators want or need such a high level of security. Some may wish to create or modify wills more informally, without having to go to the trouble and expense of hiring a lawyer. If someone is not particularly concerned about the possibility of a will contest after her death, why not allow her to express her testamentary desires in any way she wishes, as long as we have adequate evidence of those intentions?

To some extent, holographic wills are already an informal means of creating a will that functions more like a record of the testator's intentions, rather than formally textualizing them. In stark contrast to attested wills, holographs do not need to be witnessed and can usually be changed by the testator after the will is signed, with or without formalities.[82]

The law of holographic wills is useful as far as it goes. But the technology of writing and the textual conventions of society are certain to change. It will become increasingly archaic to maintain that the only alternative to a formal textualized will is one fixed on paper in the handwriting of the testator.

The reason for allowing holographic wills (which are a clear exception to the textual conventions of the law) is generally held to be that handwriting analysis can provide strong evidence that it really was written by the person in question. Many such wills, incidentally, consist of letters sent to family members. But if an ordinary letter can be a will, why should the same principle not apply to electronic mail, as long as its authenticity can be established with equal certainty? Handwriting will probably never completely disappear, but many younger people today are more comfortable with writing on some kind of keyboard. It may well be that handwriting will largely be supplanted by typing or keying in text. As new forms of writing develop, it will be increasingly unrealistic to insist on handwritten wills as the only alternative to the formal and highly textualized variety.

A Modest Proposal

I propose that we need to rationalize the law of wills. Currently, we have detailed and to some extent archaic rules relating to the execution of wills, with a slew of exceptions that rather haphazardly recognize ordinary literary conventions but which in the process sometimes create unjustifiable inconsistencies. Instead, we should recognize two basic categories of wills, one formal and the other informal.

My proposal differs in important respects from reforms suggested by other scholars. Some, including John Langbein and Lawrence Waggoner, support retaining at least some of the formalities while giving courts the power to dispense with them on an ad hoc basis in appropriate cases.[83] Others would dispense with most formalities in all cases. James Lindgren has argued that the only requirements for will making should be writing and a signature.[84] Adam Hirsch has made a similar proposal.[85] While I am sympathetic to this idea, it implies that all wills would be relatively informal and more consistent with ordinary textual conventions.

Yet I hope to have made the point—a point borne out by long practice—that the literary practices of the legal profession, and especially textualization, can sometimes be useful. My proposal is therefore that we reduce the formalities of execution when they are not necessary but allow people the option of expressing their intentions in a more formal manner if they prefer to do so.

People who wish to make their estate plan as fixed and secure as possible would thus be able to go to a lawyer to make a formal will. Currently this requires the attestation of two witnesses and the other formalities of execution that we previously discussed, but the nature of those formalities might very well change as new means to fulfill their functions become available. What is critical is that such wills provide a high level of protection against fraud or undue influence, strong evidence of the testator's desires, and a certain amount of ritual to emphasize the importance of the transaction. In addition, the resulting text should be regarded as the definitive expression of the testator's intentions. Informal changes would undermine the integrity of the text and should therefore be discouraged. Because these textual practices are foreign to the average person, they should be clearly explained before the will is executed. In fact, it might not be a bad idea to include in a formal will a notice, in plain English, explaining that it can only be revoked or changed by following a prescribed procedure (such as going to a lawyer and executing a new will).

Informal wills would follow a much more relaxed set of rules. As mentioned, the only such option these days is holographic wills. One problem is that they are not valid in many jurisdictions. Also, the requirement that they be entirely handwritten or that the material provisions be in the testator's handwriting is a continual source of litigation when part of the text is typed or printed.[86] Finally, it seems likely that handwriting will soon be to some extent supplanted by new technologies of writing or recording speech.

A broader category of informal wills could address many of these issues. Borrowing a phrase from copyright law, we should probably insist that such a will be "fixed" in a "tangible medium of expression," a flexible phrase that should accommodate future technological developments. And the person who makes it should intend it to be her will. People should be able to make changes, even after the will is made, using normal textual conventions. And it should be interpreted as ordinary language with the aim of carrying out the testator's actual intentions.

While practitioners of estate planning may find this a fairly radical proposal, it is worth pointing out that living trusts, which are increasingly being used to transfer assets at death, can already be created and amended with far fewer formalities than wills. Ironically, lawyers draft almost all trusts. In contrast, a person who does not have a large enough estate to justify going to a lawyer is much more likely to try to write a will on his own. The textual practices of the legal profession are therefore most likely to stymie the intentions of those who are least familiar with them and who are least able to hire the services of a lawyer.

My proposal differs from alternative suggestions by leaving it up to the testator to decide the degree to which he would like to textualize his testamentary intentions. If the proposal is adopted, the textual practices relating to wills would become more similar to those governing contracts, which we discuss in the next chapter. Parties who enter into a contract generally have the option of making a purely oral agreement, or making an oral agreement with a writing that records the more important terms, or textualizing their contact by creating a writing that is regarded as the definitive and complete repository of the terms of the agreement. In modern wills law, testators have only the third option. If parties to a contract can generally choose whether to textualize a contract, why should testators not be allowed to decide whether or not to textualize their wills?

In other words, the testator should be able to choose how much protection he would like to have against the possibility of fraud, undue influence, and so forth. If a family is riven by dissent or cursed by greed, or if a testator is wealthy and without apparent heirs, fully textualizing his intentions by means of a traditional will is an excellent idea. Yet if someone dies without having made such a formal will but has left behind other reliable indicators of his testamentary intentions, the textual conventions of the law should not get in the way of bringing those intentions to fruition.

4
Contracts

The word *contract*, like the word *will*, can refer either to a particular mental state (an agreement between two or more parties) or to a physical document that contains the terms of the agreement. In the case of wills, however, we observed that from a legal standpoint the written text has come to almost completely supplant the mental state or spoken words of the testator. The essence of a modern will is the written text. In contrast, once the sound waves conveying oral negotiations have dissipated, contracts may exist purely in the minds of the parties. Of course, they will often write down the critical terms of the agreement, thus creating a record or evidence of what is in their minds. And, as we shall see, a contract can also be textualized, by means of which the written text becomes the complete and exclusive statement of the terms of the agreement.

It may seem odd that oral wills are completely unenforceable in most common law jurisdictions, while oral contracts are made in massive numbers every day, often with few or no formalities. Whenever you agree to buy some apples from a vendor at a farmers' market, or order dinner in a restaurant, or leave your car in a parking lot, you have entered into a contract.

When transactions are routine, fairly conventionalized, and need to be carried out quickly, using speech to communicate is extremely efficient. Of course, once larger sums of money are at stake, writing down the terms of the agreement becomes increasingly advisable. The same is true if a transaction is likely to be repeated or if it is part of a lasting business relationship. The process of writing down the terms of contracts is useful because it creates solid evidence of the parties' agreement. It can also clarify what is part of the contract and what is not.

The printing of contracts adds another dimension: standardization. Routine transactions can thus be engaged in more efficiently. And because printing is cheap, standardized terms and conditions can be imposed even in fairly minor deals. Electronic contracting makes transactions even faster and cheaper.

Yet writing, printing, and modern technology also have their shadow side, especially when ordinary citizens are parties to a contract. Consumers may be unaware of the distinct textual practices that have developed in the realm of contract law. Lengthy printed agreements may result in information overload. The problem is intensified with electronic transactions, which make it easy to bury critical information under hyperlinks or at the bottom of a Web page.

We will discuss these and similar issues later in this chapter. Before doing so, we will set the stage by briefly reviewing the origins and current state of contract law, especially with respect to the use of writing and other technologies for storing and transmitting information.

The Rise of Contract

The Ancient World

The earliest known writing system was invented in Sumer, an area that is part of present-day Iraq, around 5,000 years ago.[1] Sumerian scribes used a stylus made from reed to imprint wedge-like marks in clay, developing a writing system known as *cuneiform*. The main impetus for creating cuneiform was apparently economic and, to a somewhat lesser extent, administrative or legal. Around 150,000 cuneiform inscriptions have been found in Mesopotamia. Of these, more than 75 percent are administrative and economic in nature, including inventories of goods and even tax returns.[2] Among the legal documents are wills, deeds of sale and purchase, and contracts relating to loans, adoption, and marriage.[3] Indeed, the oldest known legal texts involve the sale of land and were made in Mesopotamia in the third millennium BC.[4]

Private legal documents, including contracts, were generally inscribed on clay tablets, which were sometimes placed inside a clay envelope. On the envelope was a copy of the text contained on the tablet. The purpose was to deter one of the parties from changing the text because as long as the envelope was intact, the text on the tablet inside it remained inviolate and could be consulted if fraudulent changes to the envelope were suspected. The tablets normally listed the witnesses who were present, and the parties had to indicate their consent to the agreement by making an impression in the clay using a cylinder seal, seal ring, or some other object.[5] At roughly the same time in Egypt, important private contracts were also being reduced to writing.[6]

As with early wills, these ancient contracts did not constitute the transaction but were records or evidence of it. Referring to Mesopotamian legal documents, Johannes Renger has observed, "They do not have dispositive force. Mesopotamian legal documents are written in the past tense. They report in the form of a protocol about a transaction that has already taken place . . . [The clay tablet serves as] an instrument of evidence in case of a dispute."[7]

China is another civilization with a long history of writing. Written agreements or contracts can be traced back around two millennia to the Han dynasty. Many of them involve the sale of land. Surviving examples were mostly etched into durable media like stone, brick, metal, and jade. They typically named the parties and the place where the transaction occurred, the identity of the witnesses, and a recitation of the performance of formalities (such as partial payment of the price or the drinking of wine).[8]

Writing was even more central to Roman law. One of the more common forms of contract was the *stipulatio*. Originally, it involved an oral question and answer, one party asking, "*Spondesne* . . . ?" ('do you promise to . . . ') and the other responding, "*Spondeo*" ('I promise'). After some time it became customary to draw up a memorandum of the transaction, after which the importance of the oral ceremony declined.[9] The writing of such legal texts was typically done on waxed wooden tablets. It became customary to attach two or three tablets together with hinges, placing the text on the inside. A string could then be tied around it as a type of seal. At some point, people began to write a duplicate of the text on the outside of the tablet, similar to clay envelopes in Mesopotamia.[10]

The Common Law of Contracts

Britain was part of the Roman empire for several centuries, and some measure of Roman cultural and legal influence must have continued even after the last legions departed. With the Anglo-Saxon invasion, however, any remaining Roman influence disappeared, including notions of contracting and the process of writing that accompanied them.

As mentioned in the previous chapter, literacy returned to England with the arrival of Christian missionaries around the year 600. Soon thereafter, several of the Anglo-Saxon kings began to have codes of laws set down in written form (see chapter 5). We have also seen that there are a few dozen wills and transfers of land that have survived from the Anglo-Saxon period, but from all indications written contracts or agreements were scarce during this time.

Even after the Norman Conquest in 1066, there are initially few indications of contracts that are similar to what we understand by the term today (that is, an exchange of promises). Yet in the next couple of centuries, the royal courts developed a procedure, using what was called a *writ of covenant*, that required the defendant to carry out a covenant (or promise) that he had made. Typically the covenant (essentially, a promise) involved a lease of land, but it might include other types of agreements as well. Writing was important because the lawsuit was started by a *writ* (a writ in this case was an order in the name of the king to a local sheriff written on parchment in Latin). Also, the royal courts would only enforce covenants evidenced by a *deed* (a written document under seal). Actions alleging an oral agreement were relegated to the lower courts, which generally operated under local custom rather than the common law that was being developed at that time in the royal courts.[11]

Another device that had some similarity to modern contracts was the *writ of debt*, by which a plaintiff could recover money that someone owed him. The best way to prove a debt was to produce a deed, usually in the form of a *bond* (also called an *obligation*). A typical bond was written on two sides of a piece of parchment, the front containing formulaic language in Latin stating that the obligor (the debtor) was firmly bound to the obligee to pay a certain sum of money before a fixed date. On the back of the bond was a condition: that if the obligor performed a specified act (usually it required paying a sum of money), then the obligation would become void.

Bonds were popular in England for hundreds of years, in part because courts tended to enforce them relatively strictly. It is easy to see how bonds could function as a species of contract, or as a means of enforcing contracts, by making the condition of the bond not that the obligor pay money but that he perform a certain action, such as building a house for the obligee.[12] If the obligor built the house, the bond became void. Otherwise, he was on the hook for the full amount of the obligation.

Assumpsit: The Effect of a Growing Money Economy

Although writs of covenant and debt seem to have worked well enough during the later Middle Ages, they were unable to meet the demands of increasing commerce and an emerging money economy in the sixteenth and seventeenth centuries. For instance, an action to recover a debt might not allow for the enforcement of a promise, such as a person's promise to pay you a certain amount of money for a barrel of wine. If the buyer later repudiated the deal, you would be out of luck. You could only sue for debt if you delivered the wine and the recipient refused to pay for it, since there was no debt until after the wine was delivered.[13]

For this and other reasons, the old actions of covenant and debt were largely replaced by a cause of action called *trespass on the case*. Today, *trespass* is used to refer to a very specific type of wrongdoing (going on someone's property without that person's permission), but originally it referred to wrongful acts more generally.[14] Agreements came to be enforced as a particular type of trespass called *assumpsit*, a Latin word meaning 'he undertook.'

Although the details are complex, the word *contract* started to be used in its modern sense over the course of the seventeenth century. During this same period, in response to continuing demands of the marketplace, the royal courts began to enforce informal agreements, including oral agreements as well as written agreements that did not have a seal.[15]

The trend toward enforcing informal agreements solved some problems but created others. Oral contracts are hard to prove if one party claims there was a contract and the other denies it. Moreover, parties to lawsuits were often suspected of presenting false or perjured testimony on the issue.

Parliament took action by way of the Statute of Frauds, enacted in 1677. (This is the same statute that required many wills to be written, as we saw in chapter 3.) It mandated that certain categories of contracts, such as those for the sale of land, be evidenced by a writing.[16] We will discuss this statute in greater detail later in this chapter.

The Industrial Revolution: English Contract Law Comes of Age

The Industrial Revolution inspired further changes. It demanded a more sophisticated commercial law and also one that was more in line with international norms. Thus, beginning at end of the eighteenth century, a modern law of contracts began to emerge in England. It was to some extent inspired by Roman and continental ideas, and it led to the common law's adoption of concepts that are extremely familiar to today's lawyers, including, most notably, the doctrine that contracts are formed by means of offer and acceptance.[17]

Modern English contract law thus largely developed over the course of the past two or three centuries. In fact, many important contract principles derive from English decisions that were rendered in the nineteenth century and were later adopted in the United States, well after American independence. We will now explore some of those principles, especially as they relate to the creation and interpretation of the contractual text.

Contract Formation

Just about every law student learns that the basic ingredients for creating a contract are *offer*, *acceptance*, and *consideration*. The requirement that there be an offer and an acceptance is essentially another way of saying that the parties must have reached an agreement. And the requirement of consideration, roughly speaking, means that the agreement must be one that the law deems worthy of enforcement. In most cases, it means that the agreement must contain a promise by each party to do something for the benefit of the other and that these promises are part of a bargained-for exchange. As a result, most social agreements and gratuitous promises are not legally enforceable. The question of consideration does not involve many interesting textual issues, so we will not systematically discuss it.[18] Instead, we will focus in this chapter on the nature of contractual agreements, how they are created, and how we determine the terms or text of the resulting contract.

Offer and Acceptance

One of the basic principles of contract law is that the parties must agree to the terms of a bargain. In theory, there are various ways in which parties could come to agreement. Yet for many generations the common law has firmly adhered to the notion that agreements are reached in only one way: by the process of offer and acceptance.

More recently, the influential *Restatement (Second) of Contracts*, which originated as an attempt by lawyers and legal scholars to "restate" or summarize the common law of the United States, has somewhat de-emphasized the process of offer and acceptance. Its formulation refers in the first instance to mutual assent rather than offer and acceptance: "the formation of a contract requires a bargain in which there is a manifestation of mutual assent to the exchange and consideration."[19] The *Restatement*'s choice of the phrase "mutual assent" seems to contemplate that the parties have a particular state of mind. At the same time, it further specifies that the mutual assent must be manifested by overt actions.

Despite the *Restatement*'s prominence, just about every American law student is still taught the familiar mantra that the creation of a contract requires offer, acceptance, and consideration. Indeed, the *Restatement* itself maintains that mutual assent "*ordinarily* takes the form of an offer or proposal by one party followed by an acceptance by the other party or parties."[20] Thus, the process of offer and acceptance, if no longer deemed essential, is nonetheless felt to be the primary way by which potential parties to a contract reach agreement.

What, then, is an offer? The *Restatement* defines it as "the manifestation of willingness to enter into a bargain, so made as to justify another person in understanding that his assent to that bargain is invited and will conclude it."[21] As with its general statement on contract formation, which focuses on the mental state of mutual assent, the *Restatement*'s definition of *offer* once again concentrates on a state of mind ("willingness to enter into a bargain") and again requires that this mental state be manifested. The *Restatement* goes on to provide that "a manifestation of mutual assent may be made even though neither offer nor acceptance can be identified and even though the moment of formation cannot be determined."[22] What it seems to be saying is that a contract can be made even though no one made an offer!

The *Restatement*'s definition of an offer differs from the ordinary meaning of the word in another way: by requiring that there be a bargain. A normal offer simply proposes a future course of action (typically, an action that would be pleasing to the addressee). I can offer to open a door for you, or I can offer to give you some milk to put in your tea, for instance. In both cases I would have offered to do something, subject to your acceptance, but we would not say that I had offered you a bargain. Recall that a general requirement for contract formation is that there must be consideration, which normally means that the agreement must involve an exchange of promises. What the *Restatement* seems to have done here is to integrate the consideration requirement into its definition of an offer. All in all, it's a confusing and convoluted definition.

Speech Act Theory

A more straightforward approach is to say that the formation of a contract requires that (1) there be an agreement (or mutual assent, if you prefer) and (2) that the agreement must satisfy certain legal criteria for enforcement, which we traditionally call consideration. As noted above, consideration is primarily a question of policy, so we will concentrate on the requirement of mutual assent or agreement.

Although agreement can be reached in a variety of ways, it is common enough for it to occur via offer and acceptance. As developed in the work of philosophers like J. L. Austin and John Searle,[23] who articulated an approach to language use called *speech act theory*, an offer is a type of speech act. Moreover, offers belong to a particular class of speech acts known as *commissives*. As the name suggests, a commissive speech act is one that commits a person to a future course of action.[24] If I offer to take you kayaking tomorrow, and you accept, I have committed myself to this course of action.

Another feature of an offer is that it can only be performed as part of a mutual or cooperative set of speech acts. In contrast, a promise—which is also commissive—is a unilateral speech act and therefore does need not be accepted in order to be valid.[25] All it takes is a statement that is understood as committing the speaker to a future course of action. If I promise to go kayaking with you tomorrow, I have bound myself by my words alone. You need not do anything to make the promise effective. But if I offer to do so, you need to accept. If you reject my offer or fail to reply within a reasonable time, I am under no obligation to you whatsoever.[26]

Thus, promising is an act of commitment that is performed by means of a single, unilateral speech act, where P is a proposal to do something in the future:

A: I promise P.

A's utterance places her under an obligation (to carry out the proposal, or P) without any action or response by B, the addressee. In contrast, an offer is an act of commitment that requires two people to each perform a separate speech act:

A: I offer P.
B: I accept P.

Only after A and B have successfully engaged in these reciprocal acts can we say that they have agreed to the proposal that we call P.

Although promises can create obligation unilaterally, the typical contract involves two parties with reciprocal obligations. And they place these obligations upon themselves by means of agreement. Because offer and acceptance constitute cooperative and commissive speech acts, it is not surprising that the process of offer and acceptance is a natural way for two parties to reach agreement.

Nonetheless, it is a serious mistake to think that agreement or mutual assent can only be accomplished by offer and acceptance. A good illustration is what are called *unilateral contracts*. For instance, I might publish a notice that I promise to pay any licensed real estate broker a certain commission for selling my house. It would seem that I have committed myself by means of this notice: I have obligated myself to pay the commission to the first broker who sells my house. Yet the brokers who read the notice are not under an obligation to find a seller.

Judges, anxious to systematize the law of contract formation, tried to shoehorn such examples into the offer and acceptance paradigm. Thus, my public notice would be viewed as an offer that must be accepted before any commitment arises. Under orthodox contract theory, a broker could only "accept" my offer by completing a sale. As a result, I would be able to revoke my offer at any time before then because I would not yet be committed to anything. That, of course, is unfair to a broker who has started to perform. Courts eventually devised a solution to protect brokers in this situation, but for reasons that I have elaborated elsewhere, it is not very satisfactory.[27] A more straightforward solution is to acknowledge that my published notice is not an offer but is rather a promise that creates commitment as soon as I utter or print the words. Applying an offer and acceptance analysis to such cases distorts what is really happening. After all, if a broker starts to try to sell my house, he must be doing so because he believes that I am committed to paying a commission if he is successful.

Scholars have also recognized that a contract can arise without offer and acceptance if A proposes a bargain to B and C and if B and C then agree to the proposed terms. Likewise, in international relations a neutral country or international organization may propose terms for a ceasefire to two warring countries, and they may both agree to them. Even though there is clearly mutual assent if such a proposal is adopted, it does not seem to arise by offer and acceptance.[28] Neither of the parties has made an offer, and the person or organization who made the accepted proposal is not a party to the agreement.

A Discursive Approach to Offer and Acceptance

There is another way in which contracts can arise without either party making an identifiable offer or acceptance. This happens when an agreement emerges piecemeal, either during a single conversation or as a result of protracted negotiations. Especially commercial transactions often involve weeks or months of negotiation, after which the parties reach agreement and then, as a rule, jointly draft a contract that contains its terms. There is usually no identifiable offer or acceptance.

Contract law is certainly aware that it is commonplace for parties to negotiate an agreement and later write down the terms. Yet neither traditional contract doctrine nor speech act theory is able to handle such examples very well. Each discipline has tended traditionally to concentrate more on abstract principles and less on naturally occurring data. This has changed in recent years. Linguists remain interested in speech acts, but they increasingly try to base their analyses and conclusions on actual language data. This is especially true of linguists who specialize in studying conversations, often called *discourse analysts*.

Thus, a discourse analyst might point out that it is relatively rare for someone to say, "I promise to take you kayaking tomorrow." Much more likely is a conversation similar to the following:

> Bob: Hey, Anne, what's up?
> Anne: Not much, but I'm looking forward to some kayaking tomorrow.
> Bob: You have a kayak?
> Anne: As a matter of fact, I have two of them.
> Bob: Well, if you have an extra one, could I come along?
> Anne: Sure.
> Bob: What if I come by your place at noon?
> Anne: Great. I'll be waiting for you. And be sure to take a swimsuit!

Has Anne promised to take Bob kayaking tomorrow? It seems to me that she has. But nowhere does she utter the word *promise*, nor does she make any single utterance that is identifiable as such. Of course, if Bob wants to make absolutely sure that Anne is committing herself, he can ask, "Is that a promise?" and she can say "Yes." Even then, Anne herself has never said, "I promise to take you kayaking tomorrow."

The same point can be made of offer and acceptance. Linguist Michael Geis, who has tried to integrate speech act theory into conversation analysis, provides the following example of a customer buying an airplane ticket by telephone:

A: May I help you?
C: Do you have any flights to Miami on the 26th?
A: How many seats are you looking for?
C: One.
A: What time can you leave?
C: Some time in the afternoon.
A: Let me look . . . I'm not finding anything then . . . Can you leave earlier?
C: If I have to.
A: I've got a seat on an 11:00 a.m. flight on Treetop Airlines.
C: That'll be good.
A: When can I bring you back?
C: On the morning of the 30th.
A: Well, all I'm showing is a 10:00 p.m. flight.
C: Do you have anything the night before?
A: I can put you on that 10:00 p.m. flight.
C: That'll be okay.
A: The round-trip fare will be $295.
C: Okay.[29]

Clearly, the parties have reached agreement—there is mutual assent, in other words. But where exactly is the offer and where is the acceptance? Perhaps the agent's statement regarding the fare could be taken, combined with the rest of her utterances, as constituting an offer. In the alternative, we could analyze the conversation as being purely informative (that is, the customer and agent jointly working out what a possible itinerary and price would be), with the customer then offering to buy a ticket on those terms (by saying "okay") and the agent accepting the offer by issuing the ticket.

Not only is it impossible to pinpoint the offer and acceptance in this conversation with any degree of confidence, but the designation of one party as offeror and the other as offeree (or the acceptor) is almost entirely arbitrary, depending on where in the conversation we determine that the offer occurred. Did the customer offer to buy a ticket, or did the airline offer to sell him one? This is a remarkable observation because, as we will explore in greater detail below, much of the law regarding the formation of contracts depends fundamentally on the notion that it is possible to distinguish the offeror from the offeree, that the offeror is "master" of his offer, and that if there is to be a contract, the offeree must meekly agree to the terms that the offeror proposes.[30]

Bargaining via Correspondence

If it is so difficult to identify offer and acceptance in actual conversations or negotiations, and if contracts are commonly created without them, how did the law ever come to place such heavy reliance on these two speech acts? The answer, it seems to me, is that the doctrine of offer and acceptance is to a large extent the product of writing and the growth of a more literate culture. More specifically, the doctrine seems to have arisen when businesses began to negotiate by means of correspondence.

We observed in chapter 2 that when writing first enters a culture, it is very similar to speech, but that with the passage of time it begins to assume a separate identity. In particular, writing tends to become more autonomous than speech, in the sense that writers often strive to place more of their communicative intentions into the document itself. And people tend to be more explicit in writing. Information that can be assumed or implied from context or conveyed by nonverbal means during face-to-face negotiations must generally be expressed in words and placed into a text by someone communicating in writing (especially when the writing is sent to a stranger or someone removed from the author in space or time).

In terms of contracts, during oral negotiations there is little need to identify an utterance as an offer or acceptance. As Karl Llewellyn pointed out, what matters to the parties is whether at the end of the day they have a deal.[31] It is the agreement that the parties usually remember, not the exact details of who said what or when they said it. These points are consistent with an observation by Kevin Teeven that "from the sixteenth century until the early nineteenth century, there was no concern about when a contract was formed—the parties either emerged from face-to-face negotiations with an agreement or they didn't."[32] Or, as an English lawyer argued at the end of the sixteenth century, "in Contracts it is not material which of the Parties speaks the Words, if the other agrees to them, for the Agreement of the Minds of the Parties is the only Thing the Law respects in Contracts."[33]

But this all changes when parties negotiate by correspondence. Written negotiations tend to take place when the parties are not in close proximity to each other, which means that visual cues, background information, and the overall circumstances may not be known to the other party. For this reason, people involved in written negotiations almost invariably create relatively autonomous texts that express their intentions as fully as possible. It is usually not practical to send ten or fifteen letters back and forth while negotiating (at least not before e-mail existed!), so negotiating parties tend to summarize all the conditions under which they are ready to deal in one or two pieces of correspondence. And they try to be as explicit as possible, which means they are much more likely to use speech act verbs like "offer" and "accept" to clarify their intentions.

Recall the conversation regarding the airline ticket purchase. If this transaction had been done via correspondence, it would probably have resembled the following:

> C: Please advise whether you have any flights leaving for Miami on the 26th of January, preferably leaving in the afternoon, but otherwise in the morning. I would like to return the morning of the 30th of January, but if that is not possible, I will need to return the evening of the 29th.
>
> A: Responding to your letter of January 1, we can offer you a round-trip to Miami leaving on the 26th at 10 a.m. and returning on the 29th at 11 p.m. for $295.
>
> C: With regard to your letter of January 4, offering a round-trip to Miami leaving on the 26th at 10 a.m. and returning on the 29th at 11 p.m. for $295, I agree to the proposed terms and enclose payment. Please mail the tickets to . . .

This exchange seems rather artificial if we imagine it as a spoken conversation, but it is completely natural as a written exchange.

If my hypothesis is correct, it suggests that judges would not have focused on offer and acceptance until it became relatively common practice to negotiate agreements by means of written messages. The generally accepted view, articulated by A. W. B. Simpson, is that the doctrine of offer and acceptance was adopted from the civil law of continental Europe in the early nineteenth century.[34] Simpson also posits that an important impetus for this transformation in English contract law was the need to deal with "the problem of written contracts by correspondence."[35]

Teeven's history of common law contracts identifies *Kennedy v. Lee*, a case decided in 1817, as one of the earliest cases to specifically invoke the concepts of offer and acceptance.[36] Interestingly, the *Kennedy* case also seems to have been one of the first cases to address the issue of contract formation by means of correspondence. Lord Chancellor Eldon found it expedient to clarify that a contract formed by an exchange of letters could be every bit as valid as one that was agreed to orally and then written down:

> "If a correspondence is of such a nature as, according to the rules of sound legal interpretation, would amount to an agreement, the agreement so constituted will be carried into effect in the same manner as if it had been regularly drawn up in the form of articles of agreement, and signed by the parties as such . . ."[37]

If contracting by correspondence was a well-accepted practice at the time, it would hardly have been necessary to make this point.

Kennedy v. Lee has been relegated to the dustbin of legal history. But in the very next year, 1818, a major English case arose dealing specifically with the creation of contracts by correspondence. *Adams v. Lindsell* involved a letter sent by merchants in wool to a woolen manufacturer on September 2. The manufacturer did not receive the letter until the evening of September 5 because the merchants had misdirected it. The manufacturer sent an acceptance by post that same evening. The reply was also slow to arrive because it had to pass through London. Not having received an acceptance by the time that they anticipated, the merchants sold the wool to someone else on September 8. The next day, September 9, the letter of acceptance arrived. The question presented by the case was, When is an acceptance by correspondence effective? The court of King's Bench held that the offer had been accepted on September 5, when the letter of acceptance had been placed in the mail, not on September 9, when it was received. In other words, a contract arose on September 5, and the merchants breached it by subsequently selling the wool to someone else, even though they had not yet received the acceptance.[38]

This famous case established what is now called the *mailbox rule*. Although controversial, it has been adopted by most American jurisdictions.[39] It seems rather odd to say that an acceptance is effective even though the offeror has not received word of it. Unlike assent, which is primarily a mental state, offer and acceptance are speech acts and must therefore be communicated to the hearer. If someone speaks in a forest and no one hears it, the person has spoken, but nothing has been communicated. The mailbox rule becomes even stranger in light of a related principle: that a mailed offer is not effective until received. The same is true of the revocation of an offer.[40]

We need not debate the merits of these rules, which are obsolescent in today's culture of near-instantaneous communication. For our purposes, the point is that the doctrine of offer and acceptance, and many of the rules that regulate the process of contract formation, are to a large extent the result of parties beginning to engage in written negotiations. These writings tend to be more explicit than speech and therefore lend themselves to being more readily characterized as an offer or acceptance. Consider, in this regard, the language of the offer in the *Adams* case:

> We now offer you eight hundred tods of wether fleeces, of a good fair quality of our country wool, at 35s. 6d. per tod, to be delivered at Leicester, and to be paid for by two months' bill in two months, and to be weighed up by your agent within fourteen days, receiving your answer in course of post.[41]

Notice how autonomous this letter is, providing all details necessary for the recipient to decide whether to accept. And observe also that it employs the phrase, "we now offer . . . " Such use of explicit speech act verbs is not especially common in spoken conversation but is quite natural in writing.

Suppose that these businessmen had instead met in person at a county fair:

> Buyer: Have you any wool for sale?
> Seller: We have hundreds of wether fleeces. How many do you need?
> Buyer: I could use around 800 tods. What quality?
> Seller: Good fair quality of our country wool.

But by now you get the idea. After several additional utterances of this kind, the details of the transaction would have been hammered out, the businessmen would have shaken hands, and a deal would be struck.

No doubt people made offers and accepted them long before the nineteenth century and long before the law recognized them as a means of reaching agreement. It is entirely possible to make offers and acceptances orally, and people regularly do so. Yet the notion that offer and acceptance are essential to contract formation is almost certainly an artifact of the rise of negotiation by correspondence.

Not only is the doctrine of offer and acceptance closely associated historically with the development of contracting via correspondence, but the doctrine makes the most sense in that context even today. When businesses send letters to each other, they often contain readily recognizable offers and acceptances, and they are often explicitly phrased as such. Oral negotiations, as we have seen, typically consist of the gradual hammering out of terms, followed by a handshake or other indication that a deal has been struck. It is certainly possible that at the end of the negotiations one of the parties summarizes all the terms in a way that resembles a written offer, but in many cases it is neither easy nor sensible to try to impose the offer and acceptance paradigm on agreements arising from such discussions.

Thus, in response to a growing practice of negotiating by correspondence, English and later American courts developed the requirement that contracts arise by offer and acceptance. This has created a number of problems, both real and theoretical, such as the imposition of the offer and acceptance paradigm on unilateral contracts, as well as the inability of the offer and acceptance requirement to be imposed on most agreements that result from protracted negotiations. These problems have only been compounded by the widespread adoption of printing in the process of contract formation.

Printing and the Rise of Standardized Forms

The next major evolution of the contractual text occurred with the increasing use of printed forms. Over the course of the twentieth century, businesses began to make great use of such forms, especially for buying and selling goods to each other, as well as for transactions with consumers. Although a printed text is not necessarily all that different from one written by hand, it usually does not make sense to print something unless you wish to produce multiple copies. Using printed forms is therefore a very efficient way of engaging in repeat transactions of a certain kind. And the forms can all be identical. As a result, printing tends to standardize the language of texts.

The use of printed forms in commerce also promotes standardization of the transactions themselves. Of course, the forms typically have blanks where the name of the buyer or seller can be entered, along with the nature and price of the goods, as well as other details like the date and place of delivery. But the basic terms and conditions of the purchase or sale, being printed (typically in small type on the back of the form), are fixed and are usually not open to negotiation. In theory, each transaction can be made on identical terms, allowing businesses to control or eliminate potential risks and to calculate more accurately what prices they ought to charge (or pay) for the goods or services that they are buying or selling.

The Battle of the Forms

One of the areas in which forms are used to create contracts is in transactions between businesses. Commonly, each business has printed forms that it uses for certain types of deals. Standard provisions are all printed, and the forms typically contain blanks where terms relating to price and quantity can be entered (these are sometimes called the *manuscript* part of the contract, in contrast to the printed part, which mainly contains what is called *boilerplate*). Not surprisingly, most companies create forms that favor their own economic interests.

So what happens if one company, after oral negotiations, sends the other a printed contract containing numerous one-sided provisions in miniscule type on the back of the form? The other business typically fires back a different form with its own one-sided terms! This practice has come to be called the *battle of the forms*. Who wins the battle has traditionally depended on the rules of offer and acceptance.

Under the common law, the exchange of forms typically led to what is called the *last-shot problem*. Suppose that two parties negotiate a sale of goods by telephone or other communication device. The buyer sends a printed purchase agreement to the seller, filling in by hand the required amount, price, delivery date, and so on. In response, the seller sends an acknowledgment form to the buyer, once again with the same information filled in by hand. The manuscript part of each form is the same, so the parties agree on issues like quantity and price. But the printed terms and conditions on each form are different or contradict each other.

For purposes of discussion, let's say the acknowledgment form contains an arbitration cause and that the purchase agreement is silent on this issue. The parties then begin carrying out the transaction, but later a dispute arises. What are the terms of the contract? Specifically, does it require arbitration?

Using traditional offer and acceptance analysis, the buyer's purchase order (because it was sent first) is deemed to be an offer. Yet the seller's acknowledgment form is not an acceptance because it is not a mirror image of the order form. Under traditional rules of contract formation, an acceptance must be the mirror image of the offer, which means it must accept the terms of the offer "without the slightest variation."[42] After all, the offeror is master of the offer! All the offeree can do is meekly assent.

Because the second (acknowledgment) form contains terms different from the first one, the second is not an acceptance, but a counteroffer, which the buyer in turn needs to accept before a contract arises. Typically, the buyer does not expressly accept the acknowledgment and may not even have read its exact language. Instead, after exchanging forms, the parties simply proceed with the deal. Starting to perform an agreement is legally considered to be a type of acceptance. Thus, by beginning to perform the buyer is deemed to have accepted the terms of the acknowledgment form and a contract arises. The terms of the deal are those on the seller's acknowledgment form, not those in the purchase order.

Thus, under the traditional common law approach, whoever sends the last form is usually able to dictate the terms of the deal (as long as the parties proceed to performance). On the other hand, if the transaction is one that will not be performed for some time, there will be no agreement at all until performance begins, even if the parties exchanged forms and thought that the deal was on, because there has been no acceptance.

Obviously, the battle of the forms and the last-shot problem, like offer and acceptance more generally, are artifacts of the use of writing and printing to negotiate and confirm contractual relationships. When contract formation is purely oral, the parties either make a deal or they do not. They can, of course, have disputes about the terms of the transaction, but it would be relatively rare to have the parties arguing about whether or not they had an agreement.

Thus, the use of written negotiations and, later, printed forms led to a situation in which not just the substance of the agreement but the more basic issue of the existence of a contract became the subject of dispute. The terms of the agreement often depend, quite arbitrarily, on who sent the last form. And whether there even was an agreement may depend on whether the parties started to perform before the lawsuit was filed.

New Rules of Engagement

An effort to remedy problems raised by the use of printed forms was made by the *Uniform Commercial Code* (*UCC*). The *UCC* was originally a model law drafted by an influential group of lawyers, legal scholars, and judges in the 1950s. They then agitated to have it adopted by all American states, hoping in that way to codify and unify (see chapter 6) the laws relating to sales of goods throughout the country. The *UCC* has been a great success. It has facilitated commerce between states because now, with respect to the sales of goods, they all operate under the same legal regimen.

Section 2-207 is the *UCC*'s attempt to negotiate a ceasefire in the battle of the forms, or at least to reduce the number of casualties. It does so largely by defanging the mirror image rule. Its basic principle is that—unless the parties agree otherwise—an expression of acceptance operates as such even if it states additional or different terms from those contained in the offer. Recall that under the mirror image rule, such an "acceptance" would be treated as a counteroffer. So under the *UCC*, the deal is on, even if the parties' printed forms differ. Although there are important exceptions, the basic rule is that the first form to be sent is an offer and the second is an acceptance.

Of course, this approach raises a new question: assuming the deal is on, which terms are part of the contract? Logically, any provisions as to which the forms of the parties agree should be included. What about additional terms in the acceptance? Consider again the example of a purchase order containing a clause that disputes must be settled by arbitration, whereas the acknowledgment form does not address this issue. Very roughly speaking, the rule of the *UCC* is that additional terms in an acceptance become part of the contract if they do not materially alter it.[43] In contrast, if the additional terms would materially alter the agreement, they do not become part of it (unless, of course, the other party agrees to them). Thus, relatively insignificant or minor additions in an acceptance generally become part of the text, whereas more significant additions do not.

Prisoners of Print?

While the *UCC*'s solution is an improvement over the common law, it is not especially elegant. The textual details of section 2-207 are complex and have befuddled many a law student. Moreover, its application to actual transactions has caused judges a lot of headaches.[44]

Yet the fundamental error of the *UCC*, in my opinion, is that it tries to solve the problem of conflicting forms within the offer and acceptance paradigm. In most situations, the *UCC* views the first form as primary. That form is held as setting forth the basic terms of the deal, subject to nonmaterial additions by the second form. In other words, the first form is deemed an offer and the second is deemed an acceptance. This is traditional contract law, with the important exception that the mirror image rule no longer operates as strictly as in the past.

An alternative paradigm is not to apply the offer and acceptance framework to printed forms at all. Rather, judges should ask themselves whether the words and conduct of the parties indicate that they reached an agreement. The terms of the contract should include only those as to which the parties agreed. The contract would thus include any terms that appear in both forms. Other terms and conditions should be sought in the pattern of dealings between the parties, the customs or usages of their trade or business, and the default provisions in the *UCC*.[45] At least in this area of the law, it's time to storm the prison of print.

Printed Forms, Consumers, and Information Overload

The use of printed forms in deals between businesses and consumers presents additional issues. Of course, the battle of the forms is not a problem in this context. With rare exception, consumers are not in a position to print and send their own forms, full of the customary one-sided conditions, to businesses. If they tried, most enterprises would probably either ignore the forms or refuse to deal with the customers.[46] There is no battle, nor even a brief skirmish, because businesses can simply impose their take-it-or-leave-it terms and conditions on individual consumers. If you pay the price for the goods or services you need or desire, you will generally be bound by all terms and conditions in the printed forms contained in the box or on the back of a sales receipt.

Of course, competitive pressures can limit the ability of businesses to dictate conditions to consumers. And most states have enacted various kinds of consumer protection laws. Finally, courts may refuse to enforce provisions that are deemed excessively one-sided. Overall, however, in business-to-consumer transactions, the use of printed forms and standardized transactions is a rout rather than a battle.[47]

Printed forms have therefore become pervasive in transactions between businesses and consumers. By using such forms and taking advantage of the traditional rules of offer and acceptance, business enterprises can engage in commerce with the public on standardized terms that they dictate. Sales contracts, car rental agreements, residential leases, airline tickets, deposit receipts, and similar documents typically have complex stipulations printed on forms that customers must sign. If the customer tries to cross out or change a term, the variation—according to the common law—creates a counteroffer that does not go into effect unless the business accepts it, and the businesses will almost always refuse to do so. You must accept the offer exactly as printed, or you will not be able to buy the product or rent the car. Such standardized transactions between businesses and customers have come to be known as *contracts of adhesion*, and they present a formidable challenge to the notion that contracts arise via the mutual assent of the parties.[48]

The bottom line is that businesses have the power to set terms and conditions of transactions with the public, and they use printed forms to impose those conditions on their customers. In itself, the use of printing for mass contracting is not a bad thing. As we have already observed, printing can disseminate a large amount of information to many people. And the standardization of transactions reduces their cost, allowing customers to obtain goods and services at a much lower price than if each deal had to be individually negotiated and recorded.

Yet the ability of printing to cheaply disseminate large amounts of information (which is even more true of electronic publishing) is a mixed blessing in consumer transactions. Although it is easy to give customers a printed list of their rights and duties under a contract of sale, it is also very easy to overwhelm them with information. Someone who rents a car in the United States, often by telephone or the Internet, typically receives multiple pages of terms and conditions in fine print when picking it up. It would take a lot of time to read and absorb all that material, which is ordinarily phrased in convoluted and minimally comprehensible English. Most people don't bother and simply sign on the dotted line. After all, if you want to rent a car you must sign the form, and any competing rental companies use forms that are just as convoluted and one-sided.[49]

With a car rental you normally receive the form or have a chance to review it before you hand over your credit card. Yet it is becoming common practice for commerce to be transacted on the Internet. If you buy software online, there may be text containing a license for its use embedded in the software itself, where it cannot be read before you complete the purchase. Is that text part of the agreement?[50] Likewise, if you purchase something on a website that contains a hyperlink to terms and conditions of sale, are those provisions part of the contract?

Electronic Contract Formation

The amount of contracting being conducted via the Internet increases dramatically every year, raising numerous issues that are only slowly percolating through the legal system. We are concerned here with whether and how engaging in electronic commerce differs in substance from traditional contract formation, which was and often still is conducted orally, in writing, or by means of printed forms. More specifically, what are likely to be the implications of computers and the Internet for the law of contract formation?

E-commerce

Let's begin by concentrating on the buying and selling of goods, which is where e-contracting currently has its greatest impact. Obviously, in some senses the process of shopping for goods is undergoing profound changes as more and more transactions take place online. Buying online can be much more convenient than going to a store, especially when you are trying to find unusual items. Moreover, you can compare dozens of potential vendors to find the best deal. And the products can be delivered to your door. But is online commerce so revolutionary that it will force us to rethink contract law? It will certainly have a huge impact on the daily lives of merchants and on business practices in general. There is no doubt that it will transform the way in which businesses interact with each other and with consumers.

At the same time, online purchasing is in many ways more evolution that revolution. It is not so different from buying something out of a printed catalog, which has been a common practice for decades. Just as you can see a description of an item for sale on a website, accompanied by a photo, you can see the same description and photo in a printed catalog. And in both cases you need to provide the seller with your name and address, as well as your credit card information or some other means of payment. The catalog will normally have a list of terms and conditions of the sale, just as the website does. And after a few days or weeks, the item that you purchased will arrive at your door or in your mailbox. To a large extent, online commerce builds on a long tradition of remote buying and selling. Consider that contracting via correspondence seems to have been common at least two hundred years ago and probably even earlier. In that sense e-commerce is merely an incremental development in long-distance contracting, something that has been possible for centuries.

Yet it is also true that e-contracting differs in significant ways from more traditional means of contract formation. Recall that printing made it possible for businesses to create long forms containing numerous detailed provisions in small type. Computers can store and transmit vastly more information. If information overload was an illness with printed forms, it has the potential to become an epidemic with online contracts.

An actual example comes from a study of car rental agreements by Irma Russell. Such agreements when printed tend to be two or three pages (often in small print). On the Internet, however, the websites of companies renting cars contain terms and conditions that range up to sixty-three pages in length![51]

A rather extreme example of the length to which contracts can grow on the Internet is a service agreement by the AT&T telephone company. The service agreement is essentially a contract with customers, who received a printed copy of it. Although the service agreement is a modest 10,000 words long, it is not complete. For a comprehensive compilation of all terms and conditions of service, AT&T customers are referred to an online guidebook comprising around 2,500 pages![52] Obviously, overwhelming ordinary telephone customers with this much paper would be completely impractical—it's possible only with the almost limitless storage capacity of the Internet.

A related issue is the accessibility of the information. From a consumer standpoint, printed form contracts can be problematic because critical provisions may be phrased in convoluted language that is buried on the back of the form in small print. Electronic contracting does nothing to solve the comprehensibility issue, and it can actually aggravate the accessibility problem by enabling businesses to place information in out-of-the-way locations via hyperlinks or by putting it at the bottom of a page that does not appear on the customer's computer display without a lot of scrolling downward.

Consider also that one of the significant features of electronic communication is that it is dynamic rather than static. In other words, it can be almost instantly changed and updated. This can be extremely useful if you want the latest news. But the dynamic nature of online information can cause problems in the legal arena, especially in the realm of e-contracting. In our discussion of the distinction between speech and writing in chapter 2, we noted that a great advantage of writing from a legal perspective is that it is relatively permanent, making it a good medium for preserving the law (especially when carved into stone!). But electronic text is highly malleable. websites can change from one day to the next, and regular archiving of the entire Internet has, until now at least, proven elusive. So the terms and conditions that are in place on a website when you agree to buy a product may have disappeared or been changed when a problem with the product develops at some later time. Presumably, the provisions that were on the website when you bought the item govern the transaction, but unless you had the foresight to print them out, you may not be able to prove what they were.

If this concern seems overwrought, consider a provision that is at the time of this writing on the website of a video rental company:

> Blockbuster may at any time, and at its sole discretion, modify these Terms and Conditions of Use, with or without notice. Such modifications will be

> effective immediately upon posting. You agree to review these Terms and Condition of Use periodically and your continued use of this Site following such modifications will indicate your acceptance of these modified Terms and Conditions of Use. If you do not agree to any modification of these Terms and Conditions of Use, you must immediately stop using this Site.[53]

Many online companies have similar provisions. As a consequence, you can be bound by conditions that were changed after you first read them, without ever getting notice of the change!

A final observation about online contracting is that its greatest virtues—the ease and speed of engaging in transactions with minimal formalities—can also be problematic. When you rent a car, the process of being handed a long printed form and being required to sign it impresses on you that this is a transaction that may have legal consequences. Recall the importance of formalities in the execution of wills and the great reluctance of courts to make the process more convenient. Electronic contracting illustrates the opposite extreme, where it is possible to engage in serious transactions with the casual click of a mouse.

Clickwrap, Shrinkwrap, Browsewrap

Not surprisingly, e-contracting has been the subject of much discussion by legal scholars. Mark Lemly, for example, has argued that the ease of imposing terms and conditions on electronic commerce has led to vastly more transactions being subject to detailed written provisions than was the case before. Traditionally, merchants and consumers engaged in numerous transactions—in grocery stores, restaurants, bookstores, and the like—without written agreements that specified their rights and obligations. The same transactions, when they take place online, typically have lengthy and detailed terms and conditions imposed on them by the vendor.[54]

Because sellers do not want to slow down or discourage business, these provisions are often placed (or hidden, some might say) in an unobtrusive location. It is worth observing that the longer the text containing terms and conditions becomes, the less likely it is that consumers will read and understand them. And with computers, there is virtually no limit to how long texts lurking behind a single hyperlink can be.

The result, according to Lemly, is the "death of assent."[55] The reason is that with online contracting, it is a simple matter to include terms and conditions on a website, and typically it is much easier to induce consumers to "agree" to these terms than it would be to get them to sign printed forms when a similar transaction is conducted in a store made of bricks and mortar.

To date, most of the cases related to this issue have involved the sale of software and the enforceability of licenses. How do consumers accept the terms and conditions of a sale that is conducted on a website? Often by merely clicking on a box that says "I accept" or "I agree." In the case of software purchases, these are sometimes called *clickwrap* agreements or licenses. As Lemly points out, courts generally enforce such licenses, even though very few consumers have read the terms and even though the website is designed in a way that obscures the text.[56]

It is certainly troubling that people can be deemed to have agreed to text that they have never read. Still, it is worth observing that the same principle applies to printed form contracts. If you sign such a contract, you are legally presumed to have read it, no matter how long and obscure it might have been. "In the absence of fraud, one who signs a written agreement is bound by its terms whether he read and understood it or not, or whether he can read or not."[57] Hence, if you click "I accept" on a website, it is no great extension of current law to apply the same presumption to terms presented in an electronic format. As one court observed, there is "no significant difference" between printed and electronic terms in this situation.[58]

Yet if it bothers us that people can be bound by printed provisions buried in small type that no one seriously expects them to read and understand, it should concern us even more in the realm of online contracting. As mentioned, the terms and conditions can potentially be much longer and more detailed than is practical with print, making the task of reading them more onerous and the danger of information overload more serious than it would be with the typical printed form.

Moreover, while most people are aware that signing a document can have real-world consequences, computer users are constantly clicking on boxes and icons with their mouse. Clicking a mouse is usually a casual and relatively meaningless activity.[59] One of the dangers of online contracting is that it may be too informal and convenient.

Lemly makes a further point that, in the context of this book, is quite apropos. He argues that the pervasiveness of standard form contracts online has conditioned consumers and courts "to expect the retailer to set the terms of the deal in writing, even when there is no similar expectation for parallel transactions offline."[60] In the past, only more weighty transactions were evidenced by a written contract, mostly when required by the Statute of Frauds. But in online commerce, even the tiniest transaction may be subject to lengthy written provisions. There is thus a serious possibility that online commerce will lead to virtually all transactions being textualized to some degree. Whereas today most routine commerce is still conducted orally and disputes are commonly settled by custom and general legal principles, future commerce may increasingly take place in writing and disputes may be settled by the terms and conditions that the seller, via its website, imposes on consumers. In my mind, this is not an attractive prospect.

A variation on this theme is what Lemly calls the *browsewrap* license. Here the mere use of a website is deemed acceptance of any terms of use listed on the site. In reality, of course, it strains the meaning of the word to suggest that the user "assented to" or "accepted" those terms. Fortunately, courts currently enforce such licenses primarily in transactions between businesses, when actual knowledge of the terms was likely.[61] Even so, use of browsewrap licenses may be problematic, since a large company may enter into dozens or hundreds of online transactions in a day, each with a website that imposes somewhat different terms.[62]

Another problem, not unique to online contracting but exacerbated by it, is that with many modern deals the consumer does not receive the text of the terms and conditions pertaining to a transaction until after the deal has been made. One way that this happens is by means of a *shrinkwrap* license. Here a customer buys a product, often software, containing a license or other contractual provisions inside the box. There is sometimes a statement on the box that the act of opening it (by removing the shrinkwrap enclosure) constitutes agreement to the printed terms inside. Or a customer might find the license embedded in the software itself, with a statement that the act of installing or using the software will be deemed an acceptance of its terms.

What is disturbing about this method of contracting is that the customer does not have access to the terms and conditions before buying the product. Theoretically, she can buy it, take it home, read the contract, and return the product to the seller for a refund if she is unwilling to accept the terms of the license, but it can be inconvenient to do so. Moreover, many stores and websites have a general policy of refusing to take back merchandise (software in particular) if the box has been opened or the shrinkwrap removed. Amazingly, the United States Supreme Court recently held that people who had bought tickets for a cruise were bound by lengthy and detailed language in a printed form that was mailed to them after they had paid for the tickets, even though those conditions denied them a refund if the tickets were not used![63]

Lemly points out an additional problem presented by shrinkwrap licenses: customers normally open a box containing merchandise not to signal assent to the terms inside it; they merely want to use the product that they have purchased. For reasons such as these, courts were initially reluctant to validate shrinkwrap licenses, but in recent years the tide seems to have turned in favor of enforcement.[64]

I agree that all of these novel methods of imposing contractual provisions on consumers are potentially problematic. Yet it's worth observing, once again, that these issues are not unique to the Internet. It has been common practice for decades to have merchandise packaged in boxes along with a printed list of legal provisions relating to matters like the warranty and limitations of liability for certain types of damages. Similarly, the use of browsewrap licenses on websites is not really all that different from signs in stores (usually near the cash register) specifying when and how items can be returned or declaring that if you break it, you've bought it.

The challenge posed by online contracting is largely one of scale. Copying by hand is laborious and thus quite expensive. Printing made it much cheaper and easier to disseminate information, and the Internet has made it almost costless. Thus, modern technology invites businesses to impose contractual provisions on even the most routine transactions and to make those provisions ever longer and textually more complex.

A Solution: Public Standardization

The use of printed forms, as well as the practice of placing terms and conditions inside boxes, on software, or on websites, aims to standardize transactions with consumers. Standardization clearly facilitates commerce, especially with relatively small but numerous transactions. As long as courts refuse to enforce unreasonable and unexpected provisions, standardization can be a useful process.

The problem is not so much standardization per se but the fact that, for the most part, each company uses printed forms or the online equivalent to standardize its own transactions. We might call this *private standardization* because it results in a large number of differing standardized forms, even within a single trade or industry. And, as mentioned above, the forms are typically very one-sided, almost inevitably forcing judges, in cases of dispute, to make difficult decisions about which printed provisions to enforce. In addition, current standardized forms tend to be hard to understand and are often not read by, and may not even be accessible to, the consumers who are bound by them.

An alternative approach is broader standardization of routine transactions. Perhaps we should encourage a comprehensive standardization of common categories of transactions, which would apply to all businesses working within a particular trade or industry. These terms and conditions could be widely publicized and would presumptively be incorporated into all transactions of the type in question, making it unnecessary to give lengthy printed forms to customers right before (or after) they engage in a transaction.

What I am envisioning might therefore be called *public standardization*. We could turn standardized agreements into tools for promoting fairness, rather than using them as weapons in the battle of the forms or as a means of imposing one-sided terms and conditions on consumers.

For instance, there could be a standardized transaction for car rentals that sets forth, in plain language, the rights and responsibilities of both the consumer and the rental company. As a practical or political matter, it might be necessary to allow businesses to contract around these standard provisions, but it should be difficult to do so, especially in business-to-consumer contracts. Courts should presume that the standard provisions apply unless a business or corporation can prove that the consumer actually knew about, understood, and agreed to the additional or different terms.

Legal scholars like Henry Smith and Margaret Radin have pointed out that modern contracts already have many standardized provisions, which are often called *boilerplate*. According to Smith, contracts—which once had many individualized provisions—are becoming more like deeds in property law, which are highly standardized.[65] As opposed to property deeds, where the entire transaction is standardized, modern contracts tend to standardize only a number of specific clauses. The use of standardized clauses, or boilerplate, makes these provisions easier to process and understand.[66] Along similar lines, Radin argues that electronic contracting makes it even easier to use such standardized clauses.[67]

I agree that the use of standardized clauses, which allow contracts to be cobbled together in a modular fashion, can help reduce the problems presented by textual overload. This is especially true if such clauses receive a consistent interpretation, as some scholars have proposed.[68] In that case, parties to a contract need only inquire whether a particular provision is part of the text or not, without having to parse the exact language in which the clause is phrased. My proposal goes further, however, in advocating that with common types of consumer transactions, the entire agreement should be publicly standardized.

In fact, there are a number of areas in which something of this sort already occurs. Real estate sales in California are often memorialized by forms distributed by a California association of real estate agents. They are used by both buyers and sellers, and thus they are not particularly biased in favor of one side or the other. Ronald Mann has suggested a similar scheme for credit card agreements.[69] Likewise, the U.S. Department of Housing and Urban Development recently adopted rules not just requiring more meaningful disclosure of the costs connected with consumer mortgages but also mandating the use of standardized disclosure forms so that consumers could more meaningfully compare one mortgage offer with another.[70]

The crisis in the home loan mortgage market, which during the last few years has led to massive foreclosures and tremendous declines in values of houses in the United States, was to a large extent caused by the failure of consumers to understand the loans they were being offered by banks and mortgage brokers. As Lauren Willis (one of my colleagues at Loyola Law School) has explained, for two or three decades before the crisis, not only did government regulation decrease, but the variety of loan types increased and the structure of home loans became less standardized.[71] Consumers came to be confronted with a bewildering array of home loan products, making it extremely difficult for them to decide which was best in their situation.[72] Her proposed solution is to produce "simpler and more standardized loan products" so that consumers can engage in effective price shopping.[73]

What Willis means is not that each lender should offer its own printed forms, but that forms should be publicly standardized throughout the industry. They should be tested to ensure that consumers understand the language and the legal consequences. And the number of permissible loan types should be quite limited, so that people could be effectively educated on the options available to them and how they differ.

Such publicly standardized transactions might be imposed by statute, but a more attractive proposition is to encourage businesses in a specified trade or market to sit down with consumer groups and to agree on how to structure specific types of routine transactions. As this chapter was being finalized, contract scholar Joseph Perillo made a very similar proposal, with the further suggestion that a body like the American Law

Institute, a widely respected group of academics, lawyers, and judges, could take on the task of bringing together business leaders and consumer activists in order to draft and then publish what he calls "neutral standardized forms."[74]

Once the standard terms are adopted, government and public interest groups could educate the population. The Internet would be a good way to spread such information. Then you could buy software or rent a car without being confronted with pages of information in small print or the online equivalent. You could simply assume that the standard terms apply, and you would know what they are in advance.

Getting It in Writing

Despite the increasing use of writing in contract formation over the centuries (by means of correspondence, printing, and electronic communication), it is still very much possible for contracts to be made entirely by word of mouth. In fact, oral contracting remains vastly more common than contracting in writing. If an arborist comes to your house and offers to prune your trees for $250, and you agree, the two of you have entered into an enforceable agreement. You may later receive a written or printed bill or receipt, but the essence of the deal is the oral transaction.

Like the word *will*, which can refer either to a person's mental state or to the document incorporating the person's testamentary intentions, the term *contract* can refer to a mental state (the agreement or mutual assent) or to the text that contains or records the agreement. Recall the evolution of legal texts that we proposed in chapter 2. At the first stage, legal transactions are entirely oral. At the second stage the essence of the transaction is still oral, but a written record is produced as evidence. Finally, the act of writing becomes the transaction itself. Wills have fully progressed through all three stages, so that today the only valid wills are documents, produced by a carefully prescribed ritual, that are deemed to be the final and complete expression of their makers' testamentary intentions. In contrast, contracts can be entirely oral, and indeed they often are. Oral transactions are especially useful for smaller deals that need to be made quickly, but even major transactions are sometimes concluded via speech. Another possibility is for a contract to be made orally but to be evidenced by a writing. That is the topic of the next section. We will see at the end of this chapter that it is also possible to fully textualize an agreement. If this is done, the text constitutes the contract.

The Statute of Frauds

Even though most contracts are made orally, writing has many advantages. Being relatively permanent, it is more likely than human memory to preserve an accurate record of a transaction. Writing thus protects against the frailties of the human mind, and at the same time it offers some protection from those who might wish to manipulate the minds of others by means of fraud. It is for reasons such as these that the English parliament enacted the famous Statute of Frauds in 1677. As we have already noted, the statute demanded that certain types of contracts be evidenced by a writing. These include marriage contracts, promises to be responsible for someone else's debt, contracts for the sale of goods valued at over ten pounds, contracts for the sale of land, and contracts that could not be performed within a year.[75]

The statute was a compromise. On the one hand, there was a need to allow commerce via relatively informal (usually oral) transactions. On the other, writing was viewed as a means of reducing the occurrence of fraud and mistake, both of which might be facilitated by oral contracting. The solution was to require writing for more important transactions, where much money was at stake and where people would have the greatest incentive to commit fraud or perjury, as well as for contracts that would take place over a longer period of time, where failing memory would be a greater concern.

The Statute of Frauds did not directly require that contracts within its scope be in writing. It merely stated that specified types of contracts were not enforceable unless "some Memorandum or Note thereof shall be in Writeing and signed by the partie to be charged therewith."[76] In other words, someone trying to enforce a contract within the statute had to produce a written memorandum that could serve as evidence of its terms.[77] The statute imposed the second stage on certain classes of contracts, in which the writing is a record or evidence of an oral transaction. As Corbin's treatise on contract law observes, "The writing which is required need not embody the contract, but need only evidence it."[78]

The statute was only partly successful. For one thing, it enabled unscrupulous parties to enter into an oral agreement and then—if they later preferred not to go through with it—to raise the statute as a defense to its enforcement. In addition, contracts for the sale of goods worth more than ten pounds were not routinely memorialized in writing even after the statute was enacted. In England that provision was effectively repealed in

1954.[79] The provision regarding the sale of real estate was more enduring, however. In fact, in 1989 it was extended in England by a law that required sales of land to be made in writing (rather than merely being evidenced by a memorandum). In other words, this class of contracts had moved to the third stage in the evolution of legal texts. In the words of J. H. Baker, "Form [that is, writing] is no longer a matter of convenience, but is of the essence."[80]

The Statute of Frauds has also thrived in the United States. In fact, the writing requirement for contracts for the sale of goods was incorporated into the Uniform Commercial Code, which requires that when such contracts involve a price of over $500, they are not enforceable unless there is a writing "sufficient to indicate that a contract for sale has been made between the parties and signed by the party against whom enforcement is sought . . ."[81] And, of course, the statute remains in full force and effect with respect to real estate deals.

"Writing" in the Information Age

Although courts have debated the exact meaning of the terms *note* and *memorandum*, as well as how much of the substance of the agreement must be evidenced by them, there has never been any doubt that the basic terms of a contract within the Statute of Frauds must be in writing. Until relatively recently, this was almost always accomplished by means of placing ink on paper. Parchment would also suffice, but most modern examples of notes or memoranda consist of paper documents such as receipts, letters, advertisements, or record books of businesses. New technologies for transmitting such documents, including the telegraph, teletype, and mailgrams, did not, as far as I can tell, lead to serious challenges that the documents so transmitted did not constitute the required "note" or "memorandum." After all, there would almost invariably have been a hard copy that either was, or closely resembled, ink on paper.[82]

Somewhat more problematic were facsimile (fax) machines. Although they were widely used to conduct business during the latter part of the twentieth century, at least one court in Georgia expressed doubts about whether faxed documents could satisfy the statute: "the transmission of beeps and chirps along a telephone line is not a writing, as that term is customarily used. Indeed, the facsimile transmission may be created, transmitted, received, stored and read without a writing, in the conventional sense, or hard copy in the technical vernacular, having ever been created."[83] Actually, the typical fax machine requires that a piece of paper be placed into the machine, and the recipient will almost invariably have a receiving machine that will produce a relatively close copy. As a result, each party typically has a piece of paper with writing on it.

Nonetheless, the Georgia court's concern was in some sense prescient. A notable feature of e-mail and electronic messages is that they are not just transmitted but also stored electronically. Placing ink on paper can be, and often is, dispensed with. There may never be a printout or hard copy on either the sending or receiving side. The only physical manifestation of such a document may be its temporary appearance as pixels on a computer monitor and, if saved, magnetic or electrical charges on a hard disk or other storage device. This being so, can we say that an e-mail or other electronic document constitutes a "writing"?

Recall from our discussion in chapter 3 that wills must also be in writing and that courts have to date been extremely resistant to allowing the probate of wills that were not fixed on paper or a similar medium. Of course, it may take a few decades before a person dies and his or her will is offered for probate, so the issue may not become salient for some time. Yet given the uncertainty of the law on this question, it is hard to imagine any lawyer trying to execute a will exclusively in an electronic format.

On the other hand, contracts normally go into effect quite quickly, and therefore the issue of whether an electronic record can satisfy the writing requirement in the Statute of Frauds has already generated discussion. There seems to be broad consensus that electronic transmission of contracts should satisfy the statute. Quoting once again from Corbin's treatise, "It cannot be doubted . . . that the memorandum does not have to be written on 'paper,' or that the words may be traced in something other than ink."[84] Moreover, Corbin's treatise goes on to suggest that storing documents exclusively in an electronic format—without printing them out on paper—should likewise be permitted.[85]

To squelch any lingering doubts, Congress and some state governments have enacted legislation on this question. A federal law, known as ESIGN (the Electronic Signatures in Global and National Commerce Act), provides that a contract that comes within its scope "may not be denied legal effect, validity, or enforceability solely because it is in electronic form."[86] The statute also validates electronic signatures.[87] Interestingly, it specifically does not apply to wills, codicils, and testamentary trusts.[88] Many states have enacted a similar law, called UETA (the Uniform Electronic Transactions Act of 1999). It states that "if a law requires a record to be in writing, an electronic record satisfies the law."[89] It likewise authorizes electronic signatures and excludes testamentary documents from its scope.[90]

The law's vastly greater receptivity to e-contracts, as opposed to e-wills, suggests that when it comes to especially weighty transactions, most people are still more comfortable with traditional writing on paper or other durable medium. Besides the evidentiary value of having a written document, the act of physically signing it reinforces the significance of what we are doing. This is especially valuable in the law of wills, which often struggles to decide which of a testator's writings were meant to be legally enforceable. Likewise, I suspect that with major commercial transactions, like buying a house, most of us would strongly prefer to have a deed and other documentation in traditional written or printed form. In fact, as more and more commerce is conducted electronically, it may well be that written documents will be more highly valued as they become increasingly rare.

Textualizing Contracts: Parol Evidence and the Doctrine of Integration

As mentioned, the Statute of Frauds does not normally require a written contract. It can be satisfied by a note or memorandum that records the fact that an agreement was made. Courts generally hold that the memorandum must contain the "essential terms and conditions" of the contract, although which terms are essential has sometimes been the subject of dispute.[91]

If only the essential terms must be in writing, it follows that less significant provisions that were agreed to orally may be part of the contract. Indeed, many contracts are partly oral and partly written. Custom and usage of a particular trade or industry may also be incorporated into the contract.

Thus, even when agreements are written down, the writing is not necessarily authoritative. In other words, the Statute of Frauds did not and, to a large extent even today, does not require that contracts be textualized. The writing that it contemplates is not the complete and definitive expression of the intentions of the parties. A contract is whatever terms the parties have agreed to, whether or not they were written down. Thus, it is always possible for one party to claim that they orally agreed to additional or different terms that were not recorded in the note or memorandum made to satisfy the Statute of Frauds.

Of course, it might be useful to reduce the totality of the agreement to writing, making clear what the terms of the contract are. One of the advantages of the strict formalities of will execution is that they make explicit what is included in the will and what is not. Oral statements and informal letters are not normally part of the text, even if they purport to dispose of a person's property at death. All statements contained on a piece of paper signed by the testator and properly executed are part of the testamentary text. As a consequence, a will is invariably fully textualized: it consists of the text that was written on paper and properly executed, not what was in the mind of the deceased, nor what the deceased may have told potential heirs, nor what the deceased might have written on other pieces of paper. This textual practice is familiar to lawyers, although as we have seen it can befuddle the uninitiated.

Although contracts do not have to be textualized in the way that wills are, it is possible to do so via a process called *integration*. Unlike testators, parties to a contract have a choice. Assuming that the Statute of Frauds requires a writing, they can produce a memorandum that functions merely as evidence of their agreement. Or they can textualize their agreement by encapsulating its terms in a writing that is meant to be the definitive or authoritative expression of their intentions. In that event, the writing becomes the contract. All negotiations, oral statements, and previous writings are integrated or merged into this text. Another way of saying it is that the text replaces (or, as lawyers are wont to say, "discharges") any previous statements or writings with respect to the agreement contained in the text.

Because the text of an integrated agreement is deemed conclusive, any prior statements or writings (that is, parol evidence or extrinsic evidence) that contradict that text are legally irrelevant and are normally not admissible in court proceedings. This is the effect of the parol evidence rule. It is sometimes traced back to the Countess of Rutland's case, decided in 1604:

> [I]t would be inconvenient, that matters in writing made by advice and on consideration, and which finally import the certain truth of the agreement of the parties should be controlled by averment of the parties to be proved by the uncertain testimony of slippery memory. And it would be dangerous to purchasers and farmers, and all others in such cases, if such nude averments against matter in writing should be admitted.[92]

Modern judges throughout the common law world continue to insist that if the parties definitively write down the terms of their agreement, that is, create a writing that constitutes the "final expression of one or more terms of an agreement," that text cannot be undermined by evidence to the contrary.[93]

Recall our discussions of when literacy first enters a culture. It takes time for people to become comfortable with it. Initially, they continue to view the oral legal transaction as essential, even when a record is made. Yet eventually the written record becomes preferred over human memory. The quotation from the Countess of Rutland's case suggests that by the beginning of the seventeenth century, and probably earlier, many people in England had come to trust writing over the recollection of witnesses.

Confidence in written evidence has persisted into modern times. One of the great American contract scholars, Arthur Corbin, once argued that the doctrine of integration should not be limited to written documents. If the parties to a contract were to orally state their agreement in definitive form, why should that statement not have the same effect as a document? Why not invoke the parol evidence rule to bar any terms not stated in the definitive oral agreement?[94] Yet despite his influence, neither the *Restatement of Contracts* nor the courts have adopted Corbin's suggestion. Part of the reason is the great faith we have in writing. In addition, although it is conceivable that the parties might orally choose their words with "explicit precision and completeness," we saw in chapter 2 that precise verbal expression is much easier to achieve in writing. Speech cannot readily be edited as a written text can, and even if the parties could orally agree on a precise verbal formulation of their contract, it seems doubtful that they could recite it from memory a year or two later when a dispute regarding its terms arises. Our ability to remember verbatim what someone told us is very limited.[95] Thus the process of integration can only be accomplished by writing.[96]

How to Textualize a Contract

Not all written agreements are regarded as being textualized, that is, as integrated documents that invoke the parol evidence rule. Some, as we have seen, function merely as evidence of the contract. As a result, courts often need to figure out whether an agreement is integrated or not, and also whether it is partly or completely integrated.

It is easy to determine when a will is textualized—you can just look at the will itself to determine whether the required formalities of execution have been followed. Contracts, on the other hand, can be created with almost no formalities. Even when the Statute of Frauds requires a writing, the note or memorandum can be very informal. How then do we determine whether the parties have integrated their agreement?

Whereas textualization of wills is a question of following strict formalities, contracts are textualized or integrated only if it is the intention of the parties to do so. Oftentimes the document itself provides evidence of what the parties intended. Thus, according to the *Restatement*, if a writing is so complete and specific that it reasonably appears to be a complete statement of the parties' agreement, it should be taken as an integrated agreement unless there is evidence to the contrary.[97] If it looks and feels like an integration, it probably is one.

It may also be necessary to decide whether the parties intended a text to be fully or partially integrated. Even if we assume that the parties intended a text to be a definitive statement of their intentions, which is essential to any integration, they might in addition have intended it to be the complete statement of the terms of their agreement. In that case it is considered fully integrated, and parol evidence is inadmissible not just if it would contradict the text but also if it would add to it.

Suppose that the parties have completely integrated a contract that does not contain an arbitration clause. Later, one of the parties comes to court and claims (truthfully) that during negotiations they agreed that disputes would be arbitrated. Because the document is fully integrated, any evidence on this issue—whether written or oral—is not admissible. This is true even if the additional term is fully consistent with the contract or if it was written down on a separate piece of paper. A fully integrated text replaces or supersedes all previous dealings between the parties, oral or written. On the other hand, if a court were to decide that the contract was only partly integrated, the evidence regarding arbitration would be admissible because it only adds to (and does not contradict) the writing. A lawyer would tell you in legalese that a fully integrated agreement discharges all prior agreements, whereas a partially integrated agreement discharges only those prior agreements that are inconsistent with it.[98]

A well-known illustration is *Gianni v. Russel.* [99] Frank Gianni was a tenant in an office building owned by Russel. The lease allowed Gianni to sell only items like fruit, candy, and soda water. It expressly forbade the sale of tobacco. Some time after renewing the lease, Gianni found out that Russel had rented out another space in the building to a drugstore, which had started to compete with him in the sale of sodas and soft drinks. He filed a lawsuit against Russel, claiming that before renewing his lease, he and Russel had orally agreed that his right to sell soda water and soft drinks in the building would be exclusive.

The Supreme Court of Pennsylvania scrutinized the written contract and concluded that it appeared to be complete. If the parties had intended the right to sell sodas to be exclusive, they could easily have added this provision to the text. Because the written lease was deemed to be the complete expression of the parties' intentions, "all preliminary negotiations, conversations and verbal agreements are merged in and superseded by the subsequent written contract . . . its terms cannot be added to nor subtracted from by parol evidence."[100] Gianni therefore was not allowed to present evidence that when negotiating the renewal of his original lease, he agreed to a prohibition on tobacco sales in his shop only after Russel's agents assured him that his right to sell sodas and soft drinks would be exclusive.

Merger Clauses

Because there may be uncertainty on the issues of intent to integrate or whether a deal has been partially or fully integrated, it has become common practice to have the contract itself address the issue. Typically, lawyers insert clauses to the effect that the document constitutes the entire agreement between the parties and that any previous negotiations or understandings are merged or integrated into it. Such a clause (called a *merger* or *integration clause*) is generally treated as strong evidence that the parties intended to integrate their agreement, and some jurisdictions regard it as being conclusive.[101]

Sophisticated business parties, and certainly their lawyers, understand how the doctrine of integration works. They are, in other words, familiar with the textual practices of the legal profession. In a California case that applied the parol evidence rule, the court justified its decision in part by the observation that the parties were experienced businessmen who were presumed to know the effect of written agreements.[102] From a commercial perspective, the ability to create a definitive and complete contract can lend a great deal of predictability to business transactions, facilitating the flow of commerce and enhancing the welfare of the population. Yet we saw in chapter 3 that textualization and other literary conventions of the legal profession can create difficulties for ordinary citizens, who are generally not familiar with the textual practices that the legal profession applies to wills. This is true of contracts as well.

Conflicting Conventions of Literacy

From the perspective of the average person, one of the main problems with the doctrine of integration (and the related parol evidence rule) is that it runs counter to ordinary conventions of literacy. If you enter a computer store and buy an expensive software program, you normally assume that what the salesperson told you, what you read in a magazine advertisement about the product, what is printed on the box, and the sign on the cash register regarding returns are all in a sense part of the deal that you make with the store (or with the manufacturer). With most transactions of this kind, that would probably be true.

Now suppose that when you buy the software, you are presented with a purchase and sale agreement that in addition to blanks for inserting your name, the product, and the price, contains numerous printed terms. One of those terms is the following: "THIS AGREEMENT IS THE COMPLETE AGREEMENT BETWEEN THE PARTIES WITH RESPECT TO THE SOFTWARE AND SUPERCEDES ANY OTHER COMMUNICATION OR ADVERTISING WITH RESPECT TO THE SOFTWARE."[103] Leaving aside the misspelling of *supersede*, which occurred in the original, the point of this paragraph—a fairly typical merger clause—is to textualize or integrate the document in which it is contained. If enforced, the text of the purchase agreement will replace or override anything the software manufacturer or its agents might previously have communicated to the purchaser in speech or in writing.

Yet the statement that a written agreement "supersedes" all other communications is not likely to make a lot of sense to many people. A more honest way to say it is the following: "This document is our complete agreement. This means that we are not responsible for, and will not honor, any claims we made in our advertising, anything the salesperson told you, anything on our website, anything printed on the box, or anything our customer service personnel might have told you about the product before you bought it." Whether a court would enforce this clause as broadly as my plain English version suggests is (I hope!) questionable. The parol evidence rule only bars evidence that contradicts the terms of an integrated agreement, or in the case of a fully integrated agreement, evidence of additional terms. But it clearly seems to be the intention of the software manufacturer, in case of a later dispute, to bar any and all evidence of anything it might have claimed in its advertising, written on the box, or encouraged its sales force to say. It seems to me that quite a few people would be very surprised to discover that this is what the integration clause aims to achieve.

Because many consumers are unlikely to understand the effect of a merger clause in a legal document, the potential exists for businesses to exploit this lack of knowledge. As Lawrence Solan has observed, "Reliance on the written word is a two-edged sword. On the one hand it reduces the likelihood of dispute about what the agreement . . . really says. On the other, it empowers the party with the pen."[104]

An example that Solan cites is where the parol evidence rule interacts (or conflicts) with a doctrine called *promissory estoppel*. Under the common law, "bare" promises (where the addressee does nothing in return) are not normally enforceable. However, the doctrine of promissory estoppel states that if you make a promise knowing that the recipient is likely to rely on it, the promise may be enforced even if it would not qualify as a contract under traditional rules.

Thus, suppose that an overeager sales representative makes some promises about the capabilities of a product that his company manufactures. You then buy it. Let's say that the purchase form that you sign disclaims any warranties other than those on the form itself and that it also contains an integration or merger clause. The promises that the salesman made are not on the form. Suppose that the product does not perform as the sale representative claimed. At least some courts would uphold the integration clause and apply the parol evidence rule, refusing to consider any evidence of what the salesman said, despite the principle of promissory estoppel, which might otherwise make the promise enforceable.[105]

An example is *Globe Metallurgical, Inc. v. Hewlett-Packard Co.*[106] Globe was approached by a salesman from Hewlett Packard (HP), who convinced Globe to lease computer hardware and associated software from HP and two software vendors. After about a year, the equipment was still not working properly, forcing Globe to continue using its old system. Globe eventually sued HP and the other vendors for breach of contract, breach of warranty, and fraud.

HP defended by pointing out that its lease agreement, which Globe signed, contained the following language:

> Lessee shall have the benefit of applicable manufacturer's warranties covering the Equipment which are normally furnished to purchases of identical equipment manufactured by Lessor. THE WARRANTY REFERRED TO ABOVE IS EXCLUSIVE AND NO OTHER WARRANTY WHETHER WRITTEN OR ORAL IS EXPRESSED OR IMPLIED. LESSOR SPECIFICALLY DISCLAIMS THE IMPLIED WARRANTIES OF MERCHANTABILITY AND FITNESS FOR A PARTICULAR PURPOSE.

The warranties that Globe alleged HP had breached were admittedly not included in the lease agreement but were instead based on statements made orally to Globe by the HP salesman or were contained in written documents that HP provided (including a sales proposal and a benefits analysis). Was this extrinsic evidence part of the contract?

The answer depends upon whether the lease agreement was an integrated document. Significantly, the agreement contained an integration clause: "This Agreement, together with any Equipment Schedules executed hereunder, and any referenced attachments shall constitute the entire understanding between the parties and supersedes any previous communications, representations, or agreements whether verbal or written."[107] Because both parties were relatively sophisticated, the court held that they must have understood the implications of this paragraph. Globe, in other words, was deemed to have agreed that the contractual text expressed all the warranties that might apply and that any other warranties or promises that might have been made were superseded by the much more limited warranties in the lease agreement. Case dismissed.[108]

Another example involved a divorcing couple in California. According to the husband, before he signed a property settlement agreeing to pay the former wife $300 per month for the rest of her life, she promised that he would be relieved of this obligation if she remarried. He signed the agreement relying on this promise, but on its face the obligation was absolute. The court held that the written settlement agreement superseded the wife's oral promise, making evidence of the promise inadmissible.[109]

There is no doubt that the parol evidence rule sometimes produces harsh results that fly in the face of ordinary textual practices. To the average person, it must seem bizarre to suggest that a writing can sometimes replace or supersede anything that was previously said or written on a particular point. When strictly applied, the rule allows unscrupulous parties to misrepresent or even lie about the effect of a written agreement, knowing that what they say will not be admitted in a court of law.

Judges are not oblivious to the problem and have devised various ways to mitigate the harshness of the rule. Some state courts consider the relative sophistication of the parties and may decide that—despite the presence of an integration cause—a contract should not be deemed to be integrated if one party is an ordinary consumer.[110] In doing so, these courts are implicitly recognizing that the average person is not likely to be aware of the literary practices of the legal profession and, in particular, the consequences of textualization.

Should We Abolish the Parol Evidence Rule?

Given the problems that the parol evidence rule presents, perhaps we should just abolish it. The civil law system that is in place in most of Europe and much of the rest of the world seems perfectly content without it. The same is true for international law. The United States is a party to the Convention on Contracts for the International Sale of Goods (CISG), which operates something like the *Uniform Commercial Code* but on a global scale. Consistent with the law in most civil law jurisdictions, the CISG does not have the equivalent of a parol evidence rule.[111]

Perhaps American law should cast off the yoke of writing that has developed during the past few centuries and return to an era of greater orality. Modern written media like e-mail and text messaging seem to resemble speech more than the formal writing that reached its apex in the eighteenth and nineteenth centuries. In any event, there is substantial academic support for abolishing or watering down the rule, and some courts (most notably, the California Supreme Court) have diluted or eviscerated it.[112]

My inclination, however, is not to abolish the doctrine of integration entirely, nor the related parol evidence rule. Instead, I would advocate following a course similar to that recommended in the chapter on wills. Just as some people might want the peace of mind that arises from drafting a will that is highly textualized and difficult to change informally, parties entering into contracts may value the security and predictability that comes from fixing their agreement in a very definitive form, assured that casual comments they made during negotiations will not return to bedevil them later.

When all the parties to a contract are sophisticated business entities that either have or can hire lawyers to advise them, they should be well aware of the profession's textual practices relating to contracts. And when they integrate the agreement, both parties will be involved in negotiating which terms are part of the contract and which are not. It makes perfect sense to hold the parties to the text of an agreement that they jointly drafted and to prohibit them from later undermining it.

It is quite another matter when one of the parties to a contract is a consumer or a small business. They are likely to believe that they can rely on the assertions in a company's advertising or on claims made by a salesman, even if they later sign a purchase agreement with an integration clause. Moreover, when these contracts consist of standardized forms, as is typical with consumer transactions, the notion that a consumer or small business intended the form to constitute the complete and final statement of its agreement is a charade. Consumers in this situation never assent in any realistic way to the inclusion of a merger clause into the contract, nor are they likely to understand its effect. It makes no sense to impose the textual practices of contracts law on people who do not understand what those practices are. It's like attaching great significance to the placement of a comma in a writing by a person who is semiliterate and does not follow customary conventions of punctuation.

Judges should therefore take a very jaundiced view of claims by sophisticated businesses that an ordinary consumer should be forbidden from proving that a representative of a company told them something or gave them written documents that contradict language in the standardized form agreement that the consumer signed. It may be unrealistic to completely abolish the rule against parol evidence in business-to-consumer contracts, but before judges declare that a written text is the complete and final embodiment of the agreement of the parties, they should satisfy themselves that the parties understood at the time that this would be the case.

Admittedly, a large business may be hard pressed to monitor everything that its sales staff tells potential customers, and it has even less control when its goods are sold through independent retail outlets. But if someone is to bear the loss, it should be the more powerful party, which has the ability to train its staff and control how its goods are sold.

Moreover, to the extent that businesses publicly standardize their contracts, as suggested above, the potential of customers to make outrageous claims about what sales personnel promised them should largely disappear. Suppose that cell phone companies and consumers were to create and publicize a standardized set of rights and responsibilities of cell phone providers and users. Now suppose that a cell phone user claims that because her provider dropped an important call, she lost a million-dollar business opportunity. She alleges that when she bought the phone, the salesman told her that there would be no losses of service for any reason. Her claim would be denied not because of an obscure disclaimer of consequential damages accompanied by a merger clause in her service agreement, but because the standardized conditions of cell phone usage were available to her in advance, were widely publicized, and explained her rights in language that the average consumer can comprehend.

Interpreting the Contractual Text

The final issue that we consider in this chapter is the interpretation of contracts. For almost a century, judges and scholars have been debating whether contracts should be interpreted subjectively, focusing on the intentions of the parties, or objectively, focusing on the text. One of the themes of this book is that you cannot interpret in the abstract. You invariably interpret a specific utterance or text. How you interpret it depends on what type of utterance or text it is. My view is that a judge should concentrate on the subjective intentions of the parties. That is what we do in ordinary life, particularly in spoken conversations. But if the parties integrate their agreement, creating a definitive text containing its terms, it is reasonable for the judge to take a more objective approach.

The Role of Context and the Four Corners Rule

Judges have traditionally imposed upon contracts a relatively literal mode of interpretation, one that takes little account of context, the surrounding circumstances, and similar types of background information. Their stated aim is to divine the meaning of the text from the words that are contained within it. Only if those words are vague or ambiguous will they look at *extrinsic evidence* (that is, anything not part of the text of the document being interpreted). This is often called the *four corners rule*, in that the meaning of the contract is sought based exclusively on information contained within the four corners of the document. Another name for this principle is the *plain meaning rule*. We saw in the previous chapter that this approach is sometimes also applied to wills. Scholars tend to refer to it as an objective approach to interpretation, since it pays little attention to the actual (subjective) intentions of the parties. To be more exact, judges using this approach assume the parties have placed all their intentions into the written text. They therefore seek to determine intent solely from the words in the text.

Many modern courts continue to follow this approach, or at the least pay lip service to it. A judge in Illinois put it this way:

> The primary objective in contract construction is to give effect to the intention of the parties and that intention is to be ascertained from the language of the contract. . . . If a contract is clear and unambiguous, the judge must determine the intention of the parties "solely from the plain language of the contract" and may not consider extrinsic evidence outside the "four corners" of the document itself.[113]

A Texas court expressed similar sentiments: "In construing a written contract, the primary concern of the court is to ascertain the parties' true intentions as expressed in the instrument itself. . . . If the written instrument is so worded that it can be given a certain definite meaning or interpretation, then it is not ambiguous, and the court will construe the contract as a matter of law."[114] Kansas is in agreement: "Where a contract is complete and unambiguous on its face, the court must determine the parties' intent from the four corners of the document, without regard to extrinsic or parol evidence."[115] All of these statements date from the past decade or two.

An illustration is the New York case of *W. W. W. Associates, Inc. v. Giancontieri*, decided in 1990.[116] At issue was a contract to sell real estate. It provided that under certain conditions, "either party shall have the right to cancel this contract." When the sellers tried to cancel the contract, the buyers sued, claiming that only they—the buyers—had the right to invoke the cancellation clause. They sought to admit evidence to the effect that during negotiations, the cancellation clause was added purely for their benefit. The court refused to consider it: "Evidence outside the four corners of the document as to what was really intended but unstated or misstated is generally inadmissible." On its face, the clause plainly applied to either party, so there was no basis for interpreting it to mean something else.

The plain meaning or four corners rule has been attacked by judges and academics for over half a century.[117] Most notably, John Henry Wigmore, the great expert on evidence, derided it as resting on the myth that words have fixed meanings and are imbued with inherent potency.[118]

Justice Traynor of the California Supreme Court picked up the ball and ran with it. In a 1968 case that is still controversial, *Pacific Gas & Electric Co. v. G. W. Thomas Drayage & Rigging Co.*, he wrote that it is nonsense to try to decide whether there is an ambiguity based purely on examination of the text itself. "Rational interpretation requires at least a preliminary consideration of all credible evidence offered to prove the intentions of the parties."[119] Yet the court did not eviscerate the rule entirely. A California judge still needs to decide, after examining the extrinsic evidence that is being offered, that the text has an ambiguity. If so, the evidence can be admitted and used to determine its meaning. If not, the four corners rule applies.

Some authorities have abolished the rule entirely. For example, Alaska has held that its state courts can consider extrinsic evidence without first having to identify an ambiguity.[120] The *Restatement (Second) of Contracts* states that extrinsic evidence should be used to determine the meaning of any contractual text, whether or not it is integrated.[121]

On the other hand, there has also been a backlash against this liberalizing trend. Justice Stanley Mosk, who had joined Justice Traynor and the majority of the California Supreme Court in the *Pacific Gas and Electric* case, later became concerned that "it has become virtually impossible under recently evolving rules of evidence to draft a written contract that will produce predictable results in court. The written word, heretofore deemed immutable, is now at all times subject to alteration by self-serving recitals based upon fading memories of antecedent events."[122] A prominent federal judge, Alex Kozinski, has even more harshly criticized the California approach, stating that "it matters not how clearly a contract is written, nor how completely it is integrated, nor how carefully it is negotiated, nor how squarely it addresses the issue before the court; the contract cannot be rendered impervious to attack by parol evidence."[123] Kozinski's criticism is overwrought, it seems to me, but it does make an important point about the four corners rule: it applies only to written agreements. The name, four corners, suggests as much.

Oral versus Written Interpretation

Judges and scholars debating contract interpretation seem to pay little explicit attention to whether a contract is oral or written. Yet it would be bizarre for judges to declare that they will ignore extrinsic evidence and determine the meaning of an oral contract based exclusively on the plain meaning of the words that the parties uttered. For starters, the parties are not likely to remember those words verbatim. And when interpreting utterances made in face-to-face conversations, we take context and background information into account without even thinking about it. Young children sometimes take spoken language very literally, as when you ask a child, "Can you open that door for me?" and she replies, "Yes," but does nothing. Such literal interpretation of spoken utterances is usually the result of misunderstanding or adolescent attempts at humor.

Thus, the plain meaning doctrine or four corners rule is clearly associated with written contracts. Yet this does not mean that it should be automatically applied to all such texts. Many writings can be quite informal, including letters, e-mails, grocery lists, and so forth. If someone jots down a few informal notes, rather than creating a carefully drafted statement of his intentions, literal interpretation of the text is completely inappropriate.

Consequently, if an objective mode of interpretation has any justification at all, it should be applied only to written contracts that are highly textualized. If parties truly integrate their agreement, carefully hammering out the exact language of the text, then judges interpreting that text ought to accord their choice of words a great deal of deference.[124]

Once we limit the plain meaning rule in this way, the apparently contradictory comments of judges regarding the interpretation of contracts begin to make some sense. Recall that judges routinely begin their exegesis of contracts by saying that the primary goal of interpretation is to carry out the intentions of the parties. They then continue by saying that if the meaning of the text is clear, they will not consider any extrinsic evidence (that is, any evidence of the parties' intentions that is not in the text). Yet if the intentions of the parties are indeed paramount, why should judges exclude evidence that might throw light on those intentions? On one level, these statements appear irreconcilable: judges seem to be simultaneously embracing a subjective and objective approach.[125]

Yet if we restrict this objective approach to integrated (or textualized) documents, the contradiction largely disappears. Textualization (or integration) involves attempting to place all your communicative intentions into the text itself. While it is impossible to really do so, lawyers nonetheless try. So it makes sense for judges to presume, as an initial matter, that the parties have indeed placed all their intentions into the text. As one court remarked, "Pennsylvania contract law begins with the 'firmly settled' point that the intent of the parties to a written contract *is contained in the writing itself*."[126]

Of course, just because a principle flows naturally from the textual practices of the profession, we are not obligated to follow those conventions today. They are customs, not law adopted by a popular assembly and cut into stone. They should certainly not be followed if they frustrate the intentions of the parties.[127]

Objective interpretation is inappropriate when a writing is merely evidence of the agreement—for instance, if it is merely a note or memorandum made to satisfy the Statute of Frauds. In that case it is almost perverse to fixate on the exact words contained in the text. The essence of the contract is the agreement that the parties reached during their negotiations. When we seek to determine a speaker's communicative intentions in ordinary conversation, we use all cues and background information that are available to us. We certainly do not artificially restrict ourselves to the words of the utterance.

The same is true of a contract between a business and consumers, especially if it contains a boilerplate merger clause. It is nonsense to focus intently on a text that one of the parties has almost certainly not read, or if she has read it, does not understand. In such cases, judges should adopt a more ordinary (or even a more oral) method of interpretation that tries to determine how a reasonable consumer would have understood the language in question. Ordinary citizens do not fixate on exact words or the placement of a comma when they interpret a text. Rather, they strive to discover the gist or to get a general sense of what the writer is trying to convey.

Insurance law has been moving in this direction with respect to the interpretation of ambiguities in policies held by consumers. As the Montana Supreme Court recently stated, "We accord the usual meaning to the terms and the words in an insurance contract, and we construe them using common sense. . . . We determine whether an ambiguity exists from the viewpoint of a consumer with average intelligence, but untrained in the law or the insurance business."[128] If an ambiguity is found under this test, "we will construe the ambiguous language and apply a meaning that would ordinarily be understood by the insured."[129] Or as stated by a Rhode Island court, "When the terms of an insurance policy are unambiguous, this Court will give the words, when read in conjunction with the entire policy, their plain and ordinary meaning. . . . The test is not what the insurer subjectively intended, but rather 'what the ordinary reader and purchaser would understand [the terms] to mean.' "[130] It seems to me that these principles should apply to all consumer contracts, not just those involving insurance.

Where objective interpretation and the plain meaning rule went astray was in assuming that all written contracts are the result of a carefully negotiated drafting process by which the parties jointly expressed their agreement definitively and completely. Not every contractual writing is fully textualized. Most, in fact, are not. Thus, judges should inquire whether the writing was carefully drafted by all the parties to reflect their actual agreement. If so, they should give a great deal of respect to the language of the text and pay relatively less attention to extrinsic evidence.

Yet if the document was intended to be merely a record or evidence of what the parties agreed to, there is no rational reason to systematically exclude other relevant evidence, whether oral or written, of what the parties meant to accomplish. And if one of the parties is an ordinary consumer, unaware of the textual conventions of the legal profession, it likewise seems highly unfair to interpret a contract using those conventions, especially if they would defeat the consumer's reasonable expectations.

Contract interpretation therefore inevitably has a mix of subjective and objective elements. The subjective intentions of the parties are always primary, just as we normally seek to determine what a speaker means by an utterance, rather than focusing inordinately on the words. But where the parties are represented by lawyers, who are familiar with the textual conventions of the profession and who embody their agreement in an authoritative text that is jointly and carefully drafted, the interpreter should pay careful attention to what that text says.

Conclusion

In a world where all agreements are oral, there would be little need for contract law. Just about every dispute would boil down to a question of credibility. Did the parties reach an agreement? What were its terms? What did the parties intend to accomplish? Did each party perform? Those questions would be answered almost entirely by testimony of the parties, and the judge or jury would do little beyond deciding whom to believe.

When people began to enter into contracts via written correspondence, the situation changed dramatically. Judges began to closely scrutinize the words in the correspondence and to then categorize them as comprising an offer, or as merely requesting information, or as an acceptance or counter-offer. They began to attach important consequences to this classification.

Printed agreements posed additional difficulties. They became ammunition in the proverbial battle of the forms. The problems intensified as printed forms became common in consumer transactions. And, of course, courts today are confronted with e-contracts, e-signatures, and other challenges posed by our increasingly digital world.

The law has not always responded well to new technologies of communication. Too often it has imposed past paradigms on such innovations, with predictable consequences. I hope to have shown in this chapter that it matters whether a contract is created orally, or whether it is created orally but evidenced by a written memorandum, or whether it is completely written. And it also matters whether the writing was handwritten, printed, or produced electronically.

All of these themes will reappear (albeit with some interesting and important variations) in the next chapter, where we consider another major type of legal text: statutes or, more generally, legislation.

5
Statutes

When societies become literate, their laws are one of the first things that they begin to write down. At first writing functions merely to record custom or oral decisions, or perhaps to enhance the prestige of the monarch. But eventually governments begin to legislate by enacting written text.

In this chapter we will explore more extensively what happens when laws are set down in an authoritative textual form. In England, Parliament began to enact written text during the Tudor era, but fully accurate copies of that text were not widely available until the early eighteenth century. Not coincidentally, these developments enabled judges to interpret the words of statutes in a more textual way than had been possible previously.

In the United States, legislation has been highly textualized and accurate copies of statutes have been readily available for at least two hundred years. Nonetheless, the rigid textual interpretation that developed in England did not take hold with equal force, as evidenced by current debate between textualists and intentionalists.

The different approaches that have been taken in two closely related legal systems suggest that there may be no single best or true method of interpretation. One reason is that political and institutional concerns will always play a role, something that has received a great deal of attention in the scholarly literature.

What has received less attention is the relationship between the nature of the statutory text and the mode of its interpretation. Just as speech is interpreted differently from writing, so differing types of texts may invite a mode of interpretation that fits the kind of text in question. Thus, rather than employing a one-size-fits-all approach to interpretation, judges should consider the type of statute in question, how carefully the words of the statute were chosen, how likely it is that the legislature debated and reviewed those words, and who the intended audience is. In some cases, especially when the legislature carefully reviewed the text of a statute or when members of the public are likely to read and rely on the text, a more textual approach to interpretation will be justified. When such issues are not a concern, the courts should concentrate less on words and more on the intent behind them.

Currently, our conception of writing, text, and publication is rapidly changing. The writing in many texts is becoming more speech-like in style. Moreover, electronic texts are far less static than those that consist of ink on paper. Statutes in the future may be drafted, updated, and published in radically different ways than they are today, becoming more like information posted on a website than printing in a book. At the same time, the rule of law has a strong interest in promoting stability and predictability, which may mean that some of the traditional features of written text, such as autonomy and textualization, may continue to perform important functions in the digital age.

Oral and Written Law

In light of the advantages of literacy, which we discussed in chapter 2, it is no surprise that one of the earliest uses of writing was to set down laws. It would be tempting to suggest that writing is essential to the lawmaking process.[1] Legal norms that are not written down would then be relegated to the status of custom.

Once writing emerged in Mesopotamia around five millennia ago, it did not take long for public law to emerge in writing. The first surviving Mesopotamian law collection is ascribed to King Ur-Nammu and dates from around 2100 BC. A few hundred years later came the well-known Code of Hammurabi, which—consistent with its public nature—was inscribed on large stone stelae.[2] Perhaps the aim was to make the law known to subjects far and wide. More likely, the king's main goal was to impress the public, since most people at that time—including judges—could not read.[3]

Although the exact nature of the legal codes from the Mesopotamian period remains disputed, scholars agree that they were not legislation in the modern sense. Mesopotamian law remained essentially unwritten, despite being inscribed in clay or stone. Evidence of the relatively oral nature of these early codes is that in the many extant documents and reports of disputes from the period, there are few if any in which the wording of the text of a law is mentioned.[4] The Mesopotamian codes were not the result of kings like Hammurabi conceiving of new rules of conduct that should henceforth govern the realm, dictating those rules to scribes, and ordering that they be chiseled into stelae.[5] Instead, they were mostly descriptions or records of rules and practices that already existed, perhaps with some embellishments and improvements.

Indeed, it seems that in just about every society that begins to write law on its own initiative, the first such writings are records of laws that already exist rather than attempts to enact new law. It is generally accepted that the earliest written laws of the Hebrews reflected underlying oral or customary rules.[6] The same is true of the oldest Germanic codes.[7] In such societies, the law remains primarily oral, and the written texts are records that perform at most an evidentiary or preservative function.

Of course, just because law can exist in oral form does not mean that, in particular societies, writing might not at some point come to be viewed as essential to the validity of a law or to the lawmaking process in general. In fact, H. L. A. Hart suggests in *The Concept of Law* that reducing a rule to writing may be part of what separates the prelegal from the legal. What was previously just a matter of custom might now be recognized as a primary rule of obligation. Hart posits that historically this process may have gone through distinguishable stages. The first is to reduce hitherto unwritten rules to writing. The next step, Hart suggests, is the crucial one: "the acknowledgement of reference to the writing or inscription as *authoritative*, i.e., as the *proper* way of disposing of doubts as to the existence of the rule."[8]

Hart seems to have recognized that the act of writing down a rule does not by itself change its essentially oral nature. Even after rules are written down, they may still be transmitted primarily by word of mouth, and questions about them will generally be answered by seeking the advice of someone reputed to know the law. Eventually, however, people may start to learn the rule or answer questions by consulting the text. The rule may then come to be viewed as words on paper or some other medium, rather than as something contained in the minds and memories of elders, remembrancers, or the community as a whole.

Ancient Greece may be the earliest example of written law becoming authoritative in this sense. Alphabetic writing arose in Greece around the eighth century BC. The Greeks had borrowed the idea of consonantal writing (still used in Hebrew and Arabic) from the Phoenicians. Their innovation was to add letters for vowels, creating a truly alphabetic system, one in which writing could represent the actual pronunciation of a word.[9] Earlier systems were partly phonetic as well, but an alphabet allows for a one-to-one correspondence between written symbols (letters) and the phonemes (sounds) of a language. Because most languages have no more than thirty or forty phonemes, the number of required letters is relatively small, making an alphabetic system easy to learn.

By 700 BC alphabetic writing had made its way to the island of Crete, and around fifty years later, it was put to use in the city of Dreros for the inscription of laws.[10] A more complete code has survived from the city of Gortyn, also on Crete. It consists of 600 lines divided into twelve columns.[11] Interestingly, the magistrate at Gortyn was required to follow this written law, if it contained an applicable rule.[12] At the same time, other procedures remained overwhelmingly oral. Legal transactions were performed orally before witnesses, and if a dispute arose, the witness had to come to court to testify; written evidence was not admissible.[13]

Written law was taken a step further in Athens, where by the fifth century BC many of the laws were inscribed in stone. Eventually, the Athenian word for law (*nomos*) came to refer exclusively to written law. Magistrates were forbidden to enforce any other type of law.[14] Moreover, the decrees of the counsel or assembly could not prevail over an inscribed law.[15] By the fourth century, there are numerous indications that judges and litigants could read and were familiar with written laws that were relevant to a case. They treated such laws as authoritative.[16] For example, sections of the law would sometimes be read aloud at trials. Someone would go to the public inscription of the law, make a copy of the relevant provision, and bring it to the clerk of the court.[17]

The authority of inscribed laws resulted to a large extent from the procedures by which they were enacted. Beginning around 400 BC, the Athenians began to write the text of proposed new laws on boards, which were placed in a public area. During this time private citizens could come before the council and suggest changes. After being approved, they were inscribed in stone.[18]

It would go too far to conclude that the Athenians had adopted something akin to modern bill procedure, where a legislature enacts written text after debating its wording, or that their society was governed entirely by written norms. Much Athenian law and procedure remained oral.[19] Written law may have trumped oral law in the areas that it regulated, but oral law would still have been valid in those areas in which there were no written rules. Nonetheless, these developing textual practices reveal a concern about the wording of statutes, presaging similar developments in England nearly two millennia later.

As opposed to Athens, Sparta had less use for the written word.[20] In fact, Sparta seems for a while to have had a ban on committing law to writing.[21] A critical observation is that Sparta did not have a ban on law; it had a ban on written law. If Sparta had no laws, there would have been no way to prohibit writing them down. Clearly, the term oral law is not an oxymoron.

Perhaps the most interesting illustration of oral law is medieval Iceland. Every summer, people from around the island would gather in a place called Thingvellir to hold a national assembly, the *Althing*. The Althing, which first met in the year 930, carried out both legislative and judicial functions. The lawmaking power was held by the *lögrétta*, a legal council, over which presided the *lögsögumaðr*, or 'law speaker.' One of his functions was to publicly recite one-third of Iceland's law at the Althing each year; the entire body of the law had to be recited in a three-year cycle. Although Iceland was at least partially literate at the time, the law speaker was expected to recite the laws from memory. Not until the twelfth century did the Icelanders begin to systematically write down their laws.[22]

It would be bizarre to suggest that Iceland had no law in the tenth and eleventh centuries, given that the law speaker was reciting something that would have sounded very much like law and which for the most part had been adopted by the law council. It is equally bizarre to suggest that those same rules, or rules very much like them, were ipso facto transformed into law when they were first written down.

This is not to say that there are no differences between oral and written law. Much of this book is about those differences. In the case of preliterate Iceland, even though its oral law was recited in three-year cycles, the law speakers do not seem to have memorized it verbatim. Not only would it be very difficult to memorize exact words without access to a written text, but when the law was later written down, it did not contain mnemonic devices like alliteration or rhyme, which are almost essential for learning long segments of text word-for-word. In addition, the law speaker would sometimes consult with legal experts before the recitation to clear up uncertainties. And although the law speaker did not have the power to add new law, his recitation "must often have amounted to his own interpretation of standing laws."[23]

The point is that there is no clear-cut relationship between writing and law. Some societies, like Sparta and Iceland, got along perfectly well without feeling a need to write down their law, even when they were literate. Other societies at some point begin to view writing as essential to their conception of law. Between those extremes are many legal systems where orality and literacy peacefully coexist. Indeed, we have seen that even in modern-day America, where writing has become essential to just about every aspect of the law, orality retains a surprising vitality.

Yet although law does not need to be written, putting law and other legal transactions into written form can have important implications. In the common law tradition, this first happened in medieval England.

Writing the Law in England

The earliest inhabitants of England to leave substantial traces in the history books were the Celtic Britons. Because they were illiterate at this time, we know little about their legal system, but it appears to have been largely regulated by custom.

During the Roman occupation of Britain, from roughly AD 50 to around 400, Latin was used for administrative and legal purposes. Latin, of course, was a written language in this period. The Roman administration of Britain (which included judicial officers) would likely have been done in accordance with a written statute, called a *lex provinciae*, which laid down some basic principles on how the province was to be governed.[24] But whatever legislation might have been in effect in Britain largely disappeared when the Romans left the British Isles. For the most part, written laws seem to have departed with them.

Lawmaking in Anglo-Saxon Times

By around AD 500 Germanic tribes who had come from the continent controlled much of what is now England, organizing themselves administratively into several small kingdoms. Like the other Germanic tribes of the time, the Anglo-Saxons, as they came to be known, were largely illiterate. As far as we know they did not have written laws.

This situation began to change with the arrival of Christian missionaries around AD 600. As we have previously mentioned, Christianity reintroduced the Latin language and, more importantly for our purposes, the practice of literacy.[25] Not long thereafter, the first written English laws appeared, those of King Æthelberht of Kent. Other codes of Anglo-Saxon law followed. These compilations of law were in the Anglo-Saxon language, also known as Old English.[26]

It is generally accepted that these early English legal codes, which were usually issued in the name of a certain king, were not legislation in the modern sense. Like the Code of Hammurabi, they were written records of laws or customs that already existed in some sense, not attempts to impose new rules or change existing law. That is certainly true of the laws of King Æthelberht, which are little more than lists of compensation to victims for various offenses, such as the following:

> *Gif man mannan ofslæhđ, medume leodgeld C scillinga gebete.*
>
> [If a person kills someone, let him pay an ordinary person-price, 100 shillings.][27]

Writing down laws in the king's name no doubt imbued them with a certain authority that they might not have had before. And it is possible that in the process of recording existing law, innovations slipped in. But on the whole, Æthelberht's code is best described as a compilation of existing law or custom rather than as legislation by the king and his council. As Patrick Wormald has remarked, most of what Æthelberht put into writing was "established" rather than "innovatory."[28]

Subsequent Anglo-Saxon compilations of law contain provisions that suggest grander ambitions. Several of Æthelberht's successors issued codes of their own, sometimes adding new laws. For example, they inserted provisions to deal with the increasing influence of the church and to funnel more money into their treasuries. Moreover, the language of these later laws is syntactically more complex and the content more abstract.[29] Wormald concludes, "Law was now *made* as well as *recorded* in writing."[30]

While it is arguable that Æthelberht's laws were nothing more than custom written down, these later innovations would almost certainly qualify as law by most standards. In such cases, the king (often with the assistance or consent of spiritual and secular advisors) acted much like a modern legislator.

King Alfred, whose code is the longest set of Anglo-Saxon laws, proceeded a step further in this direction by sometimes using the first person (*we settađ*, meaning 'we fix' or 'we set down'), as when fixing the peace for a consecrated church.[31] This strongly suggests that he viewed himself as a lawmaker. Additional evidence comes from a comment by Alfred that after commanding that the laws be written down, he showed them to his wise men, who agreed to observe them.[32]

Similarly, King Ine of the West Saxons insisted in his code that his officials and subjects obey his decrees.[33] And King Edgar's Wihtbordesstan code reveals additional evidence of a developing awareness of the rule of law. It provided that multiple copies should be made and that they should be sent "in all directions" so that the law should be known to rich and poor alike.[34]

The notion that it is possible to explicitly create or modify rules governing human behavior, which resembles the modern concept of lawmaking, was clearly beginning to emerge. What is less clear is the process by which such laws were enacted, mainly because the historical record is so sparse. Alfred's code states that he gathered together rules from synod books and the laws of other kings. He rejected some, kept others, and had them written down.[35]

Despite some signs of inchoate legislation in this period, even one of the latest and most extensive collections of Anglo-Saxon law, that of Cnut the Dane, is thought to have largely codified existing law.[36] In certain other cases, the text of Anglo-Saxon laws appears to have been a written record of previous oral pronouncements or decrees made by the king. Risto Hiltunen's linguistic analysis of the Anglo-Saxon codes also suggests that many of them are oral in origin. He notes, for instance, that they sometimes contain the introductory phrase "we have pronounced" before the statement of certain rules.[37]

Although there was a slowly developing consciousness that laws ought to be written down, the validity of legislation at the time did not depend on whether it was, in fact, memorialized on paper or parchment. Kings may have been able to have innovative laws written down, but it was not the only way in which they could make law. And the fact that a rule of conduct was written did not necessarily create law where none had existed before. To quote Wormald once more, "*Legislation*, commitment of the law to writing, showed what the law was, whether in custom or as a result of royal adjudication or decree. It was not, at this stage, necessarily the same thing as *making law*."[38]

The notion that writing was not yet essential to the lawmaking process is supported by the observation that many Anglo-Saxon kings seem to have produced no written laws at all, even after Æthelberht and other Kentish kings established a precedent for doing so, and even if they had clerics at their disposal to do the drafting. Perhaps these kings simply did not legislate. They may have been content to govern entirely by custom, lacking either the will or the power to innovate. Other kings clearly did engage in legislative activity but made no effort—as far as we know—to have their product reduced to writing. Edward the Confessor, for instance, is said to have abrogated bad laws and, with the advice of his counsel, to have established good ones. But there is no evidence that he ever made written law.[39]

The Anglo-Saxon codes were therefore mainly records of the law or evidence of what the law was. Unlike modern legislation, the written codes did not constitute the law. Wormald points out that there is not a single lawsuit from this period in which one of the participants referred to written legislation.[40] Part of the reason, no doubt, was that the supremacy of written law had not yet been established. In addition, there were often severe practical problems in obtaining copies of the royal codes, so judges may not have had easy access to them.[41] Whatever the reason, resolving disputes by referring to the language of a statute was still a thing of the future.

The Normans and Beyond

In the century or so following the Norman Conquest in 1066, there was relatively little legislative activity. William the Conqueror legislated—if it can be called that—mainly by writs, which could be loosely defined at this stage as letters from the sovereign to officials or subjects, containing commands, prohibitions, declarations, and similar legal speech acts. The famous example is William's writ to the citizens of London, soon after he assumed power, in which he declared that they were to enjoy the same laws that were in effect in King Edward's time and that the existing rules of inheritance would be respected.[42] No doubt William could instead have issued an oral proclamation, which would probably have been no less effective during his lifetime. But the fact that he made his declaration in writing did have significance, if not for its validity, then certainly for its durability. The original document has been kept ever since by the City of London, and one may assume that—at least initially—it was not merely a historical curiosity.[43]

More akin to modern legislation are various *assizes* from a slightly later period. This word, which refers in the first instance to a council or court session (*assize* means something like "sitting"), later came to refer to the enactments that were made at such sessions. Thus, the Assize of Clarendon (1166) contained various rules relating to criminal procedure. The introductory language makes clear that the king and his council are acting as lawmakers: "King Henry established by the counsel of all his barons. . . ." Moreover, the contents were not always restatements of established custom but at times were innovative. The first chapter provided that the justices and sheriffs should place twelve men under oath from every *hundred* (an administrative unit), and four men from every *vill* (a village or subdivision of a hundred), and inquire whether any crimes had been committed in their hundred or vill. This is commonly thought to have given birth to the grand jury.[44]

Although these assizes were written documents, generally issued in the name of the king and his counsel, there is no indication that writing was deemed essential. The introductory formula in the Assize of Clarendon refers in the past tense to what the king established. Moreover, these assizes seem more like directions to various government officials. For the most part, they do not contain broad legal principles applicable to the population as a whole. It is thus debatable whether they should be considered lawmaking at all.[45]

In early nineteenth century, the British government made an effort to print all English laws enacted since the Conquest in a series of books called the *Statutes of the Realm*. The first statute in this series is the Provisions of Merton (1235–36) from the reign of Henry III.[46] Yet once again, the operative words of the Provisions are in the past tense (*provisum est*, or 'it has been provided'), indicating that this is more a record of decisions that have already been made rather than text that has formally been enacted. While some of the provisions sound very much like legislation meant to govern future conduct and cases, there are also clauses that resemble the minutes of a meeting. The ninth clause reports on a disagreement between the bishops and the lords, and the final clause states that the king denied a proposal by the lords concerning trespass in parks and ponds.[47]

The Provisions of Westminster (1259), which forced Henry III to give up some of his power to the barons, reveal a growing literate mentality. A French draft text was prepared for Parliament in 1259. According to historian Paul Brand, the text of the document was originally drafted in French (the language of the aristocracy at the time). It was discussed at a parliament in 1259, and the text was then translated into Latin. After being approved, it was read out in public in Westminster Hall, and copies were made for sheriffs and justices.[48]

Thus, a gradually increasing corpus of written documents that were in some sense legislative was being produced during the first half of the thirteenth century. But writing was hardly essential. Henry III is reported to have made law orally. For instance, in 1248 he "ordered it to be proclaimed as law by the voice of the crier" that from that time forward, a man could no longer castrate someone else for engaging in fornication, an exception being made for a husband who caught another man in flagrante delicto with his wife.[49]

More inclined to rule by means of written documents was Edward I (1272–1307), who instituted a number of bureaucratic and legal innovations during his reign. An example is the first Statute of Westminster, a voluminous series of laws dating from 1275. This appears to be the first English legislation recorded in French, which became the dominant legislative language during the fourteenth and much of the fifteenth centuries. It refers to itself as containing the *establisementz* of the King. The operative language remains in the past tense, however: *le Rey ordine & establi les choses desuz escrites* . . . [the King hath ordained and established these acts underwritten . . .].[50] A year later, a statute on bigamy recited that it was "heard and published before the King and his Council" and that they agreed "that they should be put in Writing for a perpetual Memory, and that they should be steadfastly observed."[51] There was clearly a growing appreciation that laws, particularly those that related to important matters, should be perpetuated as written text.

Nonetheless, there remained a great deal of uncertainty surrounding this relatively novel form of governing. As Theodore Plucknett has observed,

> Who could then say what a statute was, or be certain that any particular document was a statute? Who could say, even, what the actual words of any acknowledged statute really were? And what was the precise significance of *carta, assisa, constitutio, provisio, ordinatio, statutum, isetnysse*, all of which come before the courts for interpretation? If they were all equally statutes, why so many different titles? And if not, where do they differ?[52]

Plucknett later answered his own question by noting that at this time, the exact form of legislation seems not to have mattered much: "The great concern of the government was to govern, and if in the course of its duties legislation became necessary, then it was effected simply and quickly without any complications or formalities."[53]

Legislating via Written Statutes

Not long afterward, legislation starts to assume greater regularity. The word *statute* appears more frequently. During this same period—starting in the latter part of the thirteenth century—we also begin to see clear signs of written laws being deliberately used to establish and change legal norms, akin to modern legislation. Statutes begin to stipulate when they go into effect, for instance, suggesting that their makers view themselves as making rules that are meant to govern future behavior and to be enforced.[54]

Moreover, the proclamation of statutes seems to have become customary, though perhaps not essential.[55] The chancery sent copies of the statutes to the sheriffs with a proclamation writ attached. The writ, in the form of a letter from the king to the sheriff, commanded the sheriff to proclaim and publish the statute.[56] The Statute of Winchester, enacted in 1285, specifically required that one of its more important provisions be cried out "in all Counties, Hundreds, Markets, Fairs, and all other Places where great Resort of People is, so that none shall excuse himself by Ignorance . . ."[57]

Although the decisions of Parliament were now generally called *statutes* and were often proclaimed in public places, the word *statute* would not inevitably have suggested written law to people of this time. It derives from the Latin verb *statuo*, which literally means 'to cause to stand, put, place.' Even in classical Latin, however, it had developed a more abstract signification that referred to establishing something, settling a principle or point, giving a ruling, or deciding something.[58] A statute, therefore, was something that was established, settled, or decided. Its original meaning did not necessarily demand that it be written.[59]

Still, the rapid expansion of literacy and writing beginning in the thirteenth century would have encouraged the belief that legislation ought to be written. M. T. Clanchy observes that before this time, to record something meant to bear oral witness to it, not to produce a document.[60] "The spoken word was the legally valid record and was superior to any document."[61] Yet by the middle of the thirteenth century, the noun *record* had come to refer to a document.[62] If ordinary legal matters were increasingly memorialized in writing, one assumes that this principle would apply with even greater force to statutes. In addition, although it would have been possible for the king to send messengers with oral instructions to the sheriffs, the proclamation of new legislation would almost inevitably have required the production of written versions for them to promulgate.[63] At least on one occasion in 1306, there is a notation at the end of a statute that it is to be sent "word for word" into all the counties of England, there to be openly read and recited.[64]

Consequences of Writing Law

Initially, the main function of writing laws must have differed little from the primary function of literacy in general: to preserve words for later use. But very quickly it would have become evident that there were some ancillary effects to setting down law in writing. Some of these effects are not direct results of literacy. For instance, in the process of writing down laws (or customs), kings could leave out those they did not like and make changes to others. Wormald points out that Kentish kings after Æthelberht apparently realized that they could benefit themselves by modifying rules for personal injury to require the payment of a fine to the royal treasury, which modified the customary rule of compensating only the victim.[65] In a kingdom largely governed by custom, the power to have existing law written down could potentially be converted into a power to subtly change custom or make new law.

Yet if the process of writing or codifying law allows for subtle modification, it is equally true that once written, law becomes increasingly static and resistant to change. Writing has a permanence that spoken language lacks. An unwritten law or custom can almost imperceptibly evolve or eventually disappear through disuse or fading memory. Clanchy has observed that

> [r]emembered truth was . . . flexible and up to date, because no ancient custom could be proved to be older than the memory of the oldest living wise man. . . . Customary law "quietly passes over obsolete laws, which sink into oblivion, and die peacefully, but the law itself remains young, always in the belief that it is old."[66]

Anthropologist Jack Goody has made the same observation on the basis of work done on traditional oral African legal systems.[67]

In contrast, once law is written down, the words remain fixed as long as the writing is legible. An example is that parts of the Statute of Marlborough, dating from 1267, are still in force today.[68] Certain clauses of the first Statute of Westminster, enacted in 1275, also remain in effect.[69] The same is true for an act known as *Quia Emptores*, portions of which have been effective since 1289 or 1290.[70] It is virtually inconceivable that oral rules could have such longevity, and if they did, the exact words would long since have dissipated in the mists of time.

Related to permanence is the greater ability of writing—before modern inventions like the telephone or television—to accurately transmit a message over long distances. Of course, in a preliterate society, it is possible to summon a messenger and have him deliver an oral message to someone a substantial distance away. Yet having the messenger deliver a written document is far more likely to guarantee accurate transmission. The writ system in medieval England, under which the king was able to promulgate laws and administer a centralized system of justice by sending writs to sheriffs throughout the country, is a prime example.

Despite growing awareness of the advantages of writing during the thirteenth century, people did not yet equate law with written text. Law was less a matter of what was written on parchment and more a matter of what the king and his council desired or decreed. The king's word was still regarded as law. The first Statute of Westminster, for instance, often speaks of what the king "wills" or "commands" or "prohibits."

Relatedly, statutes were not nearly as autonomous as they are today. It appears to have been somewhat uncertain whether or to what extent statutes survived their makers. Soon after his coronation, Edward II saw fit to send a writ to his sheriffs noting that it would be useful to have the first Statute of Westminster, enacted by his father, "observed in all its Articles." The writ then proceeded to quote part of that statute and commanded the sheriffs to cause it to be proclaimed and published.[71] Just as a spoken order or command is eventually forgotten or dies with its maker, early laws—even if written down—were apparently considered effective only while their maker remained alive to enforce them.

Consider also that judges of this time were often members of the king's council and may have been present when a law was adopted. The written record of the legislation, assuming there was one and that it was readily accessible, might have mattered less to such a judge than his own recollection of what had been decided. At best, the text would have been a reminder of what had taken place, like minutes of a meeting. This is reflected by a well-known statement made by a judge to a lawyer in 1305. The lawyer was arguing why, in his view, a statute had been enacted. The judge replied, "Do not gloss the statute, for we understand it better than you; we made it."[72]

Even after the judiciary ceased to be involved in legislating, judges continued to view the law as consisting of the will or the intentions of the lawmaker, not as the text that resulted from the lawmaking process. Sometimes the judges appealed to their common knowledge or traditions regarding a statute's meaning or purpose.[73] Or they might ask the lawmakers what they intended. This is reflected in an incident from 1366, when there is a report of judges going to Parliament to ask what it meant by a recently enacted law.[74] If your job depends on pleasing your boss, then if there is any question about a statute's application, it is obviously more politic to try to find out what the king and his council actually intended to accomplish by the legislation than to focus on the text of the legislation itself.[75] It is a very oral mode of interpretation that fit the largely oral society in which it arose.

It is not surprising that during this era English courts did not have a consistent theory of how statutes should be interpreted. Sometimes they were strictly construed, sometimes loosely. Sometimes judges carved out exceptions to a statute, sometimes they extended its reach. And on occasion they ignored a relevant statute altogether.[76]

This looseness of interpretation is quite natural if we consider that statutes of the time were records made after the fact and that, in any event, judges did not have easy access to accurate copies of the text. Carlton Kemp Allen has pointed out that statutes in the twelfth and thirteenth centuries "were not so much exact formulas emanating from a supreme Parliamentary authority, as broad rules of government and administration, intended for guidance rather than as meticulous instruction, and meant to be applied on elastic principles of expediency."[77] Or, as Plucknett aptly observed, "Interpretation in this early period could not be precise. There was no sacrosanct text."[78]

Law Becomes Text

The next major phase in the evolution of English legislation was that statutes came to be conceptualized as consisting of the texts that the lawmaker produced. A statute was no longer the lawmakers' decision; rather, it was the written act that resulted from it. This transformation was not a sudden change whose occurrence can be dated with precision. It took place during the course of the fourteenth and fifteenth centuries and perhaps even beyond.

Enacting Statutes during the Fourteenth and Fifteenth Centuries

As mentioned above, when legislation was first being made in the post-Conquest period, judges often sat on the king's council and were involved in the legislative process. They would therefore have viewed legislation as something they themselves had helped enact. And they might have had personal knowledge of its purpose and the intentions of the lawmakers. By the middle of the fourteenth century, however, judges gradually became separate from the council. According to Plucknett, there was now a "radical separation" in the roles of the legislature and the judiciary: "the first legislates and establishes a text, and the second adjudicates and interprets the text."[79] Judges thus started to treat legislation as "the commands of an authority external to themselves whose will is known to them only as expressed in the written word."[80]

Although judges were no longer involved, the procedure by which statutes were enacted remained fairly flexible throughout the fourteenth century. The first Statute of Westminster had made reference to a parliament held in Westminster and noted that both lords and commonalty were present and assented.[81] But as J. H. Baker observes, the requirement that both the lords and commons had to consent to legislation was not firmly established until around 1400. In 1407, King Henry IV recognized that the proper legislative procedure was for a proposal to be separately debated and accepted by both houses of Parliament, the lords and the commons, and for it then to receive the assent of the king.[82]

While the procedure was more regular at this stage, it differed from modern lawmaking in a critical way: the text of statutes was generally fixed after the decision was made. This explains the common use of past tense verbs, as in "it was ordained and established . . ." rather than a performative phrase like "we hereby ordain and establish . . ." It suggests that lawmakers did not have the words of a proposed statute in front of them. As Baker has observed, medieval legislation "was not a text which had been pored over word for word by the lawmakers, with debates upon the wording."[83] Lawmakers of the time did not enact text into law. Rather, they adopted statutes, which were only later reduced to writing.

Not only was the writing done after the fact, but it was done by clerks or scribes, not the lawmakers themselves. This would not necessarily prevent the text from being regarded as the law. But logically the text would have greater status and authority if it had been carefully reviewed and approved by the lawmakers. Such review and approval does not seem to have happened at this stage, certainly not as a matter of course.

In addition, statutes were seldom in the first person. And they were not signed by the king or sealed with the royal seal. This is in sharp contrast to writs, which were also written by clerks but which clearly were conceptualized as though the king himself were speaking to his sheriffs through the text. Writs were almost always in the first person, present tense (*mandamus*, or 'we command . . .') and carried the king's seal. Thus, while the king and Parliament were in some sense "speaking" to their subjects when they legislated, they were not yet viewed as authors who spoke through those texts. The law remained the decisions that they made, not the words on parchment.

It is also worth bearing in mind that although statutes were recorded in French until around 1480, the proceedings in Parliament had shifted to English over a century before this time.[84] Thus, throughout most of the fifteenth century, Parliament was apparently debating statutes in English. A record of these statutes was then made in French. This observation supports the conclusion that legislators most likely did not focus on the exact text of the proposed act, since many of them would not have understood the French in which it was written.

A final consideration is that during some of this period, the king seems to have assumed that he had the power to modify or suspend statutes.[85] It is interesting that from the perspective of judges there was sometimes little distinction between a statute and the king's personal command. The judges were viewed as an extension of royal will. If the king issued an order that overrode a statute, the judges would have been expected to follow his order.[86] As long as kings successfully asserted the power to make such informal changes, the law remained what the king willed or declared.

Thus, it might be said that at this time the text of the statute contained the law, not that it was the law. The situation is nicely summarized by Plucknett:

> The King could legislate . . . without parchment, ink or wax. Even when a written text was drawn, it was merely evidence, and by no means the best evidence, of what had been done. We therefore find that the wording of a statute is not at first taken very seriously. Copies used by the profession were only approximately accurate; even government departments and the courts were no better off; the recording of statutes in the national archives was by no means regular.[87]

The Textualization of Statutes

Over the course of the fifteenth century, statutes became more textual. Legislation ceased to be "the Government's vague reply to vaguely worded complaints." Instead, it became "the deliberate adoption of specific proposals embodied in specific texts."[88] The bills or petitions requesting legislation began to contain "the exact form of words" that Parliament was being asked to adopt.[89]

It is probably not coincidental that during the 1480s the language of statutes shifted from French to English.[90] If Anglophone lawmakers were to enact written text and be considered the authors of that text, it would have to be composed in English.

Desmond Manderson has observed that the tense of the verbs in the enactment clause changed in an interesting way at around this same time. As we saw previously, early legislation generally described the enactment in the past tense: "the King hath ordained." At around 1450, the common wording began to shift to the present tense, passive voice: "it is ordained and established" or "it is enacted, ordained, and established." By the 1480s, the phrasing is quite clearly in the present tense: "the King . . . doth ordain, enact, and establish," or "the King ordaineth . . ."[91] Although one should be careful not to read too much into the words of the enactment clause, which can easily become fossilized, the use of the past tense indicates that Parliament orally enacted legislation that was later written down. Use of the present tense, on the other hand, suggests that members of Parliament had access to the text of legislation when it was adopted.

As a result, legislating came to consist of enacting text (proposed legislation, or bills) that the legislators had in front of them or, at least, that someone had read aloud to them. The legislators began to speak through the document in words that were deemed to be their own. Even though in practice the text might have been written by someone else, the process of enactment transformed it into the words of the legislature. At this point, the word *statute* no longer refers to a legislative decision; a statute is now the text of the proposal or bill that the legislature enacted.

In addition, questions regarding whether statutes outlived their makers or might simply disappear through desuetude (lack of use) were put to rest. If a law is simply a decision by its maker or an expression of the sovereign will, then it seems logical that when the sovereign dies, the law dies with him. Once written law becomes autonomous, however, the possibility that the text can survive its maker becomes very real. At least in England, most statutes are now deemed to be perpetual, in the sense that they remain in force until repealed.[92] Custom and oral proclamations can fade away or be forgotten, but written law is far more permanent.

Recall also that in the early fifteenth century, it came to be settled that the proper way to enact legislation was for a proposal to be adopted by both houses of Parliament and to receive the monarch's assent. The establishment of this procedure not only systematized the legislative process, but it also helped determine what was statutory law and what was not. Proposals that had been through this process were statutory law. Any other discussions, decisions, or debates in Parliament were not.

By the end of the fifteenth century, according to Baker, England was a limited monarchy where even the king was subject to law. Similar to modern procedure, bills could be produced in either house of Parliament, usually received three readings, and were debated. They were not drawn as petitions but were verbatim texts of proposed statutes.[93]

Thus, statutes gradually became textualized during the course of the fourteenth and especially the fifteenth century. They became increasingly autonomous. The writing containing a statute was no longer just a record of what Parliament had enacted into law; it became the law itself. As a result, the text of the statute became authoritative in a sense that it had never been before.

Interpretation Becomes Stricter

Once legislating was viewed as enacting a proposed text or bill, it logically followed that lawmakers would pay closer attention to how the legislation was worded. As Plucknett points out, because "Parliament considered not merely the general policy, but the exact wording of the proposed statute," it became "inevitable that the words of the statute should acquire a new significance from the fact that they had been so often examined and finally adopted after prolonged deliberation."[94] Predictably, the text of statutes also became longer and contained more and more enumerations, exceptions, provisions, and so on.[95]

Statutes were coming to viewed as the *ipsissima verba* of the lawmaker. Baker writes that in the Tudor period (roughly the sixteenth century), there was a "new reverence for the written text . . . Legislative drafting was now carried on with such skill . . . that the judges were manifestly being discouraged from the creative exegesis they had bestowed on medieval statutes."[96]

As a result, it would be natural for those interpreting a statute—particularly judges—to pay close attention to the words of the text. Understanding those words would require judges to use the internalized rules of grammar that every speaker of a language possesses, although we usually apply those rules unconsciously. Sometimes, however, the judges would discuss these grammatical rules more explicitly. Thus, there is a record of a sixteenth-century judge expounding on the tense of a verb.[97] Tense in English often depends on nothing more than the addition or modification of a single letter. Relying on such a minute distinction requires great confidence in the accuracy of the text.

Not only did judges use ordinary rules of grammar, whether explicitly or not, but they developed aids to interpretation that depended on the grammatical structure of the text, principles that are often referred to as *maxims of interpretation* or *canons of construction*.[98]

One of these canons, *ejusdem generis*, still occasionally applied today, provides that when a list of specific words is followed by a broader or more general term, the broader term is interpreted to include only potential members of a class similar to those denoted by the specific words.[99] An example from the sixteenth century is the *Archbishop of Canterbury's Case*, in which the King's Bench used the principle in interpreting a statute that contained a list of "inferior" means of conveyance, followed by the phrase "or any other means." Even though "any other means" would seem to include all other types of conveyance, the court limited this catchall phrase to other inferior means of conveyance, and held that it did not include a superior conveyance by an act of Parliament.[100] Obviously, these canons or maxims presuppose both a careful drafting of the text and a close reading by the judges interpreting it.

Although it may be natural to focus on the exact words after statutes became textualized, it does not follow that interpretation must inevitably be what we might call "literal." According to the *Discourse upon the Exposicion & Understandinge of Statutes*, written in the sixteenth century, a judge should consider "the wordes, the sentence, & the meanynge therof, for sommetymes it shalbe construed straictelie—that is, accordinge to the wordes & no further." Yet the words can also be extended: "Sommetymes the wordes are by equytye stretched to lyke cases." Or the meaning of the words can be narrowed: "Sommetymes they are expounded againste the wordes."[101] The writer of the *Discourse* also mentions the importance of the mind of the legislators (the *mens legislatorum*).[102] His views can perhaps best be summed up by the observation that "wordes were but invented to declare the meanynge of men, [and therefore] we muste rather frame the wordes to the meanynge than the meanynge to the wordes."[103] While the text of legislation had become increasingly important, it did not reign supreme.

Consider also the position of another sixteenth-century observer, Edmund Plowden (1518–85), who reported many of the more important court decisions of his time. More than one-third of Plowden's reported cases were concerned with statutes and their application.[104] Plowden argued that equity could enlarge or diminish the words of an act: "It is not the words of the law but the internal sense of it that are the law . . . the letter of the law is the body of the law, but the sense and reason of the law is its soul."[105] Others of the time likewise argued against the "violence of the letter." And some felt that a man could "break the words of the law and yet not break the law itself."[106]

Plowden's suggestion that the equity of a statute could override its language may not have reflected the actual judicial practice of his time. Allen points out that Plowden's examples of equity tend to go back to the earlier period of free interpretation.[107] Whatever the case, the doctrine of the equity of the statute gradually receded into the background. In 1639, an English judge criticized it as "too general a ground" for the construction of a statute.[108]

As the courts were paying less attention to the equity of a statute, they turned their attention to its goal or purpose. Often the goal of legislation would be readily apparent. Parliament could also make its purpose clear by means of a preamble, which lays out the motivation or purpose behind an act.[109] Lengthy preambles remained customary into relatively modern times, although recently their use is receding. Preambles have been used to help interpret legislation since at least the fourteenth century.[110] Sir Edward Coke, an eminent judge in the early seventeenth century, remarked that "[t]he preamble of a statute is a good means to find out the meaning of the statute, as it were a key to open the understanding thereof."[111]

An example is *Chudleigh's Case*, dating from the late sixteenth century, in which the King's Bench noted that to determine the "true interpretation of the letter and meaning" of an act, it was necessary to consider, first, "the mischiefs that were before this Act" and, second, "what manner of remedy they have provided for it."[112] The court then proceeded to observe that to find the mischiefs, it needed to look at the preamble.[113] A somewhat more elaborate formulation of this principle appears in *Heydon's Case*, decided in 1584. The case reported that a group of judges known as Barons of the Exchequer had determined that for the "sure and true interpretation of all statutes," they would look at (1) what was the common law before the act and (2) the "mischief and defect" in the common law that the statute was aimed at correcting; they would then (3) determine the remedy that Parliament had adopted to cure the mischief and (4) the true reason of the remedy. The office of judges was to construe the statute in a way that would suppress the mischief and advance the remedy.[114]

Thus, after Parliament began to enact written text, judges started paying greater attention to the text of statutes than they had previously. In cases of doubt, they might apply various maxims of interpretation. And they might consider a statute's purpose, as stated in its preamble. Nonetheless, judges were far from being textualists in the modern sense. A large part of the reason is that for many centuries they simply did not have access to fully accurate copies of the legislative text.

Printing and the Rise of Plain Meaning

As we have seen, the textualization of statutes seems to have taken off in a serious way at the end of the fifteenth century. The language of legislation became English around 1480, making it possible for legislators to concern themselves with the exact words they were adopting. The enactment clause began to speak in the present tense.

Right around this same period of time, a very important technological development took place: printing came to England. Printing is much easier to do on paper than on parchment, and paper is also cheaper. Fortuitously, the technology for making paper was already known in Europe. These developments had important implications for lawmaking. By around the middle of the sixteenth century, bills were no longer presented to Parliament on parchment, which was quite expensive, but on paper. Identical printed copies could be given to all members, making it possible to debate the exact wording of the proposed statute. Only afterward was the final version written, or engrossed, on parchment.[115]

Printing also gave the legal profession access to affordable copies of the legislation that Parliament had enacted. Before printing, making copies of statutes was laborious and expensive. Moreover, because each copy was made individually, no two were ever going to be exactly the same.[116] As important a document as the Magna Carta of King John, which has been described as "the great precedent for putting legislation into writing,"[117] has survived in several copies that are not identical. Scribes not only made mistakes, but they sometimes endeavored to improve upon or update the original language. According to Clanchy, they were more concerned about the "gist" than the "exact words."[118]

Also, at least during much of the thirteenth century, there was no official copy of any particular statute. Lawyers often had their own private collections, of course, but in this period there was no definitive version that one could consult to determine the accuracy of one's private copy.[119] Beginning in 1299, an official roll containing the statutes was kept in the chancery, but it was incomplete. And there were apocryphal statutes.[120] It was therefore impossible in this era to establish a canon of authentic statutes.

Even judges may not have had a complete set of current statutes available for reference. For this reason, litigants sometimes brought a copy of a statute to court. Because of problems in accessing an accurate version of the text, courts often "wildly misquoted" the statutes that they endeavored to apply.[121] And they seem to have consulted statutes only sporadically.[122]

Furthermore, the process of citing statutes was initially very haphazard. Courts often referred simply to "the statute" or described it by its initial or most important words (as in the statute called *Quia Emptores*). Or they might refer to the place where the statute was made, as in "the statute lately made at Westminster," a description that could refer to at least four different documents.[123] Such vague and inconsistent citation practices are a further indication that lawyers and judges had not yet developed a fully literate mentality and seldom relied on the exact text of an enactment.

Printing Statutes

The invention of printing created the potential for solving these problems by making available to the legal profession and to the public a large number of identical copies. The first printed statutes were published in 1484.[124] Printers soon found that they had a ready market for their wares in the legal profession and printed more and more compilations of statutes.[125]

The earliest printings of legislation were private profit-making ventures. The more copies of statutes they could sell, the more money printers could make, a calculation that led less scrupulous members of the trade to include laws of questionable authenticity in their collections. Plucknett mentions that "early printers greatly increased the list of pseudo-statutes in their endeavours to bring out ever bigger and more complete collections."[126] Nor was there any guarantee that a printed version was an accurate copy of the legislation. Finally, although printed copies of a text should normally be identical, there could still be discrepancies if there was more than one printing or if a statute was published by more than one printer. Consider that numerous editions of Shakespeare's work have been published, and it has been estimated that over 24,000 variations of the King James Bible were printed between 1611 and 1830.[127] The variations among printed versions of statutes would have been far fewer, but as long as private printers were in charge, it would have been risky to focus too terribly closely on the text.

The printing and distribution of statutes eventually became more regular. Official versions of statutes were printed under the authority of the government in the early eighteenth century.[128] In 1796 it was ordered that printed statutes should be distributed throughout the realm as quickly as possible after enactment. Soon thereafter, the Commons decided that the King's Printer should publish at least 5,000 copies of each public general act.[129] An official record of past enactments became available when the Record Commission published the *Statutes of the Realm* in the beginning of the nineteenth century.[130]

The Plain Meaning Rule

With the adoption of what is now called the *plain meaning rule*, the text of a statute became even more critical to its interpretation. As mentioned, it had become established that the legislature spoke through properly enacted text. Logically, the meaning of a statute must therefore be determined, at least in the first instance, from its language.

The plain meaning rule went a step further. It required not just that judges determine the meaning of statutes from the text but that they determine the meaning only from the text. An early statement of the rule was made in 1769, when a judge declared that "[t]he sense and meaning of an act of parliament must be collected from what it says when passed into law, and not from the history of changes it underwent in the house where it took its rise."[131]

While not always strictly observed at first, the rule thrived in the next century or two. Lord Chief Justice Nicolas Tindal expressed it thus in 1844:

> The only rule for construction of Acts of Parliament is, that they should be construed according to the intent of the Parliament which passed the Act. If the words of the Statute are in themselves precise and unambiguous, then no more can be necessary than to expound those words in that natural and ordinary sense. The words themselves alone do, in such case, best declare the intention of the law giver.[132]

One reason sometimes given for the rise of the rule is that it developed at a time when legislation was becoming longer and more detailed. Medieval statutes were often fairly vague, forcing judges to fill in gaps and omissions. More modern statutes tried—successfully or not—to cover every potential contingency. Thus, the fact that legislation failed to address a particular issue could be understood to mean that the legislators did not intend to address it and that therefore judges should decline to extend the statute beyond its express provisions. As Lord Evershed said in the middle of the twentieth century, "The length and detail of modern legislation has undoubtedly reinforced the claim of literal construction as the only safe rule."[133]

It is not just the length and detail of legislation but also the increasing quality and reliability of copies of the text that has encouraged or enabled a literalistic approach. Surely it is no accident that the development of the plain meaning rule roughly coincides with the increasing availability of highly accurate printed copies of the text of statutes, especially in the late eighteenth and early nineteenth centuries.

The judicial committee of the House of Lords (Great Britain's highest court until quite recently) relaxed the plain meaning rule somewhat during the 1990s by allowing reference to parliamentary debates under certain circumstances, but it remains a guiding principle of interpretation in England. Reference to legislative materials is allowed only when (1) the legislation is ambiguous or obscure or its literal meaning leads to an absurdity; (2) the material consists of statements made by a government minister or other promoter of the bill; and (3) the statements relied on are clear.[134]

It is interesting to note that the evolution of the statutory text during the past millennium or so mirrors developments in written language more generally. Naomi Baron, a linguist who has surveyed the role of writing in the English-speaking world, has observed that throughout the Middle Ages writing served mainly to transcribe or record speech.[135] This corresponds to what was happening in the legal world, where statutes were merely evidence of a decision that the king or Parliament had made orally.

Starting in the seventeenth century, Baron continues, the written word began to develop its own autonomous identity. In this regard she refers to the work of Carey McIntosh, who pointed out that during the second half of the eighteenth century, grammars and dictionaries, as well as magazines and newspapers, proliferated in England. Language and spelling became more standardized, and English prose became more polite, more elegant, more bookish, more carefully planned, more precise, and overall more distinctly "written" in style.[136] Not surprisingly, the latter half of the eighteenth and the early part of the nineteenth century is also when the plain meaning rule, which required a relatively textual approach to statutes, was dominant. A literal mode of interpretation is a relatively natural development in such a literate era.

As we observed in other areas of the law, there is a close relationship between the nature of a text and how that text tends to be interpreted. As the text becomes more authoritative, there is increasing pressure to interpret it in a more textual way. What has also turned out to be quite significant is whether the interpreter has access to an accurate, authentic copy of the text. Because someone interpreting a private legal text, like a contract or will, can virtually always examine the original document, the need for an authentic copy is seldom an issue. With English statutes, in contrast, it was a serious concern that for centuries made it difficult to rely on the exact words of the text, even after Parliament began to speak through the text in an authoritative way.

It is also important to emphasize that while the availability of an authoritative text enables a relatively literal interpretation, it does not require it. There were many other social and political forces in England that must have played a role in these developments.

Statutes in the United States

The American states based their legal systems on the common law of England. They also adopted enactment procedures similar to those in England, as well as the canons of construction and other principles for interpreting statutes. For the most part, however, American judges have not adhered to the strictly literal mode of statutory interpretation that held sway in England for much of the nineteenth and twentieth centuries.

The Enactment and Publication of American Statutes

As in modern England, American statutes consist of text that has, in theory at least, been closely examined by legislators before they vote to approve it. Although the U.S. Constitution does not specifically require the enactment of written text into law, its reference to "bills" and the requirement that they be presented to the president for "signature" clearly presupposes a procedure of this kind.[137] State constitutions, like that of California, often stipulate that the legislature may make law only by means of statutes and that statutes may be enacted only by bill. Moreover, a bill in California must be printed and distributed to legislators before it can be passed into law.[138]

In the United States, therefore, legislation has been viewed as the enactment of written text from the very beginning of the republic. These texts have also been widely available in authoritative format. The first Congress in 1789 authorized the publication of new federal statutes in several newspapers. A couple of years later, in 1791, Congress appointed a printer to publish all the laws of the United States and required certification that they had been compared with the "original rolls."[139] The first congressionally authorized compilation of laws, known as the Folwell edition, was published in 1796. It contained statutes that had been given a number and title, and it omitted statutes that had expired or been repealed.[140]

Efforts to consolidate federal laws into a code, while at the same time correcting errors and omissions, began in the mid-nineteenth century. Currently, federal statutes can be located in a series of volumes, organized by topic, and known as the *United States Code*.[141] Thus, accurate copies of the text of American laws have been available since the country was founded.

We have seen that authoritative legal texts are ordinarily executed or enacted with certain formalities, and this is certainly true of American statutes. Typically, after a bill is introduced in each chamber of a legislature, it must be adopted in identical form by each of them. The resulting text is called the "enrolled bill." It is then usually printed and, at least on the federal level, signed by the presiding officer of each house. The enrolled bill is then presented to the president or governor of a state for his or her signature. At the end of a legislative session, all the statutes passed in this manner are officially published.[142] On the federal level, at least, the officially published version of statutes (in the *Statutes at Large*) is legal evidence in all courts of the United States.[143]

Theories of Interpretation

American statutes were thus, at an early stage, not only textualized but widely available in authentic copies. We observed that in England, this set the stage for a very literal mode of interpretation. Interestingly, this did not happen in the United States. There were certainly judges or courts that applied strict or literal interpretation, which as a matter of principle looked only at the text to determine its meaning. Other judges preferred a more intentionalist approach, however, that looked beyond the text to discover the intentions of the legislature.

Chief Justice John Marshall of the United States Supreme Court said in 1805 that "[w]here the mind labors to discover the design of the legislature, it seizes everything from which aid can be derived."[144] Whether Marshall was an intentionalist in the modern sense is debatable, since in the same case he remarked that if "the meaning of the legislature be plain . . . it must be obeyed."[145] Still, Marshall certainly understood that words do not always have a fixed or plain meaning. As he noted in the famous case of *McCulloch v. Maryland*, "Such is the character of human language, that no word conveys to the mind, in all situations, one single definite idea; and nothing is more common than to use words in a figurative sense."[146]

A later chief justice took a more textual approach. Justice Roger Taney rejected the use of legislative history in determining the meaning of a statute:

> In expounding this law, the judgment of the court cannot . . . be influenced by the construction placed upon it by individual members of Congress in the debate which took place on its passage. . . . The law as it passed is the will of the majority of both houses, and the only mode in which that will is spoken is in the act itself; and we must gather their intention from the language there used.[147]

Many state courts agreed with these sentiments. As articulated by the Rhode Island Supreme Court, "It is an elementary proposition that courts only determine, by construction, the scope and intent of a law when the law itself is ambiguous or doubtful. If a law is plain . . . it declares itself, and nothing is left for interpretation.[148] This is very similar to Martin Luther's view that scripture interprets itself, as discussed in chapter 2. Of course, legislation is not divinely inspired.

The Supreme Court took a decidedly intentionalist turn in *Holy Trinity Church v. United States*, a case decided in 1892.[149] A federal statute made it illegal to assist in or encourage the importation of a foreigner to the United States under a contract "to perform labor or service of any kind." The church had arranged for an English cleric to cross the Atlantic and become its rector. The Court admitted that the employment of the Englishman came "within the letter of this section." But it continued, "a thing may be within the letter of the statute and yet not within the statute, because not within its spirit, nor within the intention of its makers."[150]

Significantly, the Court referred to legislative history—reports of congressional committees—to bolster its conclusion that the statute was aimed at those who work with their hands, not those who work with the mind.[151] But although preaching may not be labor, it clearly is service. If the court had applied a plain meaning approach, it would surely have held that the church violated the statute. The case is thus famous for allowing the intent of Congress to override the text of the law.

At around the same time, however, Judge Oliver Wendell Holmes could write, "We do not inquire what the legislature meant; we ask only what the statute means."[152] And roughly two decades after the *Holy Trinity* case, the Supreme Court decided a case that posed a very similar issue: *Caminetti v. United States*. Instead of involving a church that took a minister across an international border to perform religious services, it dealt with a man who took his mistress across a state border for an "immoral purpose," in violation of another federal statute (called the White Slave Traffic Act). The Court refused to consider evidence that Congress's intent and purpose was to fight prostitution, not immorality in general. "It is elementary that the meaning of a statute must, in the first instance, be sought in the language in which the act is framed, and if that is plain, and if the law is within the constitutional authority of the law-making body which passed it, the sole function of the courts is to enforce it according to its terms."[153] Ministers are treated differently than mistresses.

Despite such contradictory statements, Lawrence Solan has shown that during the first half of the twentieth century the Supreme Court increasingly took legislative history into account when construing the meaning of statutes.[154] Judges during this period made memorable and sometimes elegant comments about the nature of language. Judge Cardozo, while on New York's highest court, observed that "[t]he law has outgrown its primitive stage of formalism when the precise word was the sovereign talisman, and every slip was fatal. It takes a broader view today."[155] According to Learned Hand, another renowned judge of the period, "Words are not pebbles in alien juxtaposition; they have only a communal existence; and not only does the meaning of each interpenetrate the other, but all in their aggregate take their purport from the setting in which they are used."[156] A few years later he wrote that a court should "not make a fortress out of the dictionary; but . . . remember that statutes always have some purpose or object to accomplish, whose sympathetic and imaginative discovery is the surest guide to their meaning."[157] By 1983, a respected federal judge, Patricia Wald, could conclude that although the Supreme Court still refers to it, the plain meaning rule has "effectively been laid to rest."[158]

Justice Scalia's Textualism

Judge Wald's conclusion turns out to have been premature. The plain meaning rule was not dead, or if it was, it was at least partly resurrected by the appointment of Justice Antonin Scalia to the Supreme Court in 1986. Scalia is the principal architect of what is sometimes called the "new textualism."[159] He views statutes as heavily textualized and highly autonomous, in the sense that they are not mere evidence of legislative intentions with respect to the law but actually constitute the law. Congress is therefore expected to place all its communicative intentions into the words of the statute, and judges should ignore any evidence of congressional intent that is not expressed in the text. "We are governed by laws, not by the intentions of legislators."[160]

Recall that a consequence of textualization in the law of wills is that, for the most part, changes or additions to a will cannot be made informally. Although this principle has weakened a bit in recent years, courts remain reluctant to help a testator who tried to make informal changes to a will. You are expected to amend a will by properly executing a codicil, thus maintaining the integrity of the text. Scalia would apply a similar principle to statutes. If a federal statute turns out not to work as intended, courts should not fix the problem. Rather, Congress should formally amend it. According to Scalia, it is best for courts to "apply the statute as written, and to let Congress make the needed repairs."[161] This approach is very similar to the traditional plain meaning rule.

Scalia has not yet persuaded a majority of the Court to join him. He once noted rather wistfully:

> I thought we had adopted a regular method for interpreting the meaning of language in a statute: first, find the ordinary meaning of the language in its textual context; and second, using established canons of construction, ask whether there is any clear indication that some permissible meaning other than the ordinary one applies. If not and especially if a good reason for the ordinary meaning appears plain we apply that ordinary meaning.[162]

Since he was writing a dissenting opinion, his "regular method" had not been as widely adopted as he hoped. Nonetheless, Scalia remains a force to be reckoned with.

Based on this brief history of statutory interpretation in the United States, it might seem that American judges have never adopted a consistent theory.[163] Sometimes they fixate on the text, to the exclusion of contradictory evidence of legislative intent. On other occasions they dig through musty archives to find evidence of intent that they can use to amplify upon, or even override, the words of the statute. It may be that judges simply pick the approach that best fits their ideological views. Or perhaps they flip from one approach to another, depending on the result that they hope to accomplish.

Yet what may also play a role is how judges, often without conscious reflection, take into account the nature of the text that they have before them. Indeed, we should reject efforts to adopt a single mode of interpretation that applies to all legal documents. A better approach is one that adapts itself to the type of the text that is being interpreted.

Interpreting the Statutory Text

The way in which judges interpret statutes is one of the most important of all textual practices of the legal profession. It is also one of the most contentious. Of course, neither the field of linguistics nor the study of writing and literacy can dictate a theory of interpretation to judges. To a large extent, the issue is a political one that revolves around the respective roles of the judiciary and the legislature. Yet there are a few sensible things that one can say about the process from a textual perspective. After all, legislation is simply another type of legal text that is not fundamentally different from the wills, contracts, and other genres that we have already examined.

Who Is the Author?

When statutes are enacted into law, they are normally preceded by an enactment clause. In California, it reads, "The People of the State of California do enact as follows." Many other states have similar clauses.[164] The reality, of course, is that the people of the state do not really "speak" through the statutes enacted in their name. Just as it is a fiction that a testator speaks through her will or that the parties to a contract speak through the written text of an integrated agreement, the notion that the people enact and speak through legislation is a fiction.

A more realistic view is that the people have delegated this task to the legislature. Thus, the legislators may be deemed the authors, acting as agents for the people. Of course, this view is also largely fictional. It may have been true in the past, when legislation was simpler and shorter, and it may still be true today in some instances, but modern statutes are usually written by (or, at least, heavily edited by) professional drafters. Just as a will is drafted by lawyers for clients, who are deemed to have spoken the words that the lawyer wrote, statutes today are usually written by legislative drafters, who are almost always lawyers.

The mere fact that someone ghostwrote something for you does not, of course, mean you cannot be considered the author in a broader sense. If you have told the ghostwriter what to write and then carefully read the work and actively edit it to ensure that you approve of the final product, it might not be too far-fetched to suggest that you are the author of the book in question. Fiction turns to farce, however, if you are deemed to be the author of something that you have never read or which you tried to read but did not understand.

One of the reasons that Justice Scalia rejects the use of legislative history in interpreting statutes, especially as contained in reports by congressional committees, is that legislators usually do not write the reports themselves. Because it is usually staffers that draft these reports, Scalia believes that courts should not consult them since they may not accurately reflect the intent of Congress.[165] In his book, *A Matter of Interpretation*, Scalia quotes Senator Bob Dole, chairman of the Senate Finance Committee, who admitted that he had not written a committee report that accompanied a tax bill and moreover that he had not even read it entirely.[166] If the chairman of the responsible committee had not read the complete report, it is likely that many or most of the senators voting for the bill had not read all of it either. Thus, according to Justice Scalia, judges interpreting a statute should not consult committee reports to help determine the legislature's intentions.

But if committee reports are suspect because they were not written by, and perhaps not even read by, members of Congress, then the legislation itself is subject to exactly the same criticism. As mentioned, much modern drafting is done by professionals who are not members of the legislature. And it seems highly likely that many statutes are enacted into law by legislators who have not read them or who have read only parts of them. Stephen Field, who drafted some of the early California codes, wrote that the Criminal Practice Act, consisting of over six hundred sections, was never read before the legislature.[167] In fact, the multiple "readings" of acts to the legislature before their enactment has largely become a fiction.[168] The presumption seems to be that legislators are currently all literate and can read a bill in the privacy of their offices. How often they do so is open to question, especially when legislation is highly technical and—as was the case with one recent federal statute—over 2,000 pages long.[169]

Scalia addresses this problem in his book. He admits that members of Congress are probably less likely to have read the text of a statute before them than to have read the committee report (which is in plainer English and shorter than the statute). His response is that, unlike committee reports, a statute enacted through the procedure prescribed by the Constitution is law, whether or not members of Congress have read it or understand it.[170]

Scalia is essentially saying that statutes, once they are textualized by having been properly enacted, are deemed to be the definitive and complete expression of the intentions of the legislature. It is the same process as the execution of a will, where the will is deemed to speak for the testator and to be the authoritative statement of his intentions with respect to his estate, even if it was written by a lawyer in language that the testator may not have read entirely and may not have understood if he had. Likewise, consumers are legally presumed to have read and understood lengthy form contracts written in convoluted legalese. The system may sometimes need to maintain this fiction. But as we concluded in our discussion of wills and contracts, these textual conventions should be modified or abandoned when they produce unfair or perverse results.

Insisting on a textual reading of the exact words of statutes makes little sense when most legislators cannot honestly be regarded as the authors of the text. The reason that Protestants adopted a relatively literal interpretation of the Bible during the Reformation is that they viewed scripture as coming from "God's own sacred mouth," even though it was written down by ordinary mortals. But Congress is not God, and legislative drafters are not divinely inspired to write exactly what is on Congress's mind.

It thus seems to me that when a legislature has closely examined and thoroughly debated the wording of a statute, so that it can truly be considered the author of the legislation, courts should accord a great deal of deference to those words. If the text of the legislation did not get as much scrutiny, perhaps because the statute was long or highly technical, the exact words of the text should be less critical, although they obviously remain important. It makes sense for courts in such cases to focus more closely on the intent and purpose of the legislature, and correspondingly less on the text.

Who Is the Audience?

We have noted that most modern statutes are drafted in a highly autonomous style. An autonomous style of writing is often necessary when writer and reader are separated by distance and time, rather than being in face-to-face interaction. Thus, the drafter can assume less shared background knowledge and must explicitly place more information into the text. The same is true of speech, incidentally. In conversations with close friends, we can assume a great deal of shared background information. When conversing with strangers, we need to make such information more explicit. This is even more true of formal speeches to a large audience.

Thus, the nature of the audience is very relevant to how much information we need to place into a message.[171] If one spouse gives the other a grocery list with the word "beer" on it, it may be perfectly obvious to both of them that "beer" in this situation means a six-pack of Dos Equis amber beer in bottles, because that is what they always drink. The list is more like speech than written text because much information is already known or can be assumed without being explicitly stated. In contrast, if you order beer from a professional shopping service, via fax or e-mail, or if you give the shopping list to a helpful neighbor who is going shopping, you will have to specify "a six-pack of Dos Equis amber beer in bottles." You will have to place all relevant intentions into the text of your note, and your note will be interpreted relatively literally.

One might think that of all types of legal text, statutes are the most autonomous, since they reach a large audience over a widespread geographical space and can remain in force for decades or even centuries. Most are, indeed, drafted in a highly autonomous style. But other statutes are more administrative in nature and are aimed at a relatively small audience of lawyers and government bureaucrats, who form a fairly cohesive interpretive community. In that event, the statute can be drafted less autonomously and can be a bit more speech-like. The authors can assume that the audience shares a fair amount of contextual and background information. The text need not be as explicit as it might otherwise have to be. This is similar to a shopping list that just has the word "beer" on it; the spouse who goes shopping knows what to buy. When legislation is more speech-like, especially when speakers and audience share background assumptions and information, it is natural to focus less on the precise words and more on the intentions of the speaker.

In contrast, if the audience is larger and more dispersed, and if a message is likely to have to be interpreted in the future, greater autonomy and explicitness is required. Most criminal laws address everyone within the applicable jurisdiction. Such legislation should be written very autonomously. A criminal code that instructs judges to fine or imprison anyone who has committed a crime, without further specification, would be woefully inadequate. It might work in a small and technologically simple community where everyone knows what is punishable as a crime. In a large and complex society, however, greater explicitness is essential. Judges should not be allowed to fine citizens or deprive them of their liberty unless an offense is expressly forbidden, in clear and understandable terms. This principle is an essential component of the rule of law.

Taking Text Seriously

Textualists properly demand respect for the text of our laws. At the same time, when it comes to interpretation, not all statutes are the same, from a textual point of view. Textualism (or a plain meaning approach) makes the most sense when legislators are, in fact, the authors of the text of a statute and have paid careful attention to its exact words. It also makes sense if a statute is expected to communicate a legal norm to an audience that may be far removed in distance and time. If the legislature has extensively debated and then enacted a detailed and autonomous text, judges should give that text great deference.

In contrast, where the audience is a small group with shared background information, such as bureaucrats in a particular governmental agency, a less textual approach may be more appropriate. The legislature may have intended to give some deference to the agency in question. If I ask a friend to buy me a beer, without specifying a brand, I either expect that he knows what I normally drink, or I trust his judgment to buy me a beer that I will enjoy. We might call this a more oral style of interpretation.

In either event, the nature of the text is an important determinant in how it is, or ought to be, interpreted. Because most statutes may be in force and are addressed to an audience that is widely dispersed (usually the entire population), legislators will be inclined to draft them as explicitly and autonomously as possible, because all of their message must be communicated by means of the text. And judges will be inclined to presume, as an initial matter, that the legislature successfully expressed its intentions by means of that text. We might call this the "textualist presumption."

Much of the debate about the proper method of statutory interpretation seems to boil down to how strong this presumption ought to be. Justice Scalia has tremendous confidence in the ability of Congress to accurately and completely place its intentions into the text of legislation. For him, the presumption is almost impossible to rebut. Other judges are more skeptical. They would probably admit that Congress tries to embody all of its intentions on a particular issue into a statute but point out that it is impossible to write a completely autonomous text, and therefore they quickly go beyond the text of a statute in search of other indications of Congress's intent.

My position is somewhere between these extremes. It is certainly possible to write legislation in a relatively autonomous way. Moreover, there is great value in having the laws written down so that anyone can read them and requiring judges to follow those written norms, as the ancient Greeks recognized over two thousand years ago. Judges should therefore give appropriate deference to the text of a statute and start with the textualist presumption: that it contains all of the legislature's intentions regarding its subject matter.[172] This is a common method of interpreting almost any formal writing, since the text is usually the only thing we have before us.

Yet we must remain realistic. No text can ever be completely autonomous. Even if Congress placed all relevant intentions into a statute, they cannot anticipate how the statute might need to be applied in the future. In individual cases, a statute might have been drafted sloppily or in haste, or it might be so complex that legislators never even read the text. Or a statute might have addressed a smaller audience and might not have been drafted very autonomously in the first place. In such situations a judge should look outside the text for indications of what the legislature intended to accomplish. That, as mentioned, is a more oral mode of interpretation.

So far we have assumed that we are dealing with modern printed statutes. For the past centuries, legislatures have made their intentions known by enacting written bills that were later printed as acts or statutes and distributed to the public. Much of the previous discussion may rapidly become outdated with the advent of new technologies for storing and communicating information.

Peering into the Future

As outlined above, the eighteenth and nineteenth centuries constituted a high point in English literacy. By this I do not mean that the average person could or did read and write, but that the dominant culture (or the elite) was highly literate. Our current culture, on the other hand, owing to democratization and the rise of modern media, has become more oral. Research by linguists Douglas Biber and Edward Finegan suggests that during the past two centuries, writing has again begun to reflect speech more closely, narrowing the gap between spoken and written English.[173]

Moreover, orality is making a comeback as new technologies (especially the telephone) make it possible to communicate by speech over long distances, as well as to a vast audience (radio and television). Although computers and the Internet have in some sense reinvigorated the practice of writing, the style of such writing is often quite informal. E-mail is the quintessential example of a means of communication that is conducted in writing but that in many respects seems very oral.

So, what impact will these developments in speech, writing, and communication have on the statutory text? It is impossible to predict the future with any accuracy, of course, but some trends are beginning to emerge.

Dynamic Statutes (or E-Law)

Writing and especially printing were extremely static processes in the past. Once a book or statute was published, it was quite cumbersome to change anything without reprinting it, which was a costly proposition. Many of us remember the list of errata that might accompany a book or the stickers with corrections that needed to be pasted somewhere within it. More substantial changes required printing a second edition or at least a supplement. Loose-leaf publications in binders, commonly used in the legal profession, made it easier to update topical materials, but this solution was also far from ideal.

Modern technology is rapidly making writing and publication more dynamic. Information that is available online, in the form of a cybertext, can be modified or updated with minimal effort. Someone who maintains a website can almost instantly correct mistakes, add newly found material, or adapt the website to address changes in circumstances. Legal publishers who provide electronic access to statutes take full advantage of this dynamism. As soon as the legislature enacts a new statute, it can be posted online. And when amendments are passed, the changes can very quickly be incorporated into the electronic version of the statute. It used to be necessary to find a statute in a book and then do a further search to see whether it had—after the book was printed—been amended or repealed. If amended, it was usually necessary to photocopy both the original statute and the amendment and then to create the current version of the statute by cutting and pasting. On websites currently maintained by legal information providers, the text is almost always an accurate and current copy of statutes as enacted and amended by the legislature.

The dynamic quality of the Internet can take this process one step further. At present, the official text of a statute is the enrolled bill, which is printed on paper or parchment and typically preserved in a government archive. In the American Congress, after a bill is passed by both houses in identical form, it is enrolled, printed on parchment or paper, certified by the clerk of the house where it originated, and signed by the speaker of the House and the president pro tempore of the Senate. After the president signs it, the new statute is preserved in the National Archives.[174] In the United Kingdom, an official copy of enacted statutes is printed on vellum and lodged in the House of Lords Record Office.[175]

In an age when most lawyers and virtually all members of the public will access statutes online, there is always the danger that a law in a commercial legal database, or even on the legislature's official website, differs in some way from the text of the statute as originally enacted. Since most legislatures have official websites, and since the public is increasingly obtaining almost all information online, why not make official the version posted on the legislature's website? The shelves bending under the weight of statute books, which currently decorate many law offices and judicial chambers, could then be replaced by an official online version of statutory law that is by definition completely up-to-date and authoritative.

Moreover, if the legislature discovers a mistake or ambiguity in the statute, it could be fixed immediately. Placing the official version of statutes on a government website could eliminate the bulky amendment procedure that is presently required for even the most minute corrections and changes. If a new statute is enacted, it could almost instantaneously become the law of the land simply by posting it online. And if a law is repealed, the act of removing it from the website would stop in its tracks any mischief that its continued operation might cause. Currently, it can take many weeks or months for these sorts of changes to take effect.

Perhaps an even more provocative idea is to give judges the power to edit the authoritative statute on the legislature's website. Judges would no longer have to write lengthy opinions explaining what is wrong with a statute. They could simply fix the problem adding or deleting a word or two or by inserting a definition or clarification. If the statute is unconstitutional, they could remove it from the website entirely. Judges are sometimes accused of rewriting statutes. Why not change this vice into a virtue? Currently, lawyers spend a great deal of time researching whether and how judges might have interpreted a statute, a process that often requires reading numerous judicial opinions. If judges could just edit the statute directly on the legislative website, it would save lawyers and the public a vast amount of time and money.

As exciting as these possibilities may seem, we should probably step back and take a deep breath. Even though the dynamic nature of the Internet is one of its great blessings, it is also in some respects a curse. Useful information that you find on a website can be altered or disappear overnight. In fact, the entire website might vanish or be restructured beyond recognition. One of the great advantages of traditional writing and printing is its relative permanence.

Moreover, textualization and other literary conventions of the legal profession served in the past to guarantee that the intentions of legal actors were preserved in a fixed format that for the most part could not be altered informally. By this means, traditional writing and textualization can lend a great deal of stability and predictability to the legal system, features that promote the rule of law.

Thus, it seems likely that even if statutes become e-law in the future and are preserved only in some kind of electronic format, many of the textual practices of the law will remain in effect. The process of writing and publishing laws by applying ink to paper may well be obsolescent, but my guess is that the advantages of having a relatively fixed text that is enacted with prescribed formalities will prevent statutes from becoming too terribly dynamic. It is more important for the law to be clear and certain than for it to be instantly responsive to every minor change in circumstances.

Dynamic Authorship (or Wikilaw)

Statutes are the result of collective authorship, a process largely enabled by writing. Modern technology, especially the Internet, also has implications for this process. Many current Internet users are familiar with Wikipedia and perhaps also the "wiki" movement in general.[176] Like many scholars, I have to admit that when I first heard of Wikipedia, an online encyclopedia written collectively by ordinary citizens rather than established scholars, I was quite skeptical. There are, after all, some excellent encyclopedias written by scholars that are available free or at modest cost in various electronic formats. How much trust can you place in an online encyclopedia composed and edited anonymously by anyone who wants to participate? For all we know, some of these articles are written by high school students.

Putting aside some legitimate questions about quality, what is revolutionary about Wikipedia is the way in which the information is gathered and edited. The articles in traditional encyclopedias are composed by scholars who have been commissioned to write them. Wikipedia, in contrast, is a collaborative effort by anyone who wishes to contribute. Anyone can create a new entry in Wikipedia or edit the contributions of others. As a result, its authoritativeness has been questioned, and articles on a few particularly controversial subjects have required those in charge to restrict the ability of people to make changes. Despite such problems, Wikipedia exemplifies a movement that cannot be ignored.

How long Wikipedia will last in its current incarnation is anyone's guess. For our purposes, the more interesting issue is that the wiki software makes it possible for large groups of people to collectively write and edit an online document. Clearly, this process has some very interesting potential implications for the authorship of legislation.

Instead of engaging in lengthy debates over the wording of a proposed law, legislators using wiki software, or something like it, could sit behind their computers and jointly scroll through the text of a bill. One legislator could make an edit to the text. If another legislator objected, by clicking on her "I demand a vote" icon, the software would immediately pose to all legislators the question of whether the edit should be adopted or rejected. And so it would go until they scrolled through the entire bill. That procedure would ensure that all of them had read and approved the entire bill so that the legislators could legitimately be viewed as its authors. In the alternative, the legislators could review and edit legislation individually. If another legislator later objected to a change, the software could automatically call for a vote via e-mail and incorporate the majority's decision.

Perhaps we should go a step further and eliminate the legislature altogether. Recall that in the olden days, it was common for all citizens to vote on laws in a popular assembly. Direct democracy is still practiced in some villages in New England and Swiss cantons. It is not practical for larger states, however, which is why representative democracy developed.

Modern technology could help us give the legislative power back to the people. Many jurisdictions have referenda on important legal issues, where all citizens are allowed to vote on a statute or constitutional provision. The current paper-based procedure is very expensive and time-consuming, however. Although there are security and verification issues that would need to be addressed, allowing referenda by e-mail would allow vastly more laws to be passed by the population as a whole. The function of the legislature could be reduced to proposing laws to the populace, who would then have the power to vote them up or down.

In fact, using some variant of the wiki software, legislatures could become entirely superfluous. Why not let the people also write the laws? Just as ordinary users of the Internet can collectively draft an encyclopedia article, ordinary citizens could collectively author and edit legislation. We could call it *wikilaw*.

How far we will travel along this path is highly uncertain. While the notion of wikilaw may seem intuitively attractive, the enormous complexity of much modern legislation makes it unlikely that enough citizens would take the time to educate themselves on the issues in order to write or edit statutes on a regular basis. If too few people participate, any resulting statute will not have much legitimacy. For the same reason, it seems to me that even the idea of widespread e-referenda is problematic. Of course, it seems probable that many people will be casting votes by e-mail in a number of years. But the average person does not have the time and energy to learn about and vote on every proposed law that comes before the typical legislature.

Thus, while computers and the Internet make direct democracy technologically quite feasible, and while the use of electronic voting is likely to increase, most citizens will probably be content to continue to delegate their lawmaking power to their elected representatives.

Interpreting Electronic Text

The law's increasing use of computers and the Internet may also have ramifications for interpretation. The exact implications are impossible to predict, of course. So this discussion will necessarily be somewhat speculative.

Suppose that in the future legislators do indeed start to use some type of software that allows them to collectively author the text of legislation. If so, it is likely to make interpretation more textual. This is even more likely if judges begin to edit statutes online. The reason is that the text of statutes will become much more authoritative. The online text would be completely current and accurate, having been vetted by both legislators and judges, who would all have had the opportunity to correct errors or clarify ambiguities in the language. The trend historically has been that as drafters take more time to write precise and detailed statutes, and as more authoritative copies become available, interpreters are inclined to treat the text with increasing reverence.

At the same time, there are also ways in which e-laws might promote a more intentionalist method of interpretation. As mentioned above, scholars posit that writing has become more speech-like during the past century or two, and that the Internet is intensifying this trend. If so, it should surprise no one if judges come to adopt a somewhat more oral approach to interpretation. When processing speech, we do not hesitate to access background information, including what we know about the speakers and their intentions. We concentrate more on the speaker's meaning and less on the meaning of the words. This, of course, is exactly what intentionalist judges do when they refer to evidence of legislative intent.

Modern technology has resulted in legislative history and other indications of intent (linguistically speaking, context and background) being much more accessible than before. A major reason that judges did not use such sources in the past is that they were difficult or impossible to access. Just as it's hard to be a textualist without accurate copies of the text, it's hard to be an intentionalist without accurate information about the intentions of the legislature. There are currently commercial services that can provide lawyers with materials relating to state or federal legislative history.[177] But they are quite expensive. In fact, the time and cost of researching legislative history is one of the main reasons Justice Scalia opposes its use.[178]

With the rise of the Internet, the practical impediments to finding such historical resources are fast disappearing. Many legislatures currently make a large amount of information available to the public on their websites at absolutely no cost. Searching this material is also easier than ever. When such a wealth of knowledge is available at the click of a mouse, why not use it? After all, a key to understanding just about any text is its purpose. Often enough the totality of a statute will reveal the purpose of its individual parts, but when the purpose is not obvious, and there is no preamble, evidence of legislative history might reveal it. Persuading lawyers and judges to ignore such evidence will not be easy if it is so readily accessible.

At the same time, consider the massive amount of information that is available to us electronically, the difficulties that many of us have in managing it, and the questions that often arise about its reliability. Concerns that Scalia and other textualists have expressed about the arbitrariness of choosing one source of legislative history over another, and even of the possibility of a group of legislators producing or manipulating such history to serve their purposes, are likely to increase when the information resides somewhere on the wild world of the Internet.

Such concerns are legitimate, but it seems to me that there is a way to balance respect for the text with the need to determine the intent and purpose of the legislature as a key to understanding what the text means. Although I have argued that the law at times overuses textualization, it seems to me that this is an issue that textualization can help solve. Specifically, I propose that when enacting statutes, legislatures should textualize their intentions.

Official Summaries

In the past, legislation typically began with a statement of a statute's background and purpose in the form of a preamble. We noted earlier in this chapter that preambles were often used as an aid to interpretation. It was not uncommon for the preamble to be as long as the statute proper. Today, preambles or statements of legislative purpose are less common, perhaps because courts have become accustomed to consulting committee reports, records of debates, and other sources of legislative intent.

An important advantage of the traditional preamble is that it is enacted into law as part of, or along with, the statute itself. In that sense, it is authoritative text. This means that a majority of the legislature endorsed the statement of purpose or intention contained in the preamble. We need not worry about whether the preamble really reflects the intentions of the legislature as a whole because the legislature affirmatively voted to enact it into law. The problem of collective intent is also minimized because we can assume that a majority of the legislators who voted for the statute intended to accomplish whatever purpose or intent is stated in the preamble. Moreover, any cost and difficulty of finding evidence of legislative intent disappears. If you can find the statute, you can find the preamble or statement of purpose.[179] And the endless storage capacity of computers means that it would cost almost nothing to add a substantial preamble to every statute.

I would go a step beyond the traditional preamble, however, in order to solve some other problems caused by the language and textual conventions of the profession. Legal texts, as we all know, can be dense, lengthy, convoluted, and full of language that is troublesome for ordinary citizens. In fact, they are often hard for lawyers themselves to understand, especially for those unfamiliar with the subject matter.[180] Moreover, as we have seen, the length and complexity of certain statutes also undermine confidence in whether a legislature can legitimately be viewed as the author of its legislation. A major function of committee reports is to summarize for members of Congress, in plain and ordinary English, the purpose and effect of proposed legislation. In fact, the issuance of committee reports is essentially a concession that the average legislator is not expected to actually read or understand statutes.

My proposal is that we combine the functions of the traditional preamble and the modern committee report into an official summary, written in ordinary English, that would be enacted along with the statute to which it relates. This summary would be the official statement of legislative intent regarding the statute. It would not cover all the details of the legislation, of course, so there would still be room for traditional statutory construction, such as clarifying ambiguities and filling gaps. But any judicial interpretation should be consistent with the spirit and purpose of the law, as stated in the summary.

Such a summary would be more than an aid to construction. It would have the added benefit of informing interested members of the public about the purpose and effect of the new law. Newspapers might publish it verbatim, or reporters could consult the summary and more accurately report on its likely effects. The summaries could be posted on the Internet. Official summaries would therefore also improve public access to, and understanding of, the law.

By authoritatively placing evidence of the intent and purpose of legislation into the text itself, we can be textualists and intentionalists at the same time. That, it seems to me, is exactly what we should strive to achieve. As mentioned earlier in this chapter, certain types of statutory text demand that judges give relatively more deference to the text and the words contained in it. In other cases they should pay more attention to what the speaker meant by those words. But in either case, text and intent should both get their due.

6
Judicial Opinions and the Concept of Precedent

Precedent in England

Unlike the civil law systems that arose on the continent of Europe (heavily influenced by Roman law), the common law that developed in England and its former colonies distinguishes itself by viewing judicial opinions as a source of law. In other words, a decision made by a judge on a point of law functions as a precedent that must be followed in later cases that raise the same issue.

Of course, statutes enacted by legislatures are the primary source of law in both systems. An American legislature can pass a statute that overrides a judicial opinion (unless it involves a constitutional question), and judges are bound to follow the statutes in their jurisdiction. Nonetheless, common law judges can essentially legislate in areas where there is no legislation, and they can give authoritative interpretations to statutes as well. Thus, the two major sources of law in a common law system are statutes and precedents established by judicial opinions.

Statutes, as we discussed in the previous chapter, were being written down at a relatively early stage, and they soon came to be known as "written law," or *lex scripta*. Judicial opinions, on the other hand, were long known as "unwritten law," or *lex non scripta*.[1]

Francis Bacon (Lord Chancellor of England in the early seventeenth century) wrote that the common law "is no text law, but the substance of it consisteth in the series and succession of Judicial Acts from time to time which have been set out in the books which we term Year Books."[2]

As Bacon observed, the law expounded in judicial opinions (which he called "judicial acts") was not text law, although those opinions were later written down and printed in books. The mere act of creating a record of judgments or opinions did not by itself turn precedent into written law. Judges did not issue written opinions (known as "judgments" in England) in the way that Parliament had come to enact written statutes. Traditionally, they delivered their decisions by word of mouth. In fact, even today, the common law—especially in England—remains remarkably oral, although important precedents are almost invariably written down and reported.

Yet just as there was a strong tendency for legislation to undergo textualization once the technology of writing and printing were available, the common law, especially during the past century or two, has come under similar pressure. This is particularly true in the United States. As a result, the concept of precedent is gradually becoming less conceptual and ever more textual.

Early Common Law

The term *common law* has always been somewhat vague. I will use it here to refer to the uncodified rules and principles applied by judges when deciding the cases that come before them. In other words, the term refers to judge-made law, also known as *case law*.

English judges generally claimed that the principles they used to decide cases were derived from, as Matthew Hale put it, "immemorial Usage and Custom."[3] No doubt, when there was an applicable custom that came to mind and suggested a reasonable resolution to a dispute, judges would have used it. But many issues would not have been resolvable by custom or usage, and in such cases the invocation of custom would have been a fiction that lent some legitimacy to the fact that the judges were actually making new law.

This system of adjudication and judicial lawmaking could work without requiring judges to set down its principles in written form. In fact, many judges believed that the common law, which was felt to reside mainly in the minds and memories of the legal profession, was superior to written law.[4] In medieval England, this institutional memory was embedded in a small, close-knit group of judges and barristers (or serjeants) who discussed and debated the law both in court and out.[5] What also helped was that there was simply less law to remember. During this period the common law truly was *lex non scripta*.

Although the judgments of judges were not written law, making a record of them would have been a useful aid to memory. Reports of cases began to appear, made not by the judges themselves but by other people who were present in the courtroom. These documents, which later came to be compiled into a series of volumes called *yearbooks*, reported court proceedings from the end of the thirteenth century until around 1535. They were written in Law French, which was the predominant language of the profession at the time of the earliest yearbooks.[6]

These reports were just that: they reported what happened during a judicial proceeding. They usually focused more on the arguments of lawyers than on the decision of the judges. The doctrine of precedent was still to be fully developed. Moreover, many of the reports seem to have been written by legal apprentices who observed the proceedings in order to learn how to become lawyers. They would have concentrated mainly on what the lawyers said and did, because this is what they hoped to emulate. Of course, the reaction of judges to the pleadings and arguments of the lawyers was also important, but in many of these early reports the actual decision—if reported at all—was almost an afterthought.[7] The result, as Plucknett has pointed out, is that "use of cases as sources of law" was "well-nigh impossible."[8]

The Rise of Precedent

Although the reports in the yearbooks seem to have been made largely for educational purposes, lawyers as early as the fourteenth century began to refer to decisions in earlier cases that they believed might bolster their arguments, and judges began citing cases in response. For the most part, they were referring not to written reports, but to a decision that they remembered or had heard about. Some judges seem to have had remarkably clear memories of cases decided at least a decade before. They had no citation system, of course, but might refer to "David of Fleetwick's Case" or "the Bastard's Case." And another judge or opposing counsel might attempt to distinguish the case, perhaps by retorting *n'est pas semblable* (Law French for 'it's not the same').[9]

Around the middle of the fifteenth century, there are indications that lawyers were beginning to treat descriptions of court proceedings as more than interesting or educational reports of what transpired. They were beginning to view them as sources of law. Specifically, lawyers started compiling and printing abridgments. Similar to modern digests, the abridgments consisted of alphabetical headings, like *abatement* or *battery*, followed by synopses of cases dealing with that topic. This made it much more convenient for lawyers to find and cite cases discussing a particular legal proposition.[10]

Judges in the latter half of the fifteenth century were themselves beginning to recognize the notion of precedent—the principle that once a legal issue is decided in a particular way, it ought to be decided in the same way in future cases raising the same issue. For instance, a judge observed in 1496 that "[o]ur decision in this case will be shown hereafter as a precedent" and suggested that they therefore should weigh their judgment carefully.[11]

Although a concept of precedent was beginning to develop, it did not mean that those precedents had to be fixed in writing. Reports could be oral as well as written. Just as we can make an oral report of some event today, lawyers of the time could orally report a decision made in a previous case.[12] And judges continued to have long memories. James Dyer, an Elizabethan judge, once mentioned a "report of Baron Fortescue." According to historian L. W. Abbott, this report must have consisted of passing information by word of mouth rather than by words on paper.[13] Another judge, John Spelman, noted in a proceeding from the sixteenth century that *vn case fuit remember* ('a case was remembered').[14]

Nonetheless, written reports of decisions were considered useful. Memory is fragile. Without writing, older precedents would necessarily be forgotten over time. In fact, judges might sometimes conveniently forget a precedent that they preferred not to follow. Writing, even if not essential, provided powerful evidence of what the judges had decided in an earlier case. Dyer, the Elizabethan judge, expressed doubts about the authenticity of certain cases because he had never seen references to them in any books.[15]

Written reports therefore became more common. There were many private compilations of cases before the invention of printing, and some of these manuscripts appear to have been widely copied.[16] At the same time, access to reports remained problematic. Parchment was expensive, and every copy had to be laboriously made by hand.[17] Most lawyers and judges would have had at best an eclectic sampling of cases and no easy way to find those that were most relevant to any particular point. Only the plea rolls, official records of the courts, were anywhere near complete, but they were practically inaccessible to the profession.[18]

Even when reports were available, their quality and completeness were always open to question. The apprentices or law students who made many of the early reports might not have understood the proceedings correctly, or they might have mentioned only what was of interest to them. On occasion, two reports of a case gave exactly contrary decisions.[19]

Printed Reports

The arrival of printing in England largely solved the accessibility issue. Printers soon discovered that the legal profession was a large market for their products. They printed large numbers of case reports.[20] As they became more widely available, reports ceased to be viewed primarily as learning tools and began to be seen as sources of law.

During the course of the sixteenth and seventeenth centuries, the legal profession started focusing less on the arguments of counsel and more on the decision of the judges. According to W. S. Holdsworth's *History of English Law*, the center of interest shifted from the debate in court to the decision of the judges, a change that "led to the growth of the modern view as to the authority of decided cases; and this, in turn, led to the growth of the practice of constantly citing cases in court."[21]

Once judicial decisions were considered repositories of doctrine, reports would need to be not just accessible, but accurate. The process of printing could create many identical copies of a report, but the text needed to be a reliable representation of what the judges said.[22] Accuracy increased with the advent of named reporters around 1550, as opposed to the anonymous reporters of the yearbook period. Some of these early reporters, like Edmund Plowden and James Dyer, were eminent jurists.[23] So also was another prominent reporter of this period, Edward Coke, whose first volumes of reports were printed in the early years of the seventeenth century.[24]

Coke's reports were highly regarded at the time. Through them, he tried to bring order and logic to the law. He tried to report cases that were particularly important from a legal perspective.[25] In fact, his efforts to systematize the law may have been Coke's greatest weakness, for he was sometimes accused of substituting his own opinion for that of a court with which he disagreed.[26] As Plucknett remarked, a case in Coke's reports is "an uncertain mingling of genuine report, commentary, criticism, elementary instruction, and recondite legal history."[27]

Particularly relevant from our perspective is that Coke intended his reports to be printed and designed them for use by lawyers.[28] In this sense, he may have been ahead of his time. Whatever failings Coke's reports might have had, his efforts show that the legal profession during this period was beginning to value relatively contemporaneous and accurate printed reports as a source of decisions that could function as precedents.

Throughout this period, English barristers remained free to refer to any previous case, even if not reported at all. Yet Ibbetson's examination of the arguments of contemporary lawyers shows that as early as the 1590s, they were showing a marked preference for printed reports over remembered decisions or manuscript (handwritten) reports. This was true even when the printed cases were quite old and even though more recent and more relevant cases were available in manuscript form.[29]

The Quality of Reports

The practices of reporters who followed in the footsteps of such luminaries as Plowden and Coke left much to be desired. During the seventeenth and eighteenth centuries, the quality of reports of judicial decisions fluctuated wildly. Reporting remained a private enterprise, and the results depended on the interest and care of the individual reporters and printers, whose main motive was usually to make as much money as possible. Many of them were hardly the cream of the profession.

Judges became concerned that their reputations would be injured by the poor quality of the reporting of their decisions. An exasperated Justice Holt once remarked, "See the inconveniences of these scrambling reports: they will make us appear to posterity for a parcel of blockheads."[30] Another judge described a reporter as hearing only half of what went on in court and reporting the other half.[31] Siderfin's reports were deemed "fit to be burned."[32] Justice Park is said to have actually incinerated his copy of Keble's reports.[33] Consequently, whether to follow a precedent to some extent depended on the reputation of the reporter and the quality of the report, leaving judges "at liberty to attach different degrees of weight to different authorities."[34]

Moreover, it was the reporters and printers, rather than the judges, who had control over what was published and what was not. This was problematic because there were no official reporters and few impediments on private individuals who wished to enter the business. As a result, there could be, and often were, multiple reports of a single case, none of which were complete verbatim records of what had transpired. Instead, they summarized the proceedings with varying degrees of accuracy and completeness.

By the eighteenth and nineteenth centuries, as the legal profession relied ever more on case law, the time lag to publication was reduced. At the same time, quality remained an issue. Reliance on precedents would be problematic as long as reporting was an inexact science. Lord Mansfield is said to have disregarded what he considered to be poorly reported decisions.[35] And Sir Frederick Pollock pointed out that a report can always be contradicted by a more accurate report or even by the "clear recollection of the Court or counsel."[36] Obviously, the common law of this time, though it was increasingly found in printed documents that were widely accessible, nonetheless remained largely unwritten. As a consequence, it remained conceptually distinct from statutory law.

What mattered was the court's decision and the general principle that underlay it, not the precise words in which the decision was expressed. As Mansfield said, "The law does not consist of particular cases, but of general principles, which are illustrated and explained by these cases."[37] Elsewhere he observed that "[t]he reason and spirit of cases make law; not the letter of particular precedents."[38]

Modern English Law Reporting

By the early nineteenth century, English society and its law were becoming much more complex as a result of the Industrial Revolution and related developments. Accurate reports became ever more essential. One step in this direction was to appoint authorized or official reporters. In 1865, the English bar set up a reporting system that was run by the Incorporated Council of Law Reporting. This council began issuing its own series of reports: the *Law Reports*. They have come to be treated as semiofficial and should be cited in court when possible.[39]

What also has made English case reports more authoritative is that judges now usually read and approve the text of their decisions before they appear in the *Law Reports*.[40] Unofficial reports, like those of the *All England Law Reports*, are not normally screened by the judges. Interestingly, the lack of editing by judges is sometimes felt to be a virtue. Some English lawyers prefer the unofficial reports because they are believed to be closer to what the judge actually said rather than what the judge, on reflection, would have liked to have said.[41] They are, in other words, more accurate descriptions of what happened in court.

The House of Lords further elevated the significance of the written word when it abandoned the oral delivery of its judgments in 1963.[42] The law lords began to draft their judgments after argument and provide them to reporters in written form. This seems to guarantee that there will no longer be differing reports of a case. All the reporters have to do is pick up the judgments, perhaps add some headnotes and a summary, and print the result. Judges on the Court of Appeal may also write out their opinions in some of the more important or difficult cases that come before them. But they still deliver many oral judgments, often directly after argument, which may or may not be reported.

Precedent Tightens Its Grip

We saw in chapter 5 that advances in the quality of the publishing of legislation must have been one of the factors that caused English courts to interpret statutes in a very literal fashion, particularly during the latter half of the eighteenth and most of the nineteenth centuries. Arguably, an analogous development came about with the increasing quality and accessibility of case reports.

At the end of the nineteenth century and for much of the twentieth, English appellate courts not only came to view precedent as an important source of law, but they went so far as to refuse to change their own precedents, even those they believed to be wrong.[43] As J. H. Baker has observed, the duty of "repeating errors" is a modern innovation and may have resulted from the improved quality of law reports following developments in shorthand techniques, which according to Baker "made the ipsissima verba of the judges available as an authentic text and made bold distinguishing more difficult."[44]

Precedent had long been a feature of English law, of course, but during much of the twentieth century it held courts in a tighter grip than before. Previously, judges had followed precedent if there were several cases on a point that all reached the same conclusion, or if the judges deciding a case were particularly eminent, or perhaps if they believed that the profession had come to rely on a case. But by the first part of the twentieth century, a single precedent that was on point was felt to be absolutely binding.[45]

The House of Lords unshackled itself by means of a Practice Statement in 1966, declaring that it would henceforth feel free to disregard an earlier opinion "when it appears right to do so."[46] Nonetheless, according to a study published around fifteen years later, the lords have exercised their newfound liberty quite sparingly. They have held, for instance, that it is not sufficient to overrule a previous decision just because they believe that it was wrongly decided; there has to be some additional basis for refusing to follow it.[47] This aspect of precedent—feeling oneself bound, or at least strongly encouraged, to follow one's earlier decisions—is often called *stare decisis* or *horizontal precedent*.

There is a second way in which courts are bound by precedent: lower courts must also follow precedents established by a higher court. Unlike stare decisis, which is basically a self-imposed restriction, this aspect of precedent (sometimes called *vertical precedent*) is generally felt to be mandatory in the common law system.

Of course, vertical precedent requires that there be a system in which a higher court has the power to overrule a lower court for failing to follow one of the higher court's earlier decisions. The hierarchy of English courts, with the House of Lords on the top, was not clearly established until 1876, which is another reason that the binding nature of precedent reached its apogee in the late nineteenth and early twentieth centuries. Moreover, the House of Lords did not allow the systematic reporting of its decisions until roughly the middle of the nineteenth century, making it difficult to discern the rationale for a judgment and apply it to other cases.[48]

English case reports thus went through many of the same transitions that statutes did. Yet there is at least one very critical difference. The text of statutes, as we have seen, came to be viewed as the authoritative expression of the legislature, especially after Parliament began to review and then enact written legislation. Statutes were no longer just an after-the-fact rendition by a clerk of what Parliament decided. Instead, the text came to be viewed as the law itself.

Yet throughout most of the history of England, the reports of judgments were exactly that: reports of what the judges said. The rule of law, or holding, depended not so much on what was written in the reports, but on how the case was decided. A 1940 study of reporting practices observed that "the law of England is what it is, not because it has been so reported, but because it has been so decided."[49] Case law was not really unwritten, of course. But it clearly was—and in England still is—more conceptual than verbal.

The fact that in England the common law has remained unwritten in a very real sense, that it is something to be extracted from the decisions of judges rather than by close reading of the text of a judge's opinion, may help explain why it is possible for the courts to believe themselves absolutely bound by their own previous decisions. In such a rigid system there has to be an escape valve. It turns out that English judges and lawyers have several ways to avoid the force of a precedent, many of which are aided by the vestiges of orality in the English system.

Escaping Precedent

One way to avoid the rigorous rule that precedents must be obeyed is to subtly reconceptualize the meaning of a case. For instance, English judges normally do not lay out their holding or *ratio decidendi* in an authoritative formulation. The *ratio* or holding of a case is the legal principle necessary to produce the outcome. It constitutes the precedential value of a case. Yet, important as it is, English judges traditionally do not express the *ratio* in so many words. They leave it up to later judges and lawyers to figure it out by means of legal reasoning. As a result, it is always possible to recharacterize the *ratio* retrospectively, or to broaden or narrow its reach. As Carleton Kemp Allen has stated, the *ratio decidendi* is in "a constant state of flux."[50]

In addition, even today reports of judgments are often not written by the judges themselves. And, as in earlier times, there are sometimes multiple and somewhat different reports of a case. It is therefore risky to focus too much on the exact text of an English opinion.

Moreover, it remains common for judges in England to issue multiple or *seriatim* opinions, where all the judges state their opinions one after the other, usually in order of seniority. Clearly, such opinions tend to make the determination of a holding more difficult. And, of course, they give judges in later cases a fair amount of freedom in how to characterize the holding by focusing more on one judge's opinion and less on that of another.

Finally, English courts are bound only by the *ratio* of an earlier case on the same issue. They are not obligated to follow *obiter dicta*, or comments that are not directly on point. It is easy to see how a distinction between *ratio* and dicta would arise in a system in which a reporter decides which of a judge's oral comments to memorialize for posterity. When speaking, people often say things that are not directly relevant. Writing, on the other hand, is generally planned and organized in advance. Irrelevancies and digressions, especially in formal styles of writing, tend to be frowned upon. Dismissing as dicta something that an esteemed judge has thought about and has personally reduced to writing is much more difficult than when the same thought is expressed in an oral opinion delivered right after lawyers finish their argument.

The English legal system also distinguishes between an *extempore* judgment (one that is delivered orally directly after argument) and a *reserved* judgment (where the judges have taken some time to think the matter over and deliver their judgments several weeks or even months later). A reserved judgment is not inevitably written, in contrast to an extempore judgment, which is necessarily delivered orally. But it appears to be normal practice to deliver reserved judgments in writing. In any event, a reserved judgment is felt to have greater weight than one delivered extempore because the judges had time to consider the matter.[51]

Thus, at a time when English common law was truly *lex non scripta*, rigid reliance on earlier decisions would have been unlikely to develop. Even after court proceedings came to be written down by reporters, it was possible for eminent lawyers like Francis Bacon and Matthew Hale to maintain that there was a fundamental distinction between the written law produced by Parliament and the unwritten law of judges.

As written reports became ever more accessible and accurate, a more vigorous doctrine of precedent could and did develop. Oddly enough, however, the rigidity of English precedent during the twentieth century was to a large extent made possible by the fact that English law still maintained, in some important respects, vestiges of its oral past. In fact, the English common law remains remarkably oral, as we see in the fact that precedential value is still ascribed to extempore opinions.

Residual Orality in Modern English Case Reports

Although English judgments are often reported in writing and published, there is still much evidence of orality. Even those judges who write their opinions are still to some extent operating in an oral mode. Their written opinions contain a fair amount of what linguists sometimes call *oral residue*—vestiges of oral traditions that have only recently started to die out and that retain a surprising amount of vitality even today.

For instance, judgments or opinions of the House of Lords have now been produced in writing for several decades.[52] Despite this transition, House of Lords cases are still presented in the reports as though they had been delivered orally. Each of the law lords hearing the case produces a separate opinion, in order of seniority. Often enough, it is quite brief and says nothing more than "My Lords, I have had the advantage of reading in draft the speech of my noble and learned friend Lord Hope of Craighead. For the reasons he has given I would dismiss the appeal."[53] Yet technically, the tradition of seriatim opinion delivery continues.

Another illustration of residual orality is that the lords do not hesitate to use the pronouns *I* or *my*, even though their use is generally discouraged in formal writing. In contrast, Justice Stephen Breyer recently caused a bit of a scandal by his use of the pronoun *I* in a draft opinion for the United States Supreme Court. To be exact, he wrote that "I will call" a certain decision "case two."[54] The result was a "legal frenzy" that motivated at least one law professor to send a note of complaint to the justice for his "nonstandard" usage.[55] When the opinion appeared in final form, the *I* had been replaced by *we*.[56]

There are additional vestiges of orality in judgments from the House of Lords. For example, they tend to be somewhat less formal in tone than opinions of the U.S. Supreme Court, which is roughly comparable in standing to the House of Lords. Formal language, of course, is common in writing, while speech is generally more casual.

In addition, English opinions sometimes suggest face-to-face contact with other judges or with an audience, in contrast to the impersonal tone of most U.S. Supreme Court opinions. For instance, the lords begin each opinion with the phrase "My lords," as though they were speaking to a live audience. And they often refer by name to a specific barrister who argued the case, as did Lord Goff of Chieveley: "I was at first impressed by Sir Patrick's argument, particularly as developed by him in his reply. But on reflection I find myself unable to accept it."[57]

Lord Goff's statement reveals another way in which English practice remains relatively oral: argument before the appellate courts is not subject to strict time limits, and the judges typically engage in extended interaction with the lawyers. In one Court of Appeal case, the argument seems to have gone on for three weeks.[58] This applies also to the House of Lords, where according to a study by Alan Paterson the lords base their decisions primarily on oral argument as opposed to written submissions.[59] In the United States, on the other hand, appellate judges rely far more on written briefing, and they usually impose strict time limits on oral argument, typically half an hour per side. Sometimes they refuse to allow oral argument at all.[60]

The primary reason for the much longer oral argument in English appellate cases is that English barristers do not provide the exhaustive briefs that American lawyers do. Nor do judges normally research a case beforehand (unlike American practice, in which judges and their clerks typically study the briefs, do additional research, and often reach a tentative decision before oral argument). As opposed to American judges, who typically read important precedents and have time to study their exact wording, English judges traditionally hear about them during argument.[61]

Further evidence of oral residue is that the law lords, despite having written their opinions for many years, refer to them as "speeches." Likewise, they typically remark on what a judge "said" in a previous case, rather than what he "wrote." And they admit to emotions, something considerably more common in spoken interaction than it is in formal written documents. As one of the law lords once said, "My Lords, I must own that this question has caused me considerable anxiety."[62] Such statements are unusual in an American opinion, certainly when the judge is part of the majority, as opposed to being a dissenter.

A final indication that English appellate practice is still relatively oral is that courts will recognize unreported (that is, unprinted) cases as precedents, as long as a barrister vouches for their authenticity.[63] In the House of Lords, citing to unreported cases requires leave of the court, and other courts tend to discourage it. But the mere fact that it is possible to rely on an unreported precedent indicates that the traditional view of the common law as *lex non scripta* retains remarkable vitality.[64]

As this book is going to press, the Appellate Committee of the House of Lords, England's highest court until mid 2009, was renamed the Supreme Court and separated from Parliament. It may well abandon some of its previous procedures and begin to produce more textual opinions. At present, however, English appellate practice is decidedly more oral than that of the United States.

So far the discussion may have seemed mostly of interest to legal historians or perhaps students of law and literature. I believe, however, that it has much broader implications than might at first appear. The essentially oral nature of English case law has led to a conception of precedent that is different from that in the United States. To appreciate this difference, we must examine a bit more closely the English understanding of precedent.

Finding the Ratio

When English judges say that they are bound by a precedent, they do not mean that an earlier case must be followed in all particulars. One of the basic justifications for a legal regime based on precedent is that like cases should be decided alike. Thus, the first inquiry is necessarily whether the case to be decided has similar facts or raises the same issue as a case that is a potential precedent. If the earlier case can be distinguished from the one at issue, it is not a "like" case, and judges deciding the later case need not follow it.

Assuming that a previous case is sufficiently similar, it becomes necessary to determine what the *ratio decidendi* of the previous case was. Rupert Cross and J. W. Harris provide a working definition: "The *ratio decidendi* of a case is any rule of law expressly or impliedly treated by the judge as a necessary step in reaching his conclusion . . ."[65] In the United States, we often call this the "holding."

Unfortunately, finding the *ratio*, although it is one of the most basic skills of a lawyer, can be a uncertain enterprise fraught with difficulty. Cross and Harris discuss the various approaches or methodologies proposed by legal scholars such as Wambaugh, Halsbury, and Goodhart,[66] but they end up concluding that it is "impossible to devise formulae for determining the *ratio decidendi* of a case."[67] Nonetheless, according to Lord Reid of the House of Lords, "It matters not how difficult it is to find the *ratio decidendi* of a previous case, that *ratio* must be found."[68]

Traditionally, finding the *ratio* has required close analysis of the facts and outcome of a case. In theory, it is possible to determine the holding of a case even when no reasons are given for a decision.[69] An example is the famous *Peerless* case, more precisely entitled *Raffles v. Wichelhaus* and decided in 1864. The plaintiff made a contract to sell 125 bales of Indian cotton at a specified price, to arrive from Bombay on the ship named *Peerless*. It turns out that there were at least two ships by that name, one leaving Bombay in October and the other in December. The report of the case, which consists of about one printed page, begins with a summary of the pleadings. It continues with the argument by counsel for the plaintiff seller, who was continuously interrupted by the obviously skeptical judges.

The lawyer for the buyers then started his argument by suggesting that there was evidence that the plaintiff meant one *Peerless* and that the defendant buyers intended to refer to a different *Peerless*. As a result, he argued that there was "no consensus ad idem, and therefore no binding contract." According to the reporter, the lawyer "was then stopped by the Court." With no discussion or elaboration, the judges abruptly declared, "There must be judgment for the defendants."[70]

Even though the case has no opinion, it is held to have established the important principle that there can only be a contract if there was *consensus ad idem*, or a "meeting of the minds."[71] Critically, this conclusion flows forth not just from analysis of the issue (was there an enforceable contract in this situation?) and its resolution (no) but also by considering the discourse that took place at oral argument. The judges appear to have resolved the case in the defendants' favor directly after their counsel argued that there was no meeting of the minds.[72]

Of course, English judges normally do give reasons for deciding as they do, although that does not mean that they always express the *ratio* in a succinct and understandable fashion. Cross and Harris observe, "[I]t is comparatively seldom that a judge expressly indicates the proposition on which he relies as *ratio decidendi*."[73]

Even when the judge attempts to describe the holding of a case, his or her statement of the rule of law may not settle the matter. According to A. L. Goodhart, an expert on the English concept of precedent, "it is not the rule of law *set forth* by the court, or the rule *enunciated* . . . which necessarily constitutes the principle of the case. There may be no rule of law set forth in the opinion, or the rule when stated may be too wide or too narrow."[74] Instead, according to Goodhart, the principle underlying a decision must be discovered by means of analytic thinking.[75] Eugene Wambaugh, another English scholar, likewise made the point that it is not the words or the language of judges that constitute the force of precedent.[76] Another expert on English common law, A. W. B. Simpson, has written, "[I]t is a feature of the common law system that there is no way of settling the correct text or formulation of the rules."[77] Blackstone was more blunt, stating that the law and the opinion of the judge are not the same thing, because the judge may mistake the law.[78]

Currently, there is a tendency for English judges to formulate more textual holdings, at least in certain types of cases. It is increasingly common for them to write their opinions, and in some cases they will issue an opinion that speaks for the entire court. This is especially true when clear rules are desirable.[79]

Clarity is of paramount importance in criminal matters, where the rule of law dictates that there be rules, that these rules be made and promulgated in advance, and that they be understandable to those who must follow them.[80] These efforts to promote clarity via single opinions come close to codifying the criminal law by essentially requiring that it be written down in a definitive textual form.

Yet despite some exceptions, English lawyers and judges have generally resisted the textualization (or codification) of the common law. As Lord Reid once said, "[I]t is not the function of noble and learned Lords or indeed of any judges, to frame definitions or to lay down hard and fast rules."[81] In some very real ways, the common law of England, even today, remains *lex non scripta*.

Precedent in the United States

The situation in the American colonies was originally not all that different from that in England. Colonial lawyers and judges used English common law principles and relied on law books imported from England, including case reports. There were courts in the colonies, of course, and they produced judicial decisions, but reports of those decisions were not contemporaneously published.[82]

Lawyers of the time often had manuscript reports of American cases that they either made themselves or copied from the notes of someone else who had been present in court. This practice is similar to the yearbook period in England. Also similar to earlier English developments is that lawyers commonly educated themselves by attending court sessions in colonial capitals and taking notes of the proceedings. These notes were not only useful in training them but might also come in handy in their subsequent law practices.[83]

The Formative Years

After independence, printed law reports began to appear in the American states. Not surprisingly, reliance on English cases was felt to be inconsistent with independence and the development of a distinct American legal system. But if lawyers and judges were to rely on homegrown cases, they needed accurate reports. Memory and hearsay about judicial decisions could not keep up with an expanding body of case law. An early American reporter, Ephraim Kirby, in explaining the need to report and publish cases, commented that "the principles of [judges'] decisions were soon forgot, or misunderstood, or erroneously reported from memory."[84]

These early reports were the result of private enterprise, although judges sometimes cooperated with the reporters. As in England, appellate judges delivered their opinions orally and seriatim. Thus, an American report of the time would have resulted from a private individual sitting in a courtroom, taking notes of what the lawyers argued and the opinions or judgments that the judges delivered, and publishing a synopsis of the proceedings.[85]

Early U.S. Supreme Court opinions contain clear indications of orality, even though it seems likely that the justices were speaking on the basis of notes or even reading from text they had written down beforehand. An illustration is *Georgia v. Brailsford*,[86] where the state of Georgia sought an injunction to stay a proceeding in the Circuit Court of Georgia. The report mentions that "after argument, the Judges delivered their opinions *seriatim*."[87] Justice Johnson speaks first, discloses his reasoning, and concludes that "in my opinion . . . there is not a proper foundation for issuing an injunction."[88] Next is Justice Iredell, who, after pointing out that he sat on the circuit court that decided the case at issue, ends his discussion by stating that "I think, that an injunction should be awarded."[89] Justice Blair concurs with Iredell's conclusion but adds some of his own reasoning. Wilson starts out with a personal observation that is reminiscent of the emotions and internal conflicts expressed even today by English judges: "I confess, that I have not been able to form an opinion which is perfectly satisfactory to my own mind upon the points which have been discussed."[90] He refers to what is apparently an unreported case: "I remember an action was instituted and sustained, some years ago, in the name of *Louis* XVI. king of France, against Mr. *Robert Morris*, in the Supreme Court of Pennsylvania."[91] He concludes rather timidly that he has "no objection" to the requested remedy. Justice Cushing comes out against an injunction: "I think that an injunction ought not to be awarded."[92] Finally, Chief Justice Jay, like Iredell, begins with a personal observation: "My first ideas were unfavorable to the motion; but many reasons have been urged, which operate forcibly to produce a change of opinion." His conclusion is also rather tepid: "I am content, that the injunction issue."[93]

Given that the American notion of precedent and the case law method were borrowed from the English motherland, it stands to reason that the American conception of precedent during the latter half of the eighteenth century and the first half of the nineteenth would be similar to that in England. As did the English, the early American legal profession viewed the common law as something distinct from decided cases. The cases were merely evidence of the law, which existed independently. Moreover, the opinions of judges could be stronger or weaker evidence of what the law in question was. Sometimes several cases would be needed to establish a point. On other occasions, even that was not enough. As Chancellor Kent remarked, "Even a series of decisions are not always conclusive evidence of what is law."[94] American lawyers would probably have agreed with the notion that the common law resided in the collective memory of the legal profession, rather than in the text of judicial opinions contained in printed reports.[95]

It did not take long, however, before American practice in the delivery and reporting of decisions began to diverge from its English roots in significant ways. It would eventually lead to a very different—and eventually more textual—conceptualization of the notion of precedent.

Opinions in Writing

A major American innovation is that appellate judges came to be required, often via legislation or even constitutional provision, to issue their opinions in writing. Connecticut adopted such a statute in 1785, and many states followed suit. Other courts, like the U.S. Supreme Court, adopted the practice on their own initiative.[96] Today, most states require their highest court to deliver all decisions in writing.[97] Other states, like California, require not only its supreme court but all courts of appeal to make decisions "in writing with reasons stated,"[98] a rule that mandates a full written opinion in all appellate cases. Although there might be a few isolated exceptions, the general rule in the United States today is that only written opinions have precedential value.

While the shift in the mode of delivering opinions might not seem all that significant, it signals an important development in the nature of precedent. Recall that in England, it is possible (though not common) for a case to function as a precedent without any opinion at all. *Raffles v. Wichelhaus* is the famous example. Knowing the state of existing law, it is possible to deduce a principle of decision from the facts and the outcome. In *Raffles*, the argument of counsel was also very helpful. In contrast, requiring written opinions suggests that the precedential value of a case consists not in how it was decided but in the reasons and analysis expressed in the writing. Eventually it will no longer be the outcome or decision that functions as a precedent. It will be the judge's opinion.

Official Reporters

Another American innovation is that during the first half of the eighteenth century, states began to appoint official reporters. Massachusetts did so in 1804. The statute required the reporter to obtain "true and authentic" reports of the decisions of the state's Supreme Judicial Council and to publish them annually.[99] The federal Supreme Court was authorized by Congress to appoint an official reporter in 1817.[100] By 1850, most states had official reporters for their highest courts.[101] As opposed to England, where even today there is no completely authoritative version of case reports, the practice of appointing reporters eventually led to the notion that the reports produced by that reporter—and only those reports—are deemed the official version of the court's decision. While private reporters can and do exist in the United States, the judicial opinions that they publish must be true to this official version. Thus, there can generally be only one fully authoritative text of any particular opinion.

Even though books containing judicial opinions are still called "reports" in the United States, they are no longer the result of a "reporter" going to court and "reporting" the proceedings. Because appellate judges must generally issue written opinions, the reports consist almost entirely of text drafted by the judges themselves, and they are normally published verbatim. All the reporter does is obtain a copy of the opinion from the court, add some information (typically, a summary and headnotes), and print it.[102] Any unofficial reporters do essentially the same thing, although the summary and headnotes will obviously be different. Where there are multiple reports of a single case, the only real difference in the text of the opinions consists of relatively trivial distinctions like the font used, the pagination, and the citation format. Interestingly, the use of one publisher's page numbers by another publisher has led to lawsuits for copyright infringement, which highlights how little the modern reporter contributes to the content of a report.[103] Another indication is that for the past century and a half, the reports are no longer identified by the reporters' names (for example, *Cranch's Reports*), but by the jurisdiction or court (for example, *United States Reports*).

At the same time, reporters have become more professional. The earliest American reporters were often practicing lawyers for whom reporting cases was only a sideline. Being a lawyer has the advantage that the reporter better understands what is happening, which is no doubt the reason that English reporters—while no longer having judges among their ranks—are traditionally barristers.

But problems can arise when practicing lawyers act as reporters. One is that they may have their own views on an issue involved in a case. For instance, Henry Wheaton, who reported decisions of the Supreme Court in the early 1800s, had strong opinions on admiralty law, which was one of the major preoccupations of the Supreme Court at the time. Although Wheaton's reports were generally of good repute, his views on admiralty law may have influenced how he reported a couple of cases in which he was particularly interested.[104] The difficulties are multiplied if the reporter is simultaneously arguing cases before the court. Wheaton did so on several occasions. It would only be human nature—to which Wheaton occasionally succumbed—to give greater prominence to one's own arguments in the reports and to give short shrift to those of one's opponents.[105]

The level of professionalism gradually increased, but concurrently the office became more bureaucratic and less creative. Wheaton eventually decided that the reporter's job was "mechanical drudgery" and that he was born for better things.[106] A New York reporter, George Caines, came to a similar conclusion, noting that he did little more than "arranging the materials received, and giving, in a summary manner, the arguments adduced."[107]

The reliability of the printed text remained an issue throughout the nineteenth century, however. Reporting practices were still not exact enough to allow the sort of close reading of the text that lawyers tend to do today. Judges produced handwritten manuscripts that were often hard to decipher, and printers were prone to make errors in setting the text. Around 1850, the situation began to improve when printers provided proofs of majority opinions to the justices who wrote them, allowing them to be corrected before publication.[108]

American reporters today, although they generally still have legal training, do not normally practice law and have become part of the bureaucracy of the courts. They are professionals who receive the text of opinions from the court (or sometimes directly from the judge) and are expected to reproduce them verbatim, with only minor editorial adjustments. The reporters then provide copies to the publishers (including online publishers) as well as to the public. They also generally supervise printing of the opinions in the official reports, if the jurisdiction has such a series.[109]

As a result, there is generally only one text of a judicial opinion in the United States, even if it appears in different sets of reports. The authoritativeness of the text derives not just from its accuracy, as guaranteed by professional reporters, but even more from the fact that the legal actor herself wrote the words. The judge thus speaks through the words of the text, unmediated by a reporter writing down or summarizing what the judge said. Just as Parliament at some point began to enact written text, judges in the United States create written text that represents their own words, and those words are published exactly as they drafted them.

The Elimination of Seriatim Opinions

American judges also departed from English practice by eliminating seriatim opinion delivery. We have seen that seriatim opinions are still used in some English appellate courts. In its purest form, this method of opinion delivery requires each member of the court to express his views on how the case should be decided and why. Until the early nineteenth century, the U.S. Supreme Court often delivered its opinions seriatim, even in cases raising difficult constitutional issues.[110]

Chief Justice Marshall ended the practice when he was appointed to the Supreme Court in 1801. Marshall laid heavy emphasis on producing opinions of the court in which one opinion was delivered (usually by Marshall himself) that spoke for all the judges and that was almost certainly written out beforehand. Just because Marshall delivered the opinions does not mean that he wrote them all, of course; other justices may have participated in the drafting. Nonetheless, the delivery of a single opinion lent a strong sense of cohesiveness and legitimacy to the early decisions of the Marshall era.[111]

The practice of delivering a unanimous opinion of the court began to decline in the mid-1820s, as an increasing number of concurring and dissenting opinions started to appear.[112] The Court began to speak primarily through majority opinions, as it still does today.

Although it may seem counterintuitive, the presence of concurring opinions, where a judge agrees with the outcome but differs with the majority in how that outcome should be reached, can actually make the text of majority opinions more authoritative. If judges join the majority after reading the text of a proposed opinion, with an opportunity to draft a concurring opinion, one can assume that members of the majority who did not write separately endorse the wording of the opinion. The writer of a majority opinion has to take into account the views of all judges signing on to the opinion and must therefore produce a text that has been read and approved by them all. This is not unlike legislation, where the text of a statute is debated and changed until a majority of lawmakers is willing to vote for it.

Declining Significance of Headnotes and Argument of Counsel

Reporters traditionally added value to their product by prefacing each case with one or more headnotes, as well as by summarizing the arguments of the lawyers. The headnotes (summaries of some or all of the holding) and arguments were printed as part of the case report, usually preceding the opinion itself.

Arguments of counsel were considered important not only because they provided some context to the judge's decisions, but also because they were intrinsically useful in understanding the law. The lawyers who argued before the courts were normally experts in their field and may well have known more about a specialized subject than the judges.

Reporters could likewise be quite knowledgeable about the law. As mentioned above, they were sometimes prominent lawyers. What a reporter wrote about a case might therefore be considered as important as what the deciding judges said in their opinions. At some point, the reporters' reflections on the principle of a case were formally embodied in one or more headnotes. Especially at a time when judges were issuing seriatim opinions, the synopsis of a reporter could be extremely helpful in determining the holding of the case.

The nature of headnotes underwent a subtle change after Richard Peters was appointed reporter for the Supreme Court in 1828.[113] Peters added headnotes to his reports that contained a reference to the page of the opinion where the particular point could be found.[114] His headnotes sent lawyers directly to the part of the opinion that addressed an issue of concern.

Peters's headnotes were, however, subjected to the criticism that they consisted of little more than a selection of critical sentences or paragraphs from the opinion, rather than summarizing the holding.[115] As historian G. Edward White has observed, "Peters merely copied down the Court's language," forcing readers "to make their own judgments about the precise holdings of cases, the very task that headnote summaries were supposed to perform."[116]

The implication is that it was usually not possible in those days to find a few sentences in which the court itself expressed its holding in a succinct and authoritative fashion. It was still necessary to conduct traditional legal analysis to find the *ratio decidendi*, and apparently Peters was not up to the task. But the idea of having a series of headnotes, each linked to a specific part of the case, continues to this day. It clearly fosters a more textual reading of an opinion.

During the mid-1800s, the reporters still routinely included a summary of the arguments of counsel, although whether they should do so had become a matter of debate. A reason for including the arguments was that the opinions of the court did not constitute the law, but were merely evidence of independently existing legal principles. This, of course, harked back to the view long espoused in England that the opinions of its judges were merely evidence of the common law. It had an interesting implication for how opinions should be reported. The arguments of distinguished counsel, it was suggested, or perhaps even the perceptive analysis of the reporter, might sometimes be better evidence of the state of the law than the opinion of a mediocre judge.[117] That point of view eventually lost out, of course. Today, the written opinion of a mediocre judge is the law, even if every distinguished lawyer in the country disagrees.

Thus, summaries of the arguments of counsel disappeared from the reports, as did commentary by the reporter. By the end of the nineteenth century it was clear that the American common law was no longer viewed as something contained in the minds of the legal profession. Rather, it consisted of the written words of judges.

Hierarchical Organization of the Courts

Finally, it is worth observing that the words of American appellate judges were more authoritative than those of their English counterparts in another sense. Although it is apparently less true today, English judges traditionally maintained a certain collegiality, often discussing matters in the inns of court or formally gathering in the Exchequer Chamber to collectively decide an important legal issue.[118] There were certainly disputes and rivalries between the courts, but following precedent did not normally involve one court imposing its will upon another. Instead, precedent consisted of the notion that once the royal judges decided an issue in a particular way, they and their colleagues should decide that issue in the same way in future cases. Precedent was a matter of judicial economy (not having to relitigate a question), fairness (parties in different cases would be treated the same), and predictability. This aspect of precedent, as noted earlier, is generally referred to as *stare decisis*.

American courts, in contrast, were organized hierarchically virtually from the beginning. The typical system is for a state to have trial courts, whose decisions can be reviewed by courts of appeal. Decisions by the courts of appeal are subject to discretionary review by the state's supreme court. Trial judges are not usually bound by the decisions of other trial judges, nor are they necessarily bound by their own previous decisions. For the most part, only opinions written by appellate judges can function as precedent.[119]

As we have already discussed, precedent has come to mean not just that judges, as a policy matter, should normally follow their own previous decisions (stare decisis or horizontal precedent), but that in addition lower courts must follow the decisions of judges above them (vertical precedent). Once there is a clear hierarchy of courts, the word of the higher courts—in particular, the written word—is law.

Thus, it is fair to say that by the middle of the nineteenth century, a distinct American notion of precedent and of common law decision making was beginning to form. The profession was no longer adhering to the notion that judges merely declared the common law. Rather, judges could establish principles and rules for deciding cases in their opinions. These opinions had to be in writing. Case reports contained the exact words of the judges. And increasingly, a single case on point could bind a later court.[120]

At the same time, judges did not normally write opinions in a way that made it possible to identify a specific sentence or paragraph as containing the holding of the case. It was still too soon to speak of precedent being textualized. But the essential ingredients were in place. During the twentieth century, the tendency to view precedent as textual would only intensify.

The Codification Movement

If judicial opinions were gradually becoming more textual over the years, there was another phenomenon that had the potential to transform the common law into authoritative text in one fell swoop. This was the codification movement.

European countries have been familiar with codification for centuries. The most notable example is the *Code Napoléon*, which influenced the development of the civil law throughout Europe and much of the rest of the world. Typically, civil law countries have a number of different codes, such as a civil code and a criminal code. These codes are the primary source of law in such countries. There is nothing quite like the judge-made common law on the continent. At least in theory, civil law judges do not make law; all they can do is interpret and apply the code.[121]

The great advantage of a code is that (in theory, at least) it encompasses all the law on a particular subject. If a French or German lawyer needs to research a question about the criminal law, she need only consult the penal code. In practice, of course, things are never so simple. The code may not answer the lawyer's question, forcing her to research judgments of the courts and other legal literature. The hope entertained by the French revolutionaries, among others, that a code could be made so clear that ordinary people could understand it, and that lawyers would become superfluous, has never been realized.[122] Lawyers and judges are inevitably necessary to interpret a code's provisions. But only the code is truly law.

If English or American lawyers want to know the law on a particular subject, they first must find out whether there is an act or statute that bears on the question. This is not always easy because traditionally acts were bound together into books that contain all the statutes that were enacted in a particular year, regardless of subject. And then the lawyer has to find any judicial opinions on the matter. They are also usually organized by the year in which they were delivered. Of course, the English or American lawyer's task is simplified by digests, which arrange cases according to subject matter, and private compilations of statutes, which are usually also organized by subject. Nonetheless, the concept that all the law on a particular topic should be available in one place—a code—is an attractive one.

In England, the great champion of codification was Jeremy Bentham, who is credited with inventing the term.[123] He was motivated by a strong distaste for lawyers and the common law, at one point urging citizens of the United States to "shut your ports against our *Common Law*, as you would shut them against the plague."[124] The common law, according to Bentham, was chaotic and confused, impossible for the layman to understand. His proposed remedy was to systematize the law (both statutes and common law) into orderly books of codes.[125] These codes would be enacted by the legislature, making them statutory law.

Yet codification had its critics. In particular, the English legal profession was extremely reluctant to allow the common law to be converted into a type of statute. There was a serious attempt to enact a comprehensive criminal code in the mid-nineteenth century. But judges and lawyers strenuously resisted the effort, arguing that the traditional common law was superior to written codes. As one opponent of codification said, "[T]o reduce unwritten law to statute is to discard one of the greatest blessings we have for ages enjoyed in rules capable of flexible application."[126] English judges were not giving up their treasured common law without a fight. As a result of such opposition, and despite Bentham's prodigious efforts, codification never made much headway in his native land.[127]

Codification was more successful in the United States, albeit not immediately. Some of the former colonies considered creating codes soon after independence but ultimately rejected the idea. Thomas Jefferson, who was on a Virginia law revision committee, wrote in *Notes on the State of Virginia* that his state had adopted the common law but decided it was "dangerous to attempt to reduce it to a text" and that it should be "collected from the usual monuments of it."[128]

Yet by roughly the middle of the nineteenth century, there was growing sentiment in favor of codification. Joseph Story, for example, suggested that codification would add "certainty, clearness, and facility of reference" to the law; it was therefore "desirable . . . that the laws, which govern the rights, duties, relations, and business of the people, should . . . be accessible to them for daily use or consultation."[129]

New York held a constitutional convention in 1846 which required the appointment of commissioners to "reduce into one written and systematic code the whole body of the law of this state, or so much or such parts thereof as to the said Commissioners shall seem practicable and expedient."[130] The goals of this codification were noble: "in order that the people may know the legal and equitable rules by which they must be governed—that litigation may be diminished, and justice more speedily administered."[131]

The methodology would be to collect all of the existing law, eliminate inconsistencies, improve it where needed, write it down and organize it in a logical and systematic way, and have the resulting code adopted by the legislature.[132] The New York bar, like the legal profession in England, generally opposed the idea. Nonetheless, New York eventually adopted a *Code of Procedure* (later called the *Code of Civil Procedure*) that was widely imitated by other states.[133] Efforts to codify the entire common law, or parts of it, as David Dudley Field proposed, met with far more limited success.[134]

Codification had greater appeal in the west, which did not have the established legal traditions and entrenched bar that New York did. North and South Dakota have complete systems of codes, for instance.[135] Further west, California also has a comprehensive system that includes not only codes of civil procedure and criminal law, but also some thirty separate codes bearing titles such as Business and Professions, Commerce, Corporations, Education, Elections, Finance, Fish and Game, Food and Agriculture, Government, and even Harbors and Navigation, to list just a few.

Yet despite the plethora of codes in some American jurisdictions, occupying a considerable amount of shelf space in a lawyer's office, the common law is hardly dead in states that have embraced codification. If Bentham's or Field's goal was to supplant the common law with a series of codes, the movement failed, even in places like the Dakotas and California. As a lawyer admitted to practice in California, I can attest that there are some areas of state law where the codes are extremely important and cover much of the territory. Examples are the *Code of Civil Procedure* and the *Probate Code*. But even in these areas, judicial opinions are essential not only to interpret the code but also to fill the many gaps that almost any code contains. In other areas, like the basic principles of contract and tort law, California's Civil Code does little more than provide a general framework that must be filled in by case law, with the exception of certain areas in which the legislature has taken an unusual interest.[136]

A variation on codification is the uniform laws movement. Its main objective has been to propose a body of law in specific subject areas that would be adopted verbatim by many or all states, thus making that area of law consistent across state borders. The National Conference of Commissioners on Uniform State Laws has proposed numerous such laws. Some have been widely adopted; others have been met with apathy or resistance.[137] The most successful has been the *Uniform Commercial Code* (*UCC*), which by 1968 had been enacted by forty-nine of the fifty states.[138]

Whatever the benefits of having law that is uniform throughout the states, the adoption of such acts inevitably textualizes large expanses of the law that were formerly governed by judicial decisions. Article 2 of the *UCC*, which governs sales, deals with all aspects of contract law, including offer and acceptance, the interpretation of agreements, and remedies, which were once the exclusive domain of case law in most American jurisdictions. All of these areas are now ruled by text, leaving to the common law the largely ancillary role of interpreting ambiguities and plugging gaps.[139]

Although the codification movement has been only partially successful in the United States, it has had the effect of converting broad swaths of the common law into statutory text. Judges are reduced to being interpreters of that text. Even in states that have not attempted to codify entire areas of the law, legislatures haphazardly textualize bits and pieces of the common law almost every time they enact a statute.

Restating the Law

The restatements of the law are another way in which the common law is being textualized. They are an initiative of the American Law Institute (ALI), which was founded in 1923. One of the main reasons that it was established was a perceived uncertainty that resulted from "lack of agreement on fundamental principles of the common law."[140] Lack of clarity was another concern.

The ALI therefore convened groups of legal experts, including lawyers, judges, and academics, to "restate" the law in a number of subject areas. In the next couple of decades, restatements were published on the law of agency, contracts, judgments, property, restitution, torts, and trusts.[141] Unlike the uniform law movement, the restatements cover some of the most basic areas of the common law. At the same time, it is not the expressed aim of the restatements to textualize the law. They are nothing more than the opinion of a group of experts on what the majority rule on some area of the law is, or perhaps what it ought to be.[142] The restatements are influential, but they are not sources of law, strictly speaking.

Nonetheless, they have had a certain textualizing effect on the law. There is a growing tendency by some courts to explicitly adopt portions of a restatement. In doing so, they might intend merely to embrace a principle of law contained in the restatement. But often enough, they adopt the exact language of the provision in question. The text, after all, is there for the taking. Unlike messy judicial opinions, the restatements contain carefully crafted rules. Just as the legislature can adopt some or all of a uniform act, judges can adopt sections of a restatement.

It is not unusual to find declarations such as the following in judicial opinions:

"We adopt Restatement (Second) of Judgments § 68."[143]

"We adopt Restatement (Second) of Torts § 411."[144]

An ebulliant Arizona court has gone so far as to declare that "[t]his court, when not bound by previous decisions or legislative enactments, follows the Restatement of the Law.[145]

Although adopting the rule of a restatement does not necessarily mean incorporating the exact text of that rule, it seems to be hard to resist viewing the provisions of the restatements as being similar to statutes. Sidney DeLong has observed that "[m]ost courts are inclined to treat Restatement sections as they would statutes, once they have been adopted for that jurisdiction."[146] Randy Barnett has made a similar point: "Courts are increasingly treating the Restatement as a statute."[147]

The common law is hardly dead, but there is no denying that substantial areas that were once core elements of the common law system have been textualized by means of codification, by the uniform act movement, and, to a lesser extent, by the development of the restatements. Of course, American judges continue to make new law by means of judicial opinions. Yet those opinions are also becoming more and more textual.

The Textualization of Precedent?

Half a century ago there were still prominent American legal scholars, like Roscoe Pound, who could insist that the language of judicial opinions was not authoritative, but that instead it was the result that counts.[148] Likewise, Edward Levi's influential book on legal reasoning stated that a judge "is not bound by the statement of the rule made by the prior judge even in the controlling case."[149] Henry Hart and Albert Sacks could still seriously maintain that the common law was unwritten.[150] They likewise concluded that the *ratio decidendi* of a case "is not imprisoned in any single set of words" and that it therefore "has a flexibility which the statute does not have."[151]

Yet even as these legal scholars were writing, the ground beneath them was starting to shift. The language of judicial opinions was, and still is, becoming ever more authoritative.

What was once aptly described as a case law regime is well on its way to becoming an opinion law system. In other words, the precedential value of a case is nowadays determined not so much by analysis of the facts, the issue, and the outcome, but increasingly by close scrutiny of the text of the opinion. Especially noteworthy is that American courts are beginning to state their holdings explicitly and that those statements are being treated more and more like statutes. Just as happened with other genres of legal texts over the centuries, judicial opinions—or at least the part that we regard as precedent or the holding—are gradually being textualized. The process is only in its infancy, so it is a good time to stand back and to ponder its implications.

Explicit Statements of the Holding

One sign of the gradual textualization of case law in the United States is the growing tendency of courts to explicitly state the case's holding in their own words. Recall that in the English and older American practice, finding the *ratio* or holding could be a daunting task that often required sophisticated legal reasoning. Courts certainly did not lay it out on a platter for easy consumption. Instead, lawyers had to determine the holding by analyzing the relationship of the facts to the outcome of the case, while at the same time reconciling two or three seriatim opinions explaining in somewhat different terms why the judges had decided as they did. If lawyers were lucky, a particularly able reporter would have added a headnote to the case with a good synopsis or analysis of the holding.

Traditionally, the verb "hold" in the context of a judicial decision was purely descriptive. It was almost always in the past tense. Lawyers or a reporter would try to explain what a court held in a previous case (as in, "the court held . . .").

What one does not often encounter in older cases is judges using the verb "hold" in a performative sense, where the verb is in the first person, present tense (as in "we therefore hold . . .") followed by a specific principle or rule of law. An overview of the U.S. Supreme Court cases decided in 1850 reveals that the phrase "we hold" is relatively rare, occurring only seven times. In contrast, the past tense "held" occurs no less that sixty-six times. Some of these occurrences do not describe the holding of a previous case (as in "the land was held by so-and-so"). But there are a large number of instances where "held" is used to describe something that a previous court decided.[152]

When the Court during this period expressed its own views on a proposition of law or reached a conclusion on the basis of a legal principle, it generally prefaced its statement with words or phrases such as "we are of the opinion" or "it is our opinion." Thus, the Court once observed that "we are of opinion, that the Surveyor-General had no authority to change the location of the grant, and to split up the surveys, as was done in this instance."[153] A search for the words "we are of the opinion" and related expressions revealed that such phrases occurred in twenty-three Supreme Court cases decided in 1850. Another common expression was the phrase "our opinion," as in "our opinion is," which occurred thirteen times. Also quite popular was the phrase "we think," which is found in thirty-four cases.[154]

Clearly, language referring to the mental state of the justices was vastly more common in 1850 than the phrase "we hold." This is consistent with a view of the common law as being more conceptual than textual. In fact, the very phrase "judicial opinion" suggests that it is a court's thinking that matters.

By the millennial year 2000, the Supreme Court had become much bolder about explicitly declaring a textual holding. The phrase "we hold" (sometimes separated by an adverb like "now" or "therefore") occurred in forty-six cases decided during that year. In fact, it has become common practice for the Court to state the holding of the case (usually prefaced by "we hold" or its close cousin "we conclude") in either the introductory or concluding paragraph of the majority opinion.[155]

Sometimes the Court uses the phrase "we hold" to announce a purely factual conclusion. Yet often enough the words introduce a very rule-like decision that leaves little room for traditional legal reasoning. An example comes from a 2000 case that dealt with the writ of habeas corpus and its interaction with recent legislation:

> We are called upon to resolve a series of issues regarding the law of habeas corpus, including questions of the proper application of the Antiterrorism and Effective Death Penalty Act of 1996 (AEDPA). We hold as follows:
>
> First, when a habeas corpus petitioner seeks to initiate an appeal of the dismissal of a habeas corpus petition after April 24, 1996 (the effective date of AEDPA), the right to appeal is governed by the certificate of appealability (COA) requirements now found at 28 U.S.C. § 2253(c) (1994 ed., Supp. III). This is true whether the habeas corpus petition was filed in the district court before or after AEDPA's effective date.
>
> Second, when the district court denies a habeas petition on procedural grounds without reaching the prisoner's underlying constitutional claim, a COA should issue (and an appeal of the district court's order may be taken) if the prisoner shows, at least, that jurists of reason would find it debatable whether the petition states a valid claim of the denial of a constitutional right, and that jurists of reason would find it debatable whether the district court was correct in its procedural ruling.

> Third, a habeas petition which is filed after an initial petition was dismissed without adjudication on the merits for failure to exhaust state remedies is not a "second or successive" petition as that term is understood in the habeas corpus context. Federal courts do, however, retain broad powers to prevent duplicative or unnecessary litigation.[156]

In this example, the Court is laying down the law in a way that is hard to distinguish from a federal statute or administrative rule. Its evident purpose is to establish clear procedures that the courts must follow.

Such detailed rules might be expected when the Court fulfills its role of supervising the federal judiciary, as is true with habeas corpus proceedings, where the Court has taken a particularly forceful role in attempting to limit the discretion of the lower federal courts. But textual holdings seem equally common in the far more conceptual area of constitutional law, where the Court likewise increasingly tends to pronounce very rule-like and sometimes quite detailed holdings, as in a discussion about when a lawyer must discuss a possible appeal with a client:

> We . . . hold that counsel has a constitutionally imposed duty to consult with the defendant about an appeal when there is reason to think either (1) that a rational defendant would want to appeal (for example, because there are nonfrivolous grounds for appeal), or (2) that this particular defendant reasonably demonstrated to counsel that he was interested in appealing.[157]

Not only does the Court lay out a fairly elaborate holding in its own authoritative words, but it does so by means of a two-part test.

Every lawyer has become familiar with tests of this sort. One of the best known relates to obscenity. In *Miller v. California*, the Court specifically noted that it was undertaking "to formulate standards more concrete than those in the past."[158] The Court continued:

> State statutes designed to regulate obscene materials must be carefully limited. . . . We now confine the permissible scope of such regulation to works which depict or describe sexual conduct. That conduct must be specifically defined by the applicable state law, as written or authoritatively construed. A state offense must also be limited to works which, taken as a whole, appeal to the prurient interest in sex, which portray sexual conduct in a patently offensive way, and which, taken as a whole, do not have serious literary, artistic, political, or scientific value.[159]

Although the Court did not use the phrase "we hold," it was consciously setting forth a textual standard that was meant to be implemented verbatim. The phraseology has indeed been quoted word for word in hundreds of subsequent cases.[160]

These observations are hardly novel. Robert Nagel has noted the tendency of the Court during the past few decades to use a "formulaic style" of opinion writing in constitutional cases, a style that makes much use of "elaborately layered sets of 'tests' or 'prongs' or 'requirements' or 'standards' or 'hurdles.'"[161] He suggests that the elaborateness and detail of the formulae in constitutional cases is "an obvious effort to achieve control and consistency."[162] Unlike earlier eras, when judges were subject to "simple and undefined maxims," modern courts are bound by "rules that are specific and multiple."[163]

Frederick Schauer has also addressed the notion that modern judicial opinions, especially in constitutional cases, "read more like statutes than like opinions of a court."[164] Schauer's view is that it is especially courts lower in the hierarchy that are likely to interpret a judicial opinion like a statute: "it is not what the Supreme Court *held* that matters, but what it *said* . . . one good quote is worth a hundred clever analyses of the holding."[165] The language of an opinion therefore "takes on a special significance" in the lower courts and "operates like a statute." As a consequence, the opinion's language "will be carefully analyzed, and discussions of why one word rather than another was used will be common."[166]

Likewise, Charles Collier has discussed the tendency of lawyers to view the text of judicial opinions as "direct and authoritative sources of legal rules" whose language "is studied and analyzed in much the same way that one would puzzle and agonize over the precise wording of a statute, a constitution, or a literary work."[167] He observes that the language of an opinion "begins to command authority in its own right, rather than merely as a report on how the decision was reached. Ultimately, the opinion is viewed as itself an original text or primary source."[168] Although none of these scholars uses the term, they are essentially describing the effects of textualization.

Interpreting the Holding

How judges write their opinions and establish precedents is just one side of the coin. The other side is how those who are bound by a precedent read the opinion that establishes it. In other words, if it is true that judges are expressing their opinions in a more textual way these days, is it also true that those reading the opinions are interpreting them more textually and therefore less conceptually? As we discussed in chapters 2 and 5, the nature of a text strongly influences its interpretation.

One way to approach the issue is by examining whether and how judges quote precedential opinions. It is instructive to compare American opinions with those produced by English judges. I have already suggested that the English notion of precedent is more conceptual, while the modern American notion is more textual. It turns out that both English and American judges quote extensively from the language of precedential cases. Yet the style of quotation is radically different.

Any American lawyer who reads a few English appellate opinions will immediately be struck by the lengthy quotations from precedential cases, which sometimes extend over several pages.[169] The point, of course, is to try to determine the *ratio decidendi* of the case, which can only be done by reading lengthy portions of text from the opinions of a number of judges who agreed on the outcome but for somewhat divergent reasons.

Compare the English approach to an American case, *Chambers v. Nasco*, where the U.S. Supreme Court discussed its own precedents regarding recovery of attorney's fees:

> As we explained in *Alyeska*, these exceptions [to the American rule against fee shifting] fall into three categories. The first . . . allows a court to award attorney's fees to a party whose litigation efforts directly benefit others. Alyeska, 421 U.S. at 257–258. Second, a court may assess attorney's fees as a sanction for the " 'willful disobedience of a court order.' " Id., at 258 (quoting Fleischmann Distilling Corp. v. Maier Brewing Co., 386 U.S. 714, 718, (1967)). . . . Third, and most relevant here, a court may assess attorney's fees when a party has " 'acted in bad faith, vexatiously, wantonly, or for oppressive reasons.' " *Alyeska*, supra, at 258–259 (quoting F. D. Rich Co. v. United States ex rel. Industrial Lumber Co., 417 U.S. 116, 129 (1974)). In this regard, if a court finds "that fraud has been practiced upon it, or that the very temple of justice has been defiled," it may assess attorney's fees against the responsible party, Universal Oil, supra, at 580, as it may when a party "shows bad faith by delaying or disrupting the litigation or by hampering enforcement of a court order," *Hutto*, 437 U.S. at 689, n. 14. The imposition of sanctions in this instance transcends a court's equitable power concerning relations between the parties and reaches a court's inherent power to police itself, thus serving the dual purpose of "vindicating judicial

> authority without resort to the more drastic sanctions available for contempt of court and making the prevailing party whole for expenses caused by his opponent's obstinacy." Ibid.[170]

This excerpt not only contains quotations within quotations, but the quoted segments all consist of brief snippets of text, ranging from six words to twenty-eight.

Short quotations from precedential cases appear to be the rule in American opinions. A survey of ten modern U.S. Supreme Court opinions revealed that the average quotation of language from another (precedential) case was around nineteen words long. In contrast, the average quotation in ten House of Lords opinions during the same time period contained around seventy-seven words, roughly four times as many. Moreover, in the American sample, only one quotation was over one hundred words. In the English sample there were sixteen quotations consisting of more than one hundred words, along with several over three hundred words, and one quotation containing more than four hundred words.[171]

The American custom of quoting snippets of text from a previous case suggests that the courts are approaching precedential cases as a type of authoritative text. Lower court judges seem to be looking for "sound bites" that encapsulate some or all of the holding of a case. Judges writing the precedents seem increasingly happy to provide those judicial sound bites. As noted above, they often conveniently mark the textual holding with the prefatory phrase "we hold."

Another indication of how the holding of cases is being textualized is that the rules or standards or tests developed by American courts are now often named for brief snippets of authoritative text. In other words, the test has been named for the text. Consider the "grievous wrong" standard,[172] the "outcome determinative" test,[173] or the "clear and present danger" rule articulated by Justice Oliver Wendell Holmes in *Schenck v. United States*.[174] Another celebrated Supreme Court case, *United States v. Carolene Products Co.*, contained a textual standard ("discrete and insular minorities") in a footnote,[175] but its obscure location did not hinder it from being quoted and followed in literally hundreds of cases.[176]

Even if not intended to do so, textual standards of this sort—often consisting of no more than two or three words—tend to be interpreted in a more textual and less conceptual way, as indicated and encouraged by their enclosure within quotation marks in subsequent cases. As Michael Sinclair has observed, referring specifically to the footnote in *Carolene Products*, "Legal actors in lower decision-making roles take the reasons and verbal formula of higher courts as governing, . . . following authoritative words, rather than rational analysis."[177]

Obviously, the point that I am making can be exaggerated; there are many modern cases in which American courts do not textualize their holdings so clearly, and it would be foolhardy for law schools to stop teaching traditional legal reasoning. But it is true that, in general, English judges and lawyers seem to concentrate on the concepts and reasoning contained in precedents. Their aim is to figure out what the judges meant and why they decided the cases as they did. To do so, they need as much evidence as possible, hence the lengthy quotations. Modern American judges and lawyers are looking more closely at the exact words that the judge wrote in the precedential opinion. They therefore concentrate on extracting critical excerpts of text that they regard as authoritative. More and more, American legal professionals are reading cases in a way that resembles how they read and interpret statutes.

The Publication Requirement

Recall that in England, with some limitations, unreported (that is, unpublished) decisions can be cited in most courts. The advent of online databases in England has made reference to unreported decisions even easier and induced the House of Lords to adopt a rule that discourages citing an unpublished opinion.[178] In other English courts, however, virtually any judicial decision has the potential of functioning as a precedent.

The concern of the law lords was that the rise of legal databases on the Internet, which contain many unpublished cases, would cause them to be inundated with precedents. This issue had already been raised in the United States at the end of the nineteenth and beginning of the twentieth centuries. The Internet did not exist at the time, but the book publishing industry was at the height of its glory. West Publishing Company, among others, aggressively marketed reports of cases from throughout the United States.[179] The result was that the eighteen published volumes of American reports in 1810 had grown exponentially to over 8,000 volumes a century later.[180]

Lawyers were overwhelmed by case law, and various solutions were proposed. Eventually, most jurisdictions came to address the problem by enacting rules that effectively declare that only certain appellate cases can function as precedents. These rules typically state that a case must have been published (usually in an official report) before it can be cited in court. Unpublished opinions consequently have no binding precedential value, although in some jurisdictions they may be considered "persuasive authority."[181] As opposed to the English practice, it is usually the appellate courts themselves that decide which cases merit publication—and thus function as precedents—in the United States.[182] Typically, courts do so by certifying a case for publication.[183]

The guidelines for publication usually specify that a case must present an important constitutional issue or an issue of first impression, or that it must establish new precedent or modify existing precedent.[184] Some states, like California, add that a case should also be certified for publication if it involves a legal issue of continuing public interest or makes a significant contribution to the legal literature.[185] The converse is that opinions in cases that do not raise important or novel questions, and are therefore of interest only to the parties themselves, should not be published.[186] This is sometimes called the *limited publication rule*. The name of the rule is actually somewhat of a misnomer because publication per se is not the issue. The fact that someone may have published a case does not transform it into a binding precedent. What matters is that some court, usually the one that issued the opinion, certified it for publication or ordered that it be published. The result of the publication requirement is that it is the judiciary who decide which cases function as binding precedents.

Many jurisdictions that limit publication also mandate that unpublished cases should not be cited in court. Thus, Kentucky's rules provide that such opinions "shall not be cited or used as authority in any other case in any court of this state."[187] Other jurisdictions allow litigants to refer to them in court, but hold that unpublished cases—unlike binding precedents—have only persuasive value.

Before the advent of limited publication, all judicial opinions by appellate courts counted as precedents, although the precedential value (or authority) of any opinion could vary. An old unreported decision would have relatively little precedential force, while a recent unanimous supreme court opinion would have a great deal. In jurisdictions that have adopted limited publication rules, however, the concept of precedent has turned from a sliding scale into a binary opposition. A decision either does or does not function as a precedent that binds later courts, depending on whether it was certified for publication. A precedent is thus no longer any preceding case. Rather, it is a written decision that has been authoritatively selected for publication.

The prohibitions on citation have drawn a great deal of opposition in recent years. Some lawyers have intimated that such rules raise the specter of "secret law" that is inaccessible not only to average citizens but to the legal profession as well.[188] Other critics argue that courts issuing unpublished opinions are not sufficiently explaining why they reached their decision. In the words of Judge Posner, an unpublished opinion "provides a temptation for judges to shove difficult issues under the rug."[189]

The Evolving Meaning of *Publication*

What has fomented the controversy regarding unpublished opinions is that the nature of publication has changed dramatically during the past few decades. Previously, "unpublished" was effectively a synonym of "unprinted" because printing was the only practical means of broadly disseminating text. Unpublished opinions were public records available to anyone who went to the clerk's office and paid a copying fee, but this was a cumbersome procedure. More importantly, it was virtually impossible to search through the mass of unpublished opinions to find the one or two that were relevant to a specific legal point.

Legal databases on the Internet have not only made printed legal materials more widely accessible, but they have also included many materials that would not have been printed in the past. In particular, the major online legal databases began to include in their offerings large numbers of cases that had not been certified for publication. The result was that lawyers looking for a good precedent would find what seemed to be the perfect case, only to discover on closer examination that it is not binding precedent. Those who practiced in a jurisdiction forbidding citation of unpublished cases would have felt that the rules deprived them of just the case they needed to win a lawsuit. Like Adam and Eve in the Garden of Eden, these lawyers had forbidden fruit dangling temptingly before their eyes by the online legal databases, only to be told by a panel of judges that they could not touch it.[190]

Lawyers who wished to use unpublished opinions received an important boost from the Eighth Circuit Court of Appeals. In a case that involved a routine tax matter, entitled *Anastasoff v. United States*, a three-judge panel held in 2000 that the court was bound by a previous unpublished Eighth Circuit case.[191] Under the Eighth Circuit's rules at the time, unpublished opinions "are not precedent and parties generally should not cite them," although they could be cited "if the opinion has persuasive value on a material issue and no published opinion of this or another court would serve as well."[192]

According to Judge Arnold, who wrote the opinion, Article III of the Constitution requires that every prior decision by a court, as well as any decision by a court that is above it in the hierarchy, must be obeyed. In other words, courts do not have the power to declare which of their opinions are to have precedential effect; all of their opinions must have such force.[193] According to Judge Arnold, the framers of the Constitution were familiar with the doctrine of precedent and therefore implicitly adopted the common law system of adjudication that was used when the Constitution was ratified.[194]

It is true that when the Constitution was adopted, any previous case, published or not, could probably be cited in American courts. That did not mean, however, that a single earlier decision would invariably bind a later court. Certainly in England, judges gave greater or lesser deference to a precedential decision depending on factors such as the reputation of the judge, how old the case was, the status of the court, and the quality of the report in which it appeared. Moreover, a case could function as an influential precedent even if there was no opinion at all, as we saw in our discussion of *Raffles v. Wichelhaus*. It is simply not correct that in the late eighteenth century, any previous case was binding authority in the way it is today.

Roughly the same conditions existed in the United States when the Constitution was adopted.[195] Consider the problems posed by uneven reporting, the delivery of oral seriatim opinions that were published without review by the judges who delivered them, a court system that had no clear hierarchy, and the notion that the common law was unwritten and resided in the collective memory of the legal profession. It seems unlikely that a court would consider itself strictly bound by a single decision under such circumstances and even more unlikely that it would hold itself strictly bound to follow an unreported decision.

It is bizarre to suggest that the Constitution requires the common law system of adjudication to be forever frozen in time.[196] We would have to give back to private reporters the power to decide which opinions merit publication. And we would also need to reinstate oral seriatim opinion delivery and the notion that judges do not make law but merely discover it.

The *Anastasoff* case itself soon faded from view. The Internal Revenue Service did the right thing and gave Ms. Anastasoff her refund. As a result, the case became moot and the opinion was vacated.[197] Nonetheless, the controversy lives on. Congress has recently held hearings on the issue.[198] A few jurisdictions have abolished their no-citation rules, although they generally maintain the principle of limited publication.[199] And in the federal courts, a new rule of appellate procedure prohibits courts from placing restrictions on citing "unpublished" (more accurately, nonprecedential) decisions.[200] Yet the rule merely allows citation; it does not require judges to give those cases precedential effect. It therefore fails to address what is really at the heart of the matter: whether judges should be able to decide that only certain cases or opinions can operate as precedent.

To the extent that the judiciary can maintain rules that allow them to designate only a minority of their opinions as having binding precedential force, those opinions are likely to become increasingly textual. Appellate judges currently focus most of their efforts on drafting opinions certified for publication. For lack of time, they do not devote nearly as much energy to writing unpublished opinions.[201] If the text of a limited number of precedential opinions is drafted with great care, those who read and apply those opinions will study the text quite closely.

On the other hand, if all appellate cases have precedential force, the number of precedents would grow tremendously. The Internet offers the possibility of making widely available every opinion by every judge in the country, including trial judges. Bringing this possibility to fruition seems to be the goal of the major online databases. Many of those opinions would have been drafted quickly and without the careful research and editing that commonly occurs today with regard to the much smaller number of opinions certified for publication.

Digitizing the Common Law

The shift from printed books of reports to electronic storage and communication of judicial opinions will almost certainly transform the common law and the process of legal reasoning that is so closely associated with it. We have seen that at one time lawyers could plausibly suggest that the common law resided in the minds of the legal profession rather than in the texts of reports. Until fairly recently, the number of English barristers numbered in the hundreds, and there were perhaps a dozen royal judges before whom they practiced. The judges and lawyers regularly met at the inns of court, where they debated how to resolve difficult legal issues. The situation in early America was not all that different.

As the number of courts, judges, and lawyers grew, especially in the United States, and as the legal profession left the proximity of the courts and dispersed throughout the country, the idea that the common law was common knowledge in the profession rapidly became a myth. Access to accurate written texts of opinions became essential, and the technology of printing came to the rescue. Reporters and a growing legal publishing industry supplied the ever-increasing demand. At this point, it would be fair to say that the common law resided in printed reports.

The present growth of online legal databases is rapidly undermining the supremacy of print. As the volume of cases continues to expand, online databases will grow ever more essential. If limited publication rules are eliminated and all judicial decisions function as some sort of precedent, electronic databases will be the only game in town.[202] It will not be economically feasible to print such a large mass of cases. At that point, the common law will reside in the memory banks of computers.

If all judicial opinions are available online, the rule allowing judges to designate only a small number as precedents would likely have to give way. Many opinions that would previously not have been published would become precedents. Yet because of time pressures on judges, it seems likely that such opinions would not be as carefully researched, written, and edited as was possible with the much smaller number of opinions that appellate judges traditionally certified for publication. More of the judges' words will have precedential force, but the judges will have less time than in the age of print to select those words and edit the resulting text. In theory, these less carefully crafted opinions would tend to be interpreted in a less textual way.

Yet it seems more likely that online access to a growing number of opinions will in fact have the opposite effect, making case law more textual than it was before. One reason is that with ever more opinions stored in machine-readable format, the way in which lawyers and judges research the law has begun to change. The most practical way to access such a large database is by searching for certain words or pieces of text, much like how we search the Internet for other types of information. Natural language searching, although it sounds appealing, cannot readily locate ideas or concepts. Computers cannot find the holding or *ratio decidendi* of a case (unless a human being has marked or tagged it as such). For now, at least, any search algorithm must in some way or other concentrate on strings of words. There is currently no way of escaping text.

When the law was contained in books of reports, there was no practical way to search for cases that contained specific words or strings of text. A lawyer who wished to research an issue generally had to find applicable precedents by means of a digest, a legal encyclopedia, or perhaps a treatise. All of these tools resulted from human mediation and analysis. Also important is that they were organized conceptually. If you needed to know whether in your jurisdiction a person could get a prescriptive easement against a water district, you would have to consult a treatise on property law or look at a digest or legal encyclopedia under "property" or "easement" or a related topic until you found the information you sought.

Critically, all of those research tools were compiled by human beings with legal training. In addition, each of these resources (especially legal encyclopedias and treatises) provides a great deal of context. The lawyer doing the research could easily place his search into the more general realm of easements or easements against a governmental agency. Finally, once the lawyer found some potentially relevant cases, he would look them up in the books. Then he would have an entire case before him, starting with the first page. He might not read the entire case, but he would at least skim it, once again giving him some notion of the context in which the case was decided. In reality, of course, he might not find a case on point and would have to make do with an opinion relating to easements on government property generally. He would then have to analogize that case to the issue that he needed to resolve.

I suspect that today most lawyers doing similar research would access an online database and conduct a search for the term "prescriptive easement" within a few words or within the same paragraph as "water district." The database's search engine would take him straight to the relevant paragraph of an opinion. Although digests, treatises, and tools like the West key numbering system remain available, lawyers—especially younger lawyers who have limited experience with books—tend to do the majority of their research by online searching for pieces of text.

A survey conducted in 2003 by the American Bar Association reported that around 75 percent of the respondents regularly did their legal research using printed resources. By 2008, a mere five years later, it had dropped to just over 52 percent, and 34 percent of the responding lawyers stated that they never used a traditional law library.[203] This is bound to have implications for how lawyers deal with precedent in the future.

We have already seen that the traditional analysis of the holding or *ratio decidendi* of a case, using legal reasoning, is being replaced by close reading of snippets of critical text. Clearly, the capability and convenience of doing textual searches via computers can only accelerate that trend. In fact, if we confer on all judicial decisions the status of precedent, vastly increasing the bulk of decisional law, textual searches may become the only practical way to conduct research.[204] It will be impossible, or too expensive, for traditional resources to keep up with such a mass of case law.

An additional issue is the quality of legal information. The transfer of the common law from books of reports to online databases is almost certainly unstoppable. The information age is upon us. It does not mean, however, that all information is equal. Some of the material we obtain on the Internet is of high quality and very reliable, while other information is at best worthless and at worst false, deceptive, or mendacious. Between those extremes is a vast amount of online material whose usefulness and truth is uncertain.

Traditional publishers perform a gatekeeping function with respect to information flow. Academic publishers subject proposed books and articles to peer review. Commercial printing houses are probably in some ways less rigorous in evaluating the quality and accuracy of the material they publish, but even they need to be concerned about their reputations and the reaction of the marketplace. In both settings, editors work with authors to guarantee a certain level of professionalism.

The Internet has made it possible to avoid formal publication. Virtually anyone can be a publisher, at minimal cost, by posting material on a website or on a blog or by e-mailing it to hundreds or thousands of recipients. Much of it is junk, of course, or otherwise irrelevant. Those of us who use the Internet spend a great deal of our time sifting through questionable or useless information in order to find what we need. So far, nothing has replaced the gatekeeping function traditionally performed by publication.

The relevance of these concerns to the notion of precedent should be evident. Maybe it's not such a bad idea to have someone sift through the masses of decisions and tell us which of them were carefully drafted with consideration not only of the facts in the case but of the implications that the decision might have in the future. At some point, it might have been debatable whether reporters or judges should be making that gatekeeping decision, but currently in the United States, judges seem to be the only viable option. Whether they can keep closed the floodgates is anyone's guess.

Conclusion

The digitization of judicial opinions is well upon us. Although books and printing will surely survive in some form, there is no reason for law libraries to devote massive amounts of shelf space to hundreds of printed volumes of judicial decisions, all of which can be accessed online or on an electronic storage device that fits in your pocket.

Yet while books of case reports will become far less common, and perhaps disappear, the opinions contained in those volumes will continue to be generated by judges and consumed by lawyers. And I suspect that those opinions will be fairly similar to those produced today. In particular, they will consist primarily of written text.

One of the main reasons that text will persevere is modern technology itself, which has made such large amounts of material available to the profession. Finding the needle in this haystack requires a search engine, which currently can only find specified words or collocations of text.

In addition, human language is generally a far more efficient and accurate way to convey complex information than are graphics or video. In some situations a picture may indeed be worth a thousand words, but if I had to explain to someone the California law of intestate succession, I'd much prefer a thousand words. And if I could write those words rather than spontaneously speaking, I could plan and edit the text in such a way as to produce a polished description of this area of the law. Future judicial opinions will almost certainly contain increasing numbers of links to graphics, video, and other multimedia content. But they will remain fundamentally written text.

How changes in technology will influence the textual practices of judges and lawyers who produce and read judicial opinions is harder to say. Today's college students seem to believe that writing a research paper consists of searching the Internet, copying some relevant materials, pasting them into an electronic document, doing some minimal editing, and e-mailing the result to their professors. Lawyers entering the profession may well write briefs and memoranda in the same way. Rather than reading entire cases, they may simply be jumping from one link to the other in search of the perfect sentence or paragraph to insert into their brief. They may focus so intently on text that they lose sight of the context.

As a consequence, judges may become nervous that a statement can easily be taken out of context and misinterpreted. So they may feel compelled to start drafting opinions in a more autonomous fashion, trying to create text that can stand on its own. And that, in turn, will further promote a more textual interpretation by readers.

Admittedly, lawyers steeped in the traditions of the common law will find this a rather bleak view of the future. I might well be wrong, of course—predicting the future impact of technology is an endeavor fraught with risk. And we have at least some ability to shape the future. Law schools can continue to teach and emphasize traditional legal reasoning. Lawyers can create or reinforce a professional culture where it is simply not acceptable to quote bits and pieces of a case without understanding the larger legal and social context into which it fits. And judges can write opinions that do not easily lend themselves to an overly textual exegesis.

What we cannot do is return to the days when the common law resided in the minds and memories of judges and lawyers. There are too many lawyers, and there is too much law. Yet we can hope that at least some of its orality and flexibility will endure.

7
Conclusion

Despite all the developments in the technologies of communication during the past five millennia, one thing has remained constant: the central role that language plays in our legal system and culture as a whole. It is possible to have a legal system without writing. To have one without language is inconceivable.

Although early linguists may sometimes have downplayed the value of writing, they were surely correct in claiming that the primarily means of human communication is speech. We are born with the capacity to speak and—physical impediments aside—learn to do so effortlessly. The presence of spoken language is a feature of all human societies. It's a quick and easy way to communicate not only our mundane needs and emotions but also very complex information and ideas.

As a result, every legal system makes extensive use of orality. We have seen that both wills and statutes are extremely textual in the Anglo-American tradition, but even in these areas of law the process that leads up to the final written product usually consists of discussions, interviews, debates, and other types of spoken interaction. Large numbers of contracts are concluded every day by means of speech, without a single word being written on paper. Most people enter into marriage, which is also a type of contract, merely by saying "I do" or "I will" during an oral ceremony. Even agreements that are reduced to writing are often the result of face-to-face negotiation.

Although we did not address courtroom interaction in this book, the common law tradition is that trials are almost entirely oral. It's possible to try cases mostly in writing, and they sometimes are, but generally it is much more efficient to hear and decide cases orally. Even appellate proceedings, as in the traditional English practice, can be conducted almost entirely by means of speech.

Yet writing has many advantages, as we have seen throughout this book. In the law of wills, it produces a reliable record of what the testator intended, one that is available years or decades later when those intentions must be carried out. If a will creates a charitable trust, the text of the will can potentially govern the management of the trust for hundreds of years. Likewise, there are English statutes that have been on the books for many centuries.

Although writing is sometimes just a technology for recording speech, it usually evolves into something more complex. In particular, textual practices or literary conventions tend to develop. Many of these practices have made writing far more accessible than speech. Dividing books into chapters and adding page numbers, as well as compiling an index, make it much easier to locate information. Writing also enables the creation of reference works and encyclopedias, which can organize the information contained in books and refer the reader to the original sources. Modern scholarship is unthinkable without such conventions.

The law uses ordinary textual practices, of course, but has also developed many of its own. The structure of wills and other legal documents is usually quite formulaic. This is mostly a matter of custom, rather than being legally prescribed. Wills typically start with the words, "Last will and testament" and finish with the signature of the testator and witnesses. This practice helps identify the document as a will, as well as demarcating its beginning and ending.

Consider also judicial decisions, which have functioned as precedents for hundreds of years. As long as they were oral, it was hard to remember the decisions and difficult to refer to them ("I remember a case decided in King's Bench about ten years ago . . ."). Writing not only preserves the information but also makes it readily available. It allows cases to be bound together in books of reports so that if you remember or can determine the year in which it was decided, you can probably find a report of the case. Or you can find the case using a digest, abridgment, or legal encyclopedia, all of which summarize areas of the law with citations to relevant cases.

A similar system, relying on the year of enactment, was developed for statutes. The more recent codification of statutes in many jurisdictions, placing all statutes on a certain topic into a single code, is an additional improvement. A table of contents or index makes it possible to quickly find a specific enactment.

Another textual convention of the profession is the use of a highly autonomous style of drafting, which sometimes occurs in contracts and judicial opinions but is especially common in statutes and wills. Such texts may have to be understood by people who live far in the future and who have little knowledge of the context and background. Writers of autonomous documents strive to place as much information into the text as is necessary for distant or future users to understand them simply by reading the words. The aim is to have the document, to the extent possible, stand on its own.

Perhaps the most significant and distinctive literary practice of the profession is textualization. It is a process by which authors create a text that is the definitive and sometimes also the complete statement of their intentions regarding a particular matter. Usually the process for textualizing a document is quite formal, as illustrated by the procedures for executing wills and enacting statutes. As a result, there is generally no doubt about what is part of the transaction and what is not. Formalities associated with textualization also impress on people that they are engaging in acts with great legal significance. And in the case of statutes, textualization promotes the rule of law by forcing the government to act only by means of text that has been enacted according to a prescribed procedure and that is available for all to read.

Once a transaction has been textualized, what was in the minds of the parties is generally considered secondary and perhaps even irrelevant. Informal additions or changes, whether oral or written, are usually not allowed. What matters is the text. In most common law systems, all wills and statutes must be textualized to be effective. As a result, the words *will* and *statute* today no longer refer to a person's desires regarding disposal of her property at death or to a legislature's decision regarding how to remedy a perceived problem. They refer exclusively to the text that embodies those desires and decisions.

In contrast, some contracts are textualized, but most are not. The word *contract* is therefore ambiguous. It can refer either to the agreement in the parties' heads or to the words on paper. Precedents, expressed in judicial opinions, once referred primarily to what was in the minds of judges, as the word *opinion* suggests. Although decisional law remains relatively oral, it is becoming increasingly textual, as we saw in chapter 6. For most American lawyers today, the phrase *judicial opinion* refers to what a judge writes, not to what the judge thinks.

Those who interpret legal texts are at least intuitively aware of these textual practices. With respect to statutes, for instance, judges usually presume that the legislature expressed itself carefully and completely and that the resulting text is the definitive statement of their intentions regarding the matter at hand. Problems arise if the drafters made a mistake, or were not able to foresee all possibilities or anticipate future events. There are different ways to resolve these problems, most notably intentionalism and textualism. It is important to realize that these approaches are also, for the most part, literary practices or conventions. Like all customs, they can change.

Further difficulties can arise when laypeople are confronted by the law's textual practices. In such cases, ordinary conventions of literacy should generally prevail. If a nonlawyer writes her own will or drafts a contract, it makes no sense to interpret the text using the literary conventions of the profession. It should be understood as ordinary language. When attorneys draft a will, the testator's informal changes to that will should be honored if her intentions are clear. And consumers should not be subjected to contracts with merger clauses whose effect they do not understand.

Most of the above discussion has related to the impact of writing. Other technological revolutions, particularly printing and the Internet, have had a tremendous impact on the legal system as well. The printing press had two major effects. It standardized texts by producing identical copies, and the mass production of those texts made those copies accessible to a large number of people.

Printing has not had much influence on the law of wills, which are mostly drafted by lawyers, who even today almost always write the wills, or have them written, by hand or by typewriter or on a computer. Printed fill-in-the-blank wills are sometimes used by consumers, however. As we have seen, the law on their validity is complicated and inconsistent.

The printing press has had a huge influence on contracts, on the other hand. The profession has never agreed upon a completely satisfactory solution to the "battle of the forms," in my opinion. And its regulation of the use of standardized form contracts in businesses-to-consumer transactions also leaves much to be desired. The standardization promoted by printing is potentially quite useful, but that potential can only be realized if there is broader standardization of transactions within particular industries, thereby reducing information overload rather than causing it.

Legislation has likewise been greatly influenced by printing. Combined with the introduction of paper, which is a relatively inexpensive medium, printing has made it feasible for lawmakers to have the exact texts of bills before them when they debate and vote on a proposed law. The statutes that are enacted can be widely distributed among the population, enhancing the rule of law. Printing probably also contributed to the highly textual or literal approach to interpretation taken by English judges during the eighteenth and nineteenth centuries. As we have observed, however, although writing and printing may enable and perhaps even encourage such an approach, they do not compel it.

Printing has also influenced the nature of judicial opinions. It has made the exact words of judges available to the profession. As was explained in chapter 6, English decisions or judgments remained remarkably oral until quite recently, requiring lawyers to engage in legal reasoning to find the *ratio* or holding of a case. In the United States, however, the practice of printing majority opinions, written by the judges themselves, along with the requirement that only opinions certified for publication function as precedents, has made case law much more textual. Especially younger lawyers seem to have substituted close reading of cases for traditional legal reasoning.

How the situation will respond to increasing use of computers and the Internet is difficult to predict. Wills law has until now stoutly resisted efforts to allow the electronic storage and communication of a testator's ultimate desires. Judges still want to see ink on paper. Contracting has firmly embraced the Internet. As younger generations become more comfortable using computers for increasingly important matters, wills law is likely to come under pressure to allow an electronic option, although it also seems probable that paper will be used long into the future.

Statutes, like wills, are highly textualized, and they will probably also resist some of the more far-reaching transformations in other domains. Of course, the text of statutes is already widely accessible online, and that text is usually completely up-to-date.

I am skeptical, however, that legislation will become highly malleable and full of multimedia content, as some scholars have suggested. Stability is a great virtue in this area. And although a picture may be worth a thousand words in some circumstances, most legal principles are far better communicated by means of text. Sound and graphics are at best supplements to written legislation. Finally, my own rather whimsical suggestion regarding wikilaw is almost certain to be the least likely of any predictions in this book to come to pass, except perhaps on a small, very local scale.

Just as writing materials have evolved from parchment to paper to pixels over the centuries, the technologies for storing and communicating legal information will continue to develop. Yet in some form or other, written text will remain the primary means by which lawyers and judges draft wills, create contracts, enact statutes, and express judicial opinions. Writing and text are here to stay.

Notes

Chapter One

1. David R. Olson, *From Utterance to Text: The Bias of Language in Speech and Writing*, 47 Harv. Educ. Rev. 257, 262 (1977).

2. Jack Goody and Ian Watt, *The Consequences of Literacy* in *Literacy in Traditional Societies* 27, 44 (Jack Goody ed., 1968).

3. Jack Goody, *The Domestication of the Savage Mind* 51 (1977).

4. Walter Ong, *Orality and Literacy: The Technologizing of the Word* 43–53 (1982).

5. See, for example, Wallace Chafe and Deborah Tannen, *The Relation between Written and Spoken Language*, 16 Ann. Rev. Anthro. 383, 391–99 (1987); Roy Harris, *How Does Writing Restructure Thought?*, 9 Language & Communication 99 (1989).

6. Jack Goody, *The Logic of Writing and the Organization of Society* 135 (1986).

7. See Goody and Watt, *Consequences of Literacy*, 55. For a somewhat skeptical discussion of this view in the context of ancient Athens, see Rosalind Thomas, *Written in Stone?: Liberty, Equality, Orality, and the Codification of Law*, in *Greek Law in Its Political Setting* (L. Foxhall and A. D. E. Lewis eds., 1996).

8. See Elizabeth L. Eisenstein, *The Printing Revolution in Early Modern Europe* (2d ed. 2005).

9. Jeff Gomez, *Print Is Dead: Books in Our Digital Age* 162 (2008).

10. Nicolas Carr, *Is Google Making Us Stupid?* Atlantic, July/August 2008, at 56.

11. *Id.*, 58 (quoting Scott Karp and Bruce Friedman, both frequent bloggers).

12. Available at http://www.nea.gov/pub/ReadingAtRisk.pdf. Last visited June 4, 2009.

13. University College London, *Information Behavior of the Researcher of the Future*, available at http://www.bl.uk/news/pdf/googlegen.pdf. Last visited July 18, 2008.

14. *Id.*, 10.

15. *Id.*

16. Carr, *Is Google Making Us Stupid?*, 58.

17. M. Ethan Katsh, *Law in a Digital World*, 17–18 (1995).

18. *Id.*, 23.

19. *Id.*, 31.

20. Peter W. Martin, *Reconfiguring Law Reports and the Concept of Precedent for a Digital Age*, 53 Vill. L. Rev. 1, 40–42 (2008).

21. Ronald K. L. Collins and David M. Skover, *Paratexts*, 44 Stan. L. Rev. 509 (1992).

22. *Id.*, 513.

23. Collins and Skover found only one jurisdiction in which the video record was official for purposes of appeal. *Id.*, 539.

24. Richard J. Ross, *Communications Revolutions and Legal Culture: An Elusive Relationship*, 27 Law & Soc. Inquiry 637 (2002).

Chapter Two

1. Leonard Bloomfield, *Language* 21 (1933).

2. See generally Naomi S. Baron, *Alphabet to Email: How Written English Evolved and Where It's Heading* (2000).

3. For more complete lists from a linguistic perspective, see F. Niyi Akinnaso, *On the Differences between Spoken and Written Language*, 25 Language & Speech 97 (1982); Rosalind Horowitz and S. Jay Samuels, *Comprehending Oral and Written Language* 6–10 (1987).

4. See, for example, Jack Goody, *The Logic of Writing and the Organization of Society* (1986); Jack Goody, *The Interface between the Written and the Oral* (1987); David R. Olson, *The World on Paper: The Conceptual and Cognitive Implications of Writing and Reading* (1994); Walter Ong, *Orality and Literacy: The Technologizing of the Word* (1982).

5. See Douglas Biber, *Variation across Speech and Writing* (1988).

6. Ong, *Orality and Literacy*, 32.

7. James Fallows, *File Not Found*, Atlantic Monthly, September 2006, at 142.

8. *Id.*

9. See Ronald K. L. Collins and David M. Skover, *Paratexts*, 44 Stan. L. Rev. 509 (1992).

10. See Lawrence M. Solan and Peter M. Tiersma, *Speaking of Crime: The Language of Criminal Justice* 98–104 (2005).

11. Goody, *Interface*, 178.

12. *Id.*, 171.

13. Jack Goody, *The Domestication of the Savage Mind* 44 (1977).

14. Jack K. Weber, *The Power of Judicial Records*, 9 J. Legal Hist. 180, 181–84 (1988).

15. Michael Gagarin, *Early Greek Law* 131 (1986).

16. Ivan Illich and Barry Sanders, *ABC: The Alphabetization of the Popular Mind* 49 (1988).

17. Wallace Chafe and Jane Danielewicz, *Properties of Spoken and Written Language*, in *Comprehending Oral and Written Language* 83, 88 (R. Horowitz and S. J. Samuels eds., 1987).

18. *Id.*

19. M. A. K. Halliday, *Spoken and Written Language* 51–2, 80 (1985).

20. *Cal. Penal Code* § 324. For discussion, see Peter M. Tiersma, *Legal Language* 57–59 (1999).

21. See *Mickens v. United States*, 926 F.2d 1323 (2d Cir. 1991).

22. Pictures and graphics are very useful in illustrating or clarifying text, of course.

23. *The Starr Report: The Findings of Independent Counsel Kenneth W. Starr on President Clinton and the Lewinsky Affair, with Analysis of the Staff of the Washington Post* 227–9 (1998).

24. *Id.*, 228.

25. Phil Kuntz, ed., *The Starr Report: The Evidence* 372 (1998).

26. See M. A. K. Halliday, *Spoken and Written Language*, 30–33.

27. Deborah Tannen, *The Oral/Literate Continuum in Discourse*, in *Spoken and Written Language: Exploring Orality and Literacy* 1, 2 (Deborah Tannen ed., 1982).

28. Herbert H. Clark, *Using Language* 93 (1996).

29. Glanville Williams, *Language and the Law*, 61 L.Q. Rev. 71; 179; 293; and 62 L.Q. Rev. 387 (1945) (article printed in four parts).

30. See Wallace L. Chafe, *Integration and Involvement in Speaking, Writing, and Oral Literature*, in *Spoken and Written Language: Exploring Orality and Literacy*, 35, 45.

31. S. Jay Samuels, *Factors That Influence Listening and Reading Comprehension*, in *Comprehending Oral and Written Language*, 295, 308.

32. Paul Kay, *Language Evolution and Speech Style*, in *Sociocultural Dimensions of Language Change* 21 (Ben G. Blount and Mary Sanches eds., 1977). See also Richard Posner, *The Jurisprudence of Skepticism*, 86 Mich. L. Rev. 826, 849 (1988) (a document is much harder to interpret than speech because there is no inflection or facial expression and because it may have been drafted by a committee, may have been in a foreign language, or the author may be dead).

33. Kay, *Language Evolution*, 22.

34. *Id.*, 22.

35. *Id.*, 29.

36. Ong, *Orality and Literacy*, 104.

37. Martin Nystrand, *The Role of Context in Written Communication*, in *Comprehending Oral and Written Language*, 197, 203.

38. See Paul Grice, *Studies in the Way of Words* 117 (1989); Stephen C. Levinson, *Pragmatics* 17–18 (1983).

39. Rita Watson and David R. Olson, *From Meaning to Definition: A Literate Bias on the Structure of Word Meaning*, in *Comprehending Oral and Written Language*, 329.

40. A. Hildyard and D. R. Olson, *On the Comprehension and Memory of Oral vs. Written Discourse*, in *Spoken and Written Language*, 19.

41. See Paul Campos, *That Obscure Object of Desire: Hermeneutics and the Autonomous Legal Text*, 77 Minn. L. Rev. 1065, 1091 (1993) (arguing that a text can only mean what its author intends it to mean and that there is no such thing as an autonomous text).

42. See Martin Nystrand, *The Role of Context in Written Communication*, 197.

43. James Bradley Thayer, *A Preliminary Treatise on Evidence at the Common Law*, 428–9 (1898).

44. Jack Goody, *The Logic of Writing and the Organization of Society* 136–37 (1986).

45. F. Niyi Akinnaso, *On the Differences between Spoken and Written Language*, 25 Language & Speech 97, 113 (1982).

46. See Peter M. Tiersma, *Legal Language*, 89–91 (1999).

47. *Id.*, 249.

48. *Id.*

49. *Id.*, 250.

50. For additional examples, see M. T. Clanchy, *From Memory to Written Record: England 1066–1307* 38 (2d ed. 1993); Peter M. Tiersma, *Rites of Passage: Legal Ritual in Roman Law and Anthropological Analogues*, 9 J. Legal Hist. 1 (1988).

51. Clanchy, *From Memory to Written Record*, 77.

52. On the status of Near Eastern codes, see Raymond Westbrook, *Biblical and Cuneiform Law Codes*, in *Folk Law: Essays in the Theory and Practice of* Lex Non Scripta 495 (Alison Dundes Renteln and Alan Dundes eds., 1995).

53. See Tiersma, *Legal Language*, 104–6.

54. J. L. Austin, *How to Do Things with Words* (J. O. Urmson and Marina Sbisà eds., 2d ed. 1975).

55. J. L. Austin, *Performative Utterances*, in *Philosophical Papers*, 233, 235 (J. O. Urmson and G. J. Warnock eds., 3d ed. 1979).

56. King James version of the Bible.

57. John Calvin, *Institutes of the Christian Religion* 64 (Henry Beveridge trans. 1989).

58. *Id.*, 73.

59. *Id.*, 68.

60. *Id.*, 392. In the same chapter, Calvin refers to the apostles as "sure and authentic amanuenses of the Holy Spirit." *Id.*, 395.

61. Rv 22:18–19.

62. Herald J. Berman, *Law and Revolution, II: The Impact of the Protestant Reformations on the Western Legal Tradition* 115 (2003).

63. See generally Jaroslav Pelikan, *Interpreting the Bible and the Constitution* 44–46 (2004).

64. Quoted by Werner Georg Kümmel, *The New Testament: The History of the Investigation of Its Problems* 22–23 (1972).

65. In both realms the divergent interpretations given by different schools or sects to the respective sacred texts suggests a substantial gap between theory and reality.

66. See George L. Haskins, *Law and Authority in Early Massachusetts* 141–62 (1960); Julius Goebel, Jr., *King's Law and Local Custom in Seventeenth Century New England*, 31 Colum. L. Rev. 416, 432 (1931).

67. Berman, *Law and Revolution*, 263–65.

68. See Pelikan, *Interpreting the Bible*, 56–57, 116–17.

Chapter Three

1. Russ Versteeg, *Early Mesopotamian Law* 97–106 (2000).

2. Russ Versteeg, *Law in Ancient Egypt* 140–45 (2002).

3. Alberto Maffi, *Family and Property Law*, in *The Cambridge Companion to Ancient Greek Law* 254, 257 (Michael Gagarin and David Cohen, eds., 2005).

4. W. W. Buckland, *A Text-Book of Roman Law* 283–85 (3d ed.; Peter Stein ed., 1966).

5. *Id.*, 286–88.

6. For a brief summary, see David Johnston, *Roman Law in Context* 133–36 (1999).

7. Orrin W. Robinson, *Old English and Its Closest Relatives: A Survey of the Earliest Germanic Languages* 91–99 (1992).

8. Roman law and language, as well as Christianity, were present in England during the Roman occupation, of course, but largely disappeared after the Anglo-Saxon invasion.

9. Dorothy Whitelock, *Anglo-Saxon Wills* 50–51 (1930) (will of Wulfric).

10. *Id.*, 22–23 (will of the Ealdorman Ælfheah).

11. J. L. Austin, *How to Do Things with Words* 12 (2d ed. 1975).

12. This situation is complicated by the possibility that people may speak in the third person, as is common in contracts. In that case, a performative verb can indeed be in the third person ("buyer promises . . ."), but it is really the equivalent of "I promise . . ." if the buyer is a party to the contract.

13. Austin, *How to Do Things*, 56–7.

14. *Id.*, 5.

15. Whitelock, *Anglo-Saxon Wills*, 2–3.

16. *Id.*

17. *Id.*, 30–31 (emphasis added).

18. Harold Dexter Hazeltine, *Comments on the Writings Known as Anglo-Saxon Wills*, in Dorothy Whitelock, *Anglo-Saxon Wills*, vii. See also Michael M. Sheehan, *The Will in Medieval England* 19 (1963) (describing the Anglo-Saxon will as "an oral transaction in which gifts were made which were usually completed only after the death of the donor.").

19. Brenda Danet and Bryna Bogoch, *Orality, Literacy, and Performativity in Anglo-Saxon Wills*, in *Language and the Law* 100 (John Gibbons ed., 1994).

20. *Id.*, 112, 127.

21. Sheehan, *The Will in Medieval England*, 54 (emphasis omitted).

22. M. T. Clanchy, *From Memory to Written Record: England 1066–1307* 44–80 (2d ed. 1993).

23. Sheehan, *The Will in Medieval England*, 187–88.

24. *Id.*, 144.

25. *Id.*, 186.

26. *Id.*, 189–91.

27. 32 Hen. VIII, ch. I (1540).

28. 29 Car. II, ch. 3, § V (1676).

29. *Id.*, § XVIII.

30. 7 Wm. IV & 1 Vict., ch. 26, § IX (1837).

31. William M. McGovern, Jr., and Sheldon F. Kurtz, *Wills, Trusts and Estates* 259–60 (3d ed. 2004).

32. *Id.*, 182–201.

33. In re Groffman [1969] 2 All E.R. 108.

34. Jesse Dukeminier et al., *Wills, Trusts, and Estates* 216–17 (7th ed. 2005).

35. Ashbel G. Gulliver and Catherine J. Tilson, *Classification of Gratuitous Transfers*, 51 Yale L.J. 1 (1941)

36. *Id.*, 3–4.

37. *Id.*, 4.

38. *Id.*, 4–5.

39. Sheehan, *The Will in Medieval England*, 113.

40. *Id.*, 178–9.

41. Adam Hirsch, *Inheritance and Inconsistency*, 57 Ohio St. L.J. 1057, 1103 (1996).

42. Naomi S. Baron, *Alphabet to Email: How Written English Evolved and Where It's Heading* 24 (2000).

43. David Crystal, *Language and the Internet* 31 (2d ed. 2006).

44. *Estate of Wiltfong*, 148 P.3d 465 (Colo. Ct. App. 2006). Because Colorado had adopted the dispensing power (see discussion later in this chapter), the will is likely to be carried out, despite the failure to follow formalities.

45. See Jesse Dukeminier and Stanley Johanson, *Wills, Trusts, and Estates* 274 (6th ed. 2000); see also Sir Robert Megarry, *A Second Miscellany-at-Law: A Further Diversion for Lawyers and Others* 300–301 (1973).

46. Hirsch, *Inheritance and Inconsistency*, 1058.

47. *Id.*, 1071–75.

48. For an example, see *Estate of Johnson*, 630 P.2d 1039 (Ariz. 1981).

49. The assets of a person who dies intestate (without a will) are generally distributed to close relatives according to rules established by state law. This process is called intestate succession.

50. *Johnson v. Johnson*, 279 P.2d 928 (Okla. 1954).

51. *Unif. Prob. Code*, § 2-507. This doctrine goes back to the Statute of Frauds.

52. *Board of National Missions v. Sherry*, 372 Ill. 272 (1939).

53. See *Thompson v. Royall*, 175 S.E. 748 (Va. 1934).

54. 117 Misc. 2d 669 (Sur. Ct. N.Y. 1982). See also *Patrick v. Patrick*, 649 A.2d 1204, 1212 (Md. Ct. Spec. App. 1994) (testator crossed out name of son, who was one of two remainder beneficiaries; the court held the revocation invalid).

55. For example, *Cal. Prob. Code*, § 6120.

56. See, for example, *Ruel v. Hardy*, 6 A.2d 753 (N.H. 1939).

57. 10 Cal. 2d 395 (1937). Fortunately, the court ordered that the son and daughter be made executors because they were his next of kin (not because the will appointed them!).

58. *Estate of Cumming*, 158 Cal. Rptr. 263, 265 (Cal. Ct. App. 1979).

59. See McGovern and Kurtz, *Wills, Trusts and Estates*, 260; 14 B. E. Witkin, *Summary of California Law, Wills and Probate* § 239 (10th ed. 2005).

60. 127 P. 166 (Cal. 1912).

61. *In re Lynch's Estate*, 75 P. 1086 (Cal. 1904).

62. See *Erickson v. Erickson*, 716 A.2d 92 (Conn. 1998).

63. See generally Scott T. Jarboe, Note, *Interpreting a Testator's Intent from the Language of Her Will: A Descriptive Linguistics Approach*, 80 Wash. U.L.Q. 1365 (2002).

64. 111 L.T.R. 869 (1915).

65. *Mahoney v. Grainger*, 186 N.E. 86 (Mass. 1933).

66. *Id.*, 87.

67. *In re Becker's Estate*, 75 Cal. Rptr. 359 (Cal. Ct. App. 1969).

68. For examples, see Richard F. Storrow, *Judicial Discretion and the Disappearing Distinction between Will Interpretation and Construction*, 56 Case W. Res. L. Rev. 65, 71 (2005).

69. *Unif. Prob. Code*, § 2-503.

70. For some history of this doctrine, see Jesse Dukeminier et al., *Wills, Trusts, and Estates*, 233–5.

71. *Unif. Prob. Code*, § 2-503.

72. *Estate of Reed*, 672 P.2d 829, 831 (Wyo. 1983).

73. *Id.* at 834.

74. Gerry W. Beyer and Claire G. Hargrove, *Digital Wills: Has the Time Come for Wills to Join the Digital Revolution?*, 33 Ohio N.U.L. Rev. 865, 882 (2007).

75. Ronald K. L. Collins and David M. Skover, *Paratexts*, 44 Stan. L. Rev. 509 (1992).

76. Beyer and Hargrove, *Digital Wills*, 884. See also Lisa L. McGarry, Note, *Videotaped Wills: An Evidentiary Tool or a Written Will Substitute?*, 77 Iowa L. Rev. 1187 (1992) (concluding that virtually all courts continue to insist that wills be in writing, rejecting videotaped wills, as opposed to videotaped evidence of a written will's validity, which is generally admitted); Gerry W. Beyer and William R. Buckley, *Videotape and the Probate Process: The Nexus Grows*, 42 Okla. L. Rev. 43 (1989) (listing other articles on the subject in footnote 18 and concluding that while videotape is used as evidence, its use as testamentary instrument will require legislation).

77. *Nevada Rev. Stat. Ann.* §133.085.

78. This was the case in 2002, at least, according to Christopher J. Caldwell, *Should "E-Wills" Be Wills: Will Advances in Technology Be Recognized for Will Execution?* 63 U. Pitts. L. Rev. 467, 476 (2002).

79. The case is critically discussed in Nicolas Kasirir, *From Written Record to Memory in the Law of Wills*, 29 Ottawa L. Rev. 39 (1997/1998).

80. *Taylor v. Holt*, 134 S.W.3d 830 (Tenn. Ct. App. 2003).

81. Beyer and Hargrove, *Digital Wills*, 890–97.

82. *Stanley v. Henderson*, 162 S.W.2d 95 (Tex. Comm. Appeals 1942); *Estate of Archer*, 239 Cal. Rptr. 137 (Cal. Ct. App. 1987).

83. John H. Langbein and Lawrence W. Waggoner, *Reformation of Wills on the Ground of Mistake: Change of Direction in American Law?* 130 U. Pa. L. Rev. 521 (1982); John H. Langbein, *Substantial Compliance with the Wills Act*, 88 Harv. L. Rev. 489 (1975).

84. James Lindgren, *Abolishing the Attestation Requirement for Wills*, 68 N.C. L. Rev. 541 (1990).

85. Hirsch, *Inheritance and Inconsistency*, 1075–6.

86. For examples, see Witkin, *Summary of California Law, Wills*, 12 at § 205.

Chapter Four

1. Florian Coulmas, *The Writing Systems of the World* 57 (1989). Egyptian hieroglyphs developed slightly later. *Id.*

2. *Id.*, 73–74.

3. Russ VerSteeg, *Early Mesopotamian Law* 77, 146–47 (2000).

4. Robert C. Ellickson and Charles Dia. Thorland, *Ancient Land Law*, 71 Chi.-Kent L. Rev. 321, 376 (1995).

5. VerSteeg, *Early Mesopotamian Law*, 169–71.

6. John Baines, *Literacy and Ancient Egyptian Society*, 18 Man 572, 577 (1983).

7. Johannes M. Renger, *Institutional, Communal, and Individual Ownership or Possession of Arable Land in Ancient Mesopotamia from the End of the Fourth to the End of the First Millennium B.C.*, 71 Chi.-Kent L. Rev. 269, 294 (1995).

8. Hugh T. Scogin, Jr., *Between Heaven and Man: Contract and the State in Han Dynasty China*, 63 S. Cal. L. Rev. 1325 (1990).

9. W. W. Buckland, *A Text-Book of Roman Law from Augustus to Justinian* 434–7 (3d ed.; rev. by Peter Stein, 1966).

10. Elizabeth A. Meyer, *Legitimacy and Law in the Roman World: Tabulae in Roman Belief and Practice* (2004).

11. J. H. Baker, *An Introduction to English Legal History* 361–2 (3d ed. 1990); see also Kevin M. Teeven, *A History of the Anglo-American Law of Contract* 5–7 (1990).

12. Baker, *Introduction*, 366–71.

13. *Id.*; Teeven, *History*, 7–9.

14. Consider the King James version of the Lord's Prayer ("forgive us our trespasses").

15. Teeven, *History*, 65.

16. *Id.*, 87–89.

17. *Id.*, 398–400.

18. Consideration does involve some linguistic (as opposed to purely textual) issues, as discussed by Sanford Schane, *Language and the Law* 138–79 (2006).

19. *Restatement (Second) of the Law of Contracts*, § 17 (1981).

20. *Id.*, § 22 (emphasis added).

21. *Id.*, § 24.

22. *Id.*; § 22.

23. J. L. Austin, *How To Do Things with Words* (2d ed. 1962); John Searle, *Speech Acts: An Essay in the Philosophy of Language* (1969).

24. Daniel Vanderveken, *Meaning and Speech Acts* vol. 1, 105 (1990).

25. Peter M. Tiersma, *Reassessing Unilateral Contracts*, 26 U.C. Davis L. Rev. 1 (1992).

26. Vanderveken, *Meaning and Speech Acts*, 185.

27. Tiersma, *Reassessing Unilateral Contracts*, 42–49.

28. John D. Calamari and Joseph M. Perillo, *Contracts* § 2-1, at 25 (3d ed. 1987) ("if A and B are together and C suggests the terms of an agreement for them, there would be a contract without any process of offer and acceptance if they simultaneously agreed to these terms.").

29. Michael L. Geis, *Speech Acts and Conversational Interaction* 194 (1995). The conversation is actually a composite based on a number of different taped conversations with travel agents.

30. I. E. Allan Farnsworth, *Farnsworth on Contracts* § 3.12 at 247 (2d ed. 1998).

31. K. N. Llewellyn, *On Our Case-Law of Contract: Offer and Acceptance, I*, 48 Yale L.J. 1, 30 (1938).

32. Teeven, *History*, 177.

33. *Browning v. Beston*, in Edmund Plowden, *The Commentaries or Reports of Edmund Plowden*, 140a-141 (1578) (argument of Serjeant Caitline).

34. A. W. B. Simpson, *Innovation in Nineteenth Century Contract Law*, 91 L.Q.R. 247, 258–262 (1975).

35. *Id.*, 258.

36. Teeven, *History*, 178.

37. *Kennedy v. Lee*, 36 Eng. Rep. 170, 173 (Ch. 1817).

38. 106 Eng. Rep. 250, 251 (K.B. 1818).

39. Farnsworth, *Farnsworth on Contracts*, § 3.22.

40. *Id.*

41. 106 Eng. Rep. 250, 250 (K.B. 1818).

42. Farnsworth, *Farnsworth on Contracts*, § 3.13 at 255.

43. *UCC* § 2–207(2) reads as follows:

The additional terms are to be construed as proposals for addition to the contract. Between merchants such terms become part of the contract unless:
(a) the offer expressly limits acceptance to the terms of the offer;
(b) they materially alter it; or
(c) notification of objection to them has already been given or is given within a reasonable time after notice of them is received.

44. For instance, when is a proposed addition a "material" alteration? See Farnsworth, *Farnsworth on Contracts*, § 3.21. See also *Northrop Corp. v. Litronic Industries*, 29 F.3d 1173 (7th Cir. 1994).

45. This is essentially what a revised version of *UCC* 2-207 does, but it has not been adopted by the states at this point in time. See also Victor P. Goldberg, *The "Battle of the Forms": Fairness, Efficiency, and the Best-Shot Rule*, 76 Ore. L. Rev. 155 (1997).

46. See Irma S. Russell, *Got Wheels? Article 2A, Standardized Rental Car Terms, Rational Inaction, and Unilateral Private Ordering*, 40 Loy. L.A. L. Rev. 137, 152–3 (2006).

47. See Charles L. Knapp, *Opting Out or Copping Out? An Argument for Strict Scrutiny of Individual Contracts*, 40 Loy. L.A. L. Rev. 95 (2006).

48. Friedrich Kessler, *Contracts of Adhesion: Some Thoughts about Freedom of Contract*, 43 Colum. L. Rev. 629 (1943). See also Todd D. Rakoff, *Contracts of Adhesion: An Essay in Reconstruction*, 96 *Harv. L. Rev*. 1174 (1983).

49. For some of the reasons that consumers do not read boilerplate language in standardized contracts, see Robert A. Hillman and Jeffrey L. Rachlinski, *Standard-Form Contracting in the Electronic Age*, 77 N.Y.U. L. Rev. 429, 446–54 (2002).

50. See *ProCD, Inc. v. Zeidenberg*, 86 F.3d 1447 (7th Cir. 1996) (holding that text inside box was part of the contract, even though the buyer could not read it before purchasing).

51. Russell, *Got Wheels?* 153.

52. David Lazarus, *AT&T Buries Customer Rights in 2,500-page "Guidebook,"* LA Times, September 14, 2008, at C1 (also available at http://articles.latimes.com/2008/sep/14/business/fi-lazarus14).

53. http://www.blockbuster.ca/terms.aspx (visited August 7, 2008). For discussion, see Robert L. Oakley, *Fairness in Electronic Contracting: Minimum Standards for Non-Negotiated Contracts*, 42 Houston L. Rev. 1041, 1074–5 (2005).

54. Mark A. Lemly, *Terms of Use*, 91 Minn. L. Rev. 459, 466 (2006).

55. *Id.*, 464.

56. *Id.*, 466.

57. *Cohen v. Santoianni*, 112 N.E.2d 267, 271 (Mass. 1953).

58. *Caspi v. Microsoft Network*, 732 A.2d 528, 532 (N.J. 1999).

59. See Hillman and Rachlinski, *Standard-Form Contracting*, 480–81.

60. Lemly, *Terms of Use*, 466–7.

61. *Id.*, 477.

62. *Id.*, 478–80.

63. *Carnival Cruise Lines, Inc. v. Shute*, 499 U.S. 585 (1991). On the refund issue, see the dissent of Justice Stephens at 597.

64. Lemly, *Terms of Use*, 467–70.

65. Henry E. Smith, *Modularity in Contracts: Boilerplate and Information Flow*, 104 Mich. L. Rev. 1175, 1175–76 (2007).

66. *Id.*, 1214.

67. Margaret Jane Radin, *Boilerplate Today: The Rise of Modularity and the Waning of Consent*, 104 Mich. L. Rev. 1223, 1225 (2007).

68. Stephen J. Choi and G. Mitu Gulati, *Contract as Statute*, 104 Mich. L. Rev. 1129, 1167 (2006).

69. Ronald J. Mann, *Contracting for Credit*, 104 Mich. L. Rev. 899 (2007). For additional examples, see Joseph M. Perillo, *Neutral Standardizing of Contracts*, 28 Pace L. Rev. 179 (2008).

70. See http://www.hud.gov/offices/hsg/sfh/res/respamor.cfm (visited August 6, 2008).

71. Lauren E. Willis, *Decisionmaking and the Limits of Disclosure: The Problem of Predatory Lending: Price*, 65 Md. L. Rev. 707 (2006).

72. *Id.*, 724–26.

73. *Id.*, 820.

74. See Perillo, *Neutral Standardizing*, 193–94. Trade associations and other organizations already produce quite a few standardized forms. See Kevin E. Davis, *The Role of Nonprofits in the Production of Boilerplate*, 104 Mich. L. Rev. 1075 (2007). But it is not clear to what extent consumers are involved in these efforts.

75. Teeven, *History*, 87–89.

76. 29 Car. II c.3, § IV (1677).

77. Baker, *Introduction*, 397.

78. Caroline N. Brown, *IV Corbin on Contracts*, § 22.1 at 701 (1997).

79. Baker, *Introduction*, 397.

80. *Id.*, 398.

81. *UCC* § 2–201.

82. See generally Brown, *Corbin on Contracts*, § 23.1 at 761–67.

83. *Department of Transportation v. Norris*, 474 S.E.2d 216 (Ga. Ct. App. 1996). The decision was dicta with respect to the Statute of Frauds.

84. Brown, *Corbin on Contracts*, § 23.1 at 764.

85. *Id.*, 766.

86. 15 *U.S.C.* § 7001(a)(1).

87. *Id.* at 7001(a)(2).

88. *Id.* at 7003(a)(1).

89. UETA, § 7 (c).

90. UETA, § 3 (b)(1).

91. Brown, *Corbin on Contracts*, chapter 22.

92. 77 Eng. Rep. 89, 90 (K.B. 1604).

93. *Restatement (Second) of the Law of Contracts*, § 209(1). See generally John Edward Murray, Jr., *Murray on Contracts* § 82 (4th ed. 2001).

94. Corbin, who was very influential in the drafting of the *Restatement (Second) of Contracts*, was apparently responsible for the following comment in the *Restatement*: "Indeed, the parties to an oral agreement may choose their words with such explicit precision and completeness that the same legal consequences follow as where there is a completely integrated agreement." *Restatement*, § 209 cmt. b.

95. Lawrence M. Solan and Peter M. Tiersma, *Speaking of Crime: The Language of Criminal Justice* 98–104 (2005).

96. *Restatement*, § 209 (1) (referring to a "writing").

97. *Restatement*, § 209(3); see also *Murray on Contracts*, § 83.

98. See *Murray on Contracts*, § 83 at 433–34.

99. 126 A. 791 (Pa. 1924).

100. 126 A. at 792, citing *Union Storage Co. v. Speck*, 45 A. 48, 49 (Pa. 1899).

101. *Murray on Contracts*, § 84 at 439–41.

102. *Salyer Grain and Milling Co. v. Henson*, 91 Cal. Rptr. 847, 852 (Cal. Ct. App. 1970).

103. Taken from http://www.sonicsoftware.com/web/global/xmethods/index.ssp (last visited August 8, 2008).

104. Lawrence M. Solan, *The Written Contract as Safe Haven for Dishonest Conduct*, 77 Chi.-Kent L. Rev. 87, 92 (2001).

105. Solan, *Written Contract*, 110–11. See also Charles L. Knapp, *Rescuing Reliance: The Perils of Promissory Estoppel*, 49 Hastings L.J. 1191, 1327 (1998).

106. 953 F. Supp. 876 (S.D. Ohio 1994).

107. *Id.*, 884.

108. *Id.*, 885.

109. *Cobbs v. Cobbs*, 128 P.2d 373 (Cal. Ct. App. 1942).

110. See *Sierra Diesel Injection Service, Inc. v. Burroughs Corp., Inc.*, 890 F.2d 108 (9th Cir. 1989).

111. See *MCC-Marble Ceramic Center v. Ceramica Nuova D'Agostino*, 144 F.3d 1384 (11th Cir. 1998).

112. See, for example, *Masterson v. Sine*, 436 P.2d 561 (Cal. 1968).

113. *Omnitrus Merging Corp. v. Illinois Tool Works, Inc.*, 628 N.E.2d 1165, 1167–68 (Ill. Ct. App. 1993). Interestingly, the extrinsic evidence that the court excluded was an affidavit by a linguist regarding her opinion of the contract's meaning. *Id.*, 1169.

114. *United Gas Pipe Line Co. v. Mueller Engineering Corp.*, 809 S.W.2d 597, 602 (Tex. Ct. App. 1991).

115. *LDCIRCUIT LLC v. Sprint Communications Co.*, 364 F. Supp.2d 1246, 1255–6 (D. Kan. 2005).

116. 566 N.E.2d 639 (N.Y. 1990).

117. See, for example, Margaret N. Kniffin, *Corbin on Contracts* § 24.7 (1998). For discussion, see Peter Linzer, *The Comfort of Certainty: Plain Meaning and the Parol Evidence Rule*, 71 Fordham L. Rev. 799 (2002); Lawrence M. Solan, *Contract as Agreement*, 83 Notre Dame L. Rev. 353 (2007).

118. John Henry Wigmore, *A Treatise on the Anglo-American System of Evidence* § 2461 at 187 (3d ed. 1940).

119. 442 P.2d 641, 645 (Cal. 1968).

120. *Alyeska Pipeline Serv. Co. v. O'Kelley*, 645 P.2d 767, 771 n.1 (Alaska 1982).

121. *Restatement (Second) of the Law of Contracts*, § 214(c) (1979).

122. *Delta Dynamics, Inc. v. Arioto*, 446 P.2d 785, 789 (Cal. 1968) (Mosk, J., dissenting).

123. *Trident Center v. Connecticut General Life Insurance Co.*, 847 F.2d 564, 569 (9th Cir. 1988).

124. The first *Restatement* took a similar view. American Law Institute, *Restatement of the Law: Contacts* § 230 (1932).

125. See Solan, *Contract as Agreement*, 389.

126. *Bohler-Uddeholm America, Inc. v. Ellwood Group, Inc.*, 247 F.3d 79, 92 (3d Cir. 2001) (emphasis added).

127. Solan, *Contract as Agreement*, 353.

128. *Modroo v. Nationwide Mut. Fire Ins. Co.*, 191 P.3d 389 (Mont. 2008).

129. *National Union Fire Ins. Co. of Pittsburgh, Pa. v. Maune*, 277 S.W.3d 754, 758 (Mo. Ct. App. 2009). See also *Walla Walla College v. Ohio Cas. Ins. Co.*, 204 P.3d 961, 963 (Wash. Ct. App. 2009) ("Terms in an insurance policy are given their plain, ordinary, and popular meaning as they would be understood by the average purchaser.").

130. *Metro Properties, Inc. v. National Union Fire Ins. Co. of Pittsburgh*, 934 A.2d 204, 208 (R.I. 2007).

Chapter Five

1. This appears to be the position of Michael Gagarin, *Early Greek Law* (1986) and Kevin Robb, *Literacy and Paideia in Ancient Greece* 75 (1994). For a critique of this position, see Rosalind Thomas, *Written in Stone?: Liberty, Equality, Orality, and the Codification of Law*, in *Greek Law in Its Political Setting: Justifications Not Justice* 9 (L. Foxhall and A.D.E. Lewis eds., 1996).

2. Russ VerSteeg, *Early Mesopotamian Law* 30–32 (2000).

3. Jack Goody, *The Domestication of the Savage Mind* 152 (1977).

4. VerSteeg, *Early Mesopotamian Law*, 13–15.

5. *Id.*, 15, 43.

6. See Bernard S. Jackson, *Literal Meaning: Semantics and Narrative in Biblical Law and Modern Jurisprudence*, 14 Int'l J. Sem. Law. 433 (2001).

7. C. P. Wormald, *Legal Culture in the Early Medieval West: Law as Text, Image, and Experience* 1–43 (1997).

8. H. L. A. Hart, *The Concept of Law* 92 (1961).

9. Jack Goody, *The Interface between the Written and the Oral* 40–48 (1987); Florian Coulmas, *The Writing Systems of the World* 158 (1989).

10. Robb, *Literacy and Paideia*, 84–85.

11. *Id.*, 99.

12. *Id.*, 103.

13. *Id.*, 100–101.

14. *Id.*, 125; Michael Gagarin, *Writing Greek Law* 176–83 (2008).

15. Ilias Arnaoutoglou, *Ancient Greek Laws: A Sourcebook* 91 (1998).

16. Gagarin, *Writing Greek Law*, 180–81.

17. Robb, *Literacy and Paideia*, 140.

18. Robb, *Literacy and Paideia*, 144; Gagarin, *Writing Greek Law*, 183–84.

19. Thomas, *Written in Stone?*, 25–26; Peter Goodrich, *Literacy and the Languages of the Early Common Law*, 14 J. Law & Soc'y 422, 437 (1987).

20. Rosalind Thomas, *Literacy in Ancient Greece: Functional Literacy, Oral Education, and the Development of a Literate Environment*, in *The Making of Literate Societies* 68, 70 (David R. Olson and Nancy Torrance eds., 2001).

21. Robb, *Literacy and Paideia*, 84, referring to the laws of Lycurgus. At a later period the Spartans did write law, although no inscriptions of law from the classical period have been found. See Douglas M. MacDowell, *Spartan Law* 5 (1986).

22. Knut Gjerset, *History of Iceland* 33–34 (1925); Central Bank of Iceland, *Iceland 874–1974* 34–35 (Jóhannes Nordal and Valdimar Kristinsson eds. 1975).

23. Judy Quinn, *From Orality to Literacy in Medieval Iceland*, in *Old Icelandic Literature and Society* 30, 33 (Margaret Clunies Ross ed., 2000).

24. See Peter Salway, *Roman Britain* 87 (1981); Peter Salway, *The Oxford Illustrated History of Roman Britain* 358–59 (1993).

25. The Anglo-Saxons were familiar with runes. Additionally, they had probably already had some contact with the Roman alphabet. See H. G. Richardson and G. O. Sayles, *Law and Legislation from Æthelberht to Magna Carta* 157–59 (1966). But the arrival of Christian clerics was clearly the critical impetus to the development of written culture in Anglo-Saxon England.

26. For more on the history of Æthelberht's laws, as well as a text of the laws in Anglo-Saxon and modern English, see Lisi Oliver, *The Beginnings of English Law* (2002).

27. Oliver, *Beginnings of English Law*, 66–67.

28. Patrick Wormald, *The Making of English Law: King Alfred to the Twelfth Century: Volume I: Legislation and Its Limits* 95 (1999). Wormald points out that the language is archaic in places and the syntax quite simple. *Id.*

29. *Id.*, 101–2.

30. *Id.*, 103 (emphasis added).

31. *Id.*, 272.

32. *Id.*, 106.

33. *Id.*, 104. The same is true of Edward the Elder, who commanded his reeves to follow the rules in his *domboc* or code. *Id.*, 286.

34. *Id.*, 317.

35. *Id.*

36. *Id.*, 349.

37. Risto Hiltunen, *Chapters on Legal English: Aspects Past and Present of the Language of the Law* 36 (1990).

38. Wormald, *Making of English Law*, 284.

39. *Id.*, 128.

40. *Id.*, 143.

41. *Id.*, 300.

42. *Regesta Regum Anglo-Normannorum: The Acta of William I (1066–1087)* 593 (David Bates ed., 1998).

43. Wormald, *Making of English Law*, 398.

44. Theodore F. T. Plucknett, *A Concise History of the Common Law* 112–13 (1956).

45. See Desmond Manderson, *Statuta v. Acts: Interpretation, Music, and Early English Legislation*, 7 Yale J. L. & Hum. 317, 328–31 (1995).

46. I *Statutes of the Realm* xiv, 1 (1810). Modern scholars are of the view that legislation had begun earlier. See Plucknett, *Concise History*, 318.

47. I *Statutes of the Realm*, 4.

48. Paul Brand, *Kings, Barons and Justices: The Making and Enforcement of Legislation in Thirteenth-Century England* 33–38 (2003). It is unclear if ordinary statutes were drafted in this way. *Id.*, 394.

49. M. T. Clanchy, *From Memory to Written Record: England 1066–1307* 264 (2d ed. 1993).

50. I *Statutes of the Realm*, Statutes, 26.

51. *Id.*, 42.

52. Theodore F. T. Plucknett, *Statutes and Their Interpretation in the First Half of the Fourteenth Century* 1 (1922/1980).

53. Plucknett, *Concise History*, 322.

54. Manderson, *Statuta vs. Acts*, 342, citing the second Statute of Westminster, 13 Edw. I, c. 50 (1285).

55. Plucknett, *Concise History*, 328.

56. I *Statutes of the Realm*, xlv.

57. Statute of Winchester, 13 Edw. I, c.1, reprinted in I *Statutes of the Realm*, 96. At the same time, the requirement of publication was to some extent undermined by the competing notion that every man was deemed to know what happens in Parliament, even if it had not been publicly proclaimed. Plucknett, *Statutes and Their Interpretation*, 103.

58. D. P. Simpson, *Cassell's New Latin Dictionary* 569 (1959).

59. Plucknett comments that the word *statute* in the fourteenth century means "the provision made rather than the instrument embodying it." Plucknett, *Statutes and Their Interpretation*, 12.

60. This is reflected in the Spanish word *recordar*, which in the reflexive form means 'to remember.' The root *cord* comes from the Latin word for 'heart.'

61. Clanchy, *From Memory to Written Record*, 77.

62. *Id.*

63. It might not always have been the case. At least on some occasions, the "Knights, Citizens, and Burgesses" were simply charged "upon their Return into the Country to shew and publish to the People the Matters agreed on in Parliament." *Statutes of the Realm*, xlv, fn.1.

64. The Statute of Carlisle, 35 Edw. I (I *Statutes of the Realm*, Statutes, 152).

65. Wormald, *Making of English Law*, 96, 103.

66. Clanchy, *From Memory to Written Record*, 296, citing F. Kern, *Kingship and Law in the Middle Ages* 179 (S. B. Chrimes trans., 1939).

67. Jack Goody, *The Logic of Writing and the Organization of Society* 136 (1986).

68. 52 Hen. III, c. 23 (1267). The relevant provision, which relates to waste, is set forth in 23 *Halsbury's Statutes of England and Wales* 35 (4th ed. 1997 reissue). In addition, chapters 1, 4, and 15, dealing with distress, are also still in force in England and Wales. 13 *Halsbury's Statutes*, 628–30.

There are several things that complicate identifying the oldest statute still in force. One is the very basic issue of what is a statute. I follow the table in *Halsbury's Statutes Citator 2003* and therefore accept Halsbury's judgment on this issue. Another problem is that there are some statutes of uncertain date that might well be older. An example is another statute on distress, the Statutes of the Exchequer (temp. incert.), set forth in 13 *Halsbury's Statutes* at 632–32. According to *Halsbury's* (631), this statute is also still in force and is often thought to have been enacted in the fifty-first year of Henry III, which makes it a year older than the Statutes of Marlborough. Yet *Halsbury's* also suggests that it may date from the reign of Edward I, which would make it several decades younger.

69. 3 Edw. I (1275). Chapter 5 on elections is still in force (5 *Halsbury's Statutes*, 1326), as is chapter 50 (10 *Halsbury's Statutes*, 13). The statute was cited a mere fifty years ago in *Attorney-General v. Colchester Corporation*, [1952] Ch. 586, 595 (Chancery Division).

70. 18 Edw. 1, c.1; see 37 *Halsbury's Statutes of England and Wales* 25 (4th ed. 1998 reissue). A case in 1901 referred not only to *Quia Emptores* but to a statute dating from 1315 that had never been printed but was contained in a Parliament roll. Carlton Kemp Allen, *Law in the Making* 440 (7th ed. 1964).

71. Of the Not Taking Undue Prises from Ecclesiastical Persons or Others, 2 Edw. II (I *Statutes of the Realm*, 153–54). Similar is the Statute of Stamford, 3 Edw. II.

72. J. H. Baker, *An Introduction to English Legal History* 239–40 (1990), citing Aumeye's Case (1305), YB 33–35 Edw. I, p. 82.

73. See Plucknett, *Statutes and Their Interpretation*, 50–53.

74. R. E. Megarry, *Miscellany-at-Law: A Diversion for Lawyers and Others* 358 (1958).

75. Consider the comment of one reporter that judges made a decision "more for the king's profit than for the vindication of law, and they did it through fear." Plucknett, *Statutes and Their Interpretation*, 139. And as noted previously, some kings of this time explicitly claimed the right to interpret their own laws, and it was only gradually that the power to construe statutes came to be viewed as an exclusively judicial prerogative. Plucknett, *Statutes and Their Interpretation*, 21.

76. *Id.*, 57–90.

77. Allen, *Law in the Making*, 454.

78. Plucknett, *Concise History*, 340.

79. *Id.*, 333.

80. Plucknett, *Statutes and Their Interpretation*, 56.

81. *Id.*, 26.

82. Baker, *Introduction*, 235.

83. *Id.*, 236.

84. Peter Tiersma, *Legal Language* 21 (1999).

85. Plucknett, *Concise History*, 323.

86. Pluckett, *Statutes and Their Interpretation*, 138–40.

87. Plucknett, *Concise History*, 340.

88. T. F. T. Plucknett, *Ellesmere on Statutes*, 60 L.Q.R. 242, 248 (1944).

89. Plucknett, *Concise History*, 324.

90. Tiersma, *Legal Language*, 21.

91. Manderson, *Statuta v. Acts*, 360.

92. S. G. G. Edgar, *Craies on Statute Law* 406 (7th ed. 1971).

93. John Baker, *Oxford History of the Laws of England, 1483–1558* 63–75 (vol. 6, 2003).

94. Plucknett, *Ellesmere on Statutes*, 248.

95. Plucknett, *Concise History*, 324.

96. Baker, *Introduction*, 237.

97. I *Reports from the Lost Notebooks of Sir James Dyer* 62 (J. H. Baker ed., 1994).

98. Plucknett, *Concise History*, 334.

99. *See* F. A. R. Bennion, *Understanding Common Law Legislation: Drafting and Interpretation* 110 (2001); Peter M. Tiersma, *Categorical Lists in the Law*, in *Vagueness in Normative Texts* 109 (Vijay K. Bhatia, Jan Engberg, Maurizio Gotti, and Dorothee Heller eds., 2005).

100. *Green v. Balser (Archbishop of Canterbury's Case)*, 76 Eng. Rep. 519, 520–1 [1 Co. Rep. 46a] (K.B. 1596).

101. *A Discourse upon the Exposicion & Understandinge of Statutes, with Sir Thomas Egerton's Additions* 123 (Samuel E. Thorne ed., 1942).

102. *Id.*, 151.

103. *Id.*, 140.

104. L. W. Abbott, *Law Reporting in England 1485–1585* 229–30 (1973).

105. Baker, *Introduction*, 240.

106. Abbott, *Law Reporting*, 230–31.

107. Allen, *Law in the Making*, 455.

108. *Id.*, 455. The judge was Sir William Jones, but if the date is correct this is not the Sir William Jones famous in linguistics for writing a paper that suggested a relationship

among Sanskrit, Greek, and Latin, which led to recognition of the Indo-European language family.

109. Thus, the Statute of Pleading, enacted in 1362, contained a preamble that recited all the mischief caused by the pleading and judging of cases in French, "which is much unknown in the said Realm," and further noted that a law requiring English in pleading was necessary so that "every Man of the said Realm may better govern himself without offending of the Law." 36 Edw. III stat. 1 c.15 (1362).

110. For an example from the fourteenth century, see Plucknett, *Statutes and Their Interpretation*, 44. For later examples, see Abbott, *Law Reporting in England*, 237.

111. Coke, 1 Inst. 79a, cited in Edgar, *Craies on Statute Law*, 200.

112. *Dillon v. Freine* (*Chudleigh's Case*), 76 Eng. Rep. 270, 279 [1 Co. Rep. 120a] (K. B. 1589–95).

113. *Id.*, 281.

114. 76 Eng. Rep. 637, 638 [3 Co. Rep. 7a.] (K.B. 1584).

115. Baker, *Oxford History*, 76, fn.162.

116. Judges sometimes did not have copies of relevant statutes, and even when they did, reports of cases from this period reflect that statutes were sometimes "seriously misquoted." Plucknett, *Concise History*, 327.

117. Clanchy, *From Memory to Written Record*, 264.

118. *Id.*, 264–65.

119. Baker, *Introduction*, 236.

120. *Id.* See also Plucknett, *Concise History*, 327.

121. Plucknett, *Statutes and Their Interpretation*, 105.

122. *Id.*, 103–4.

123. *Id.*, 11.

124. Allen, *Law in the Making*, 470.

125. Baker, *Oxford History*, 505–6.

126. Plucknett, *Concise History*, 327, fn.3.

127. Naomi S. Baron, *Alphabet to Email: How Written English Evolved and Where It's Heading* 57 (2000).

128. Queen's Printer's copies of all public statutes have been available since 1713. Edgar, *Craies on Statute Law*, 47.

129. Allen, *Law in the Making*, 470.

130. *Id.*, 439.

131. Plucknett, *Concise History*, 335, citing *Millar v. Taylor* (1769), 4 Burr. 2303 at 2332.

132. *The Sussex Peerage*, 8 Eng. Rep. 1034, 1057 (H.L. 1844).

133. Michael Zander, *The Law-Making Process* 93 (3d ed. 1989).

134. *Pepper v. Hart* [1993] 1 All ER 42, 69 (H.L.).

135. Baron, *Alphabet to Email*, 24.

136. *Id.* 76, citing Carey McIntosh, *The Evolution of English Prose, 1700–1800: Style, Politeness, and Print Culture* 1–38, 169–94 (1998).

137. U.S. Const. art. I § 7(2).

138. Cal. Const. art. IV, § 8(b).

139. Edwin C. Surrency, *A History of American Law Publishing* 100–1 (1990).

140. *Id.*, 103. In reality, the situation is somewhat more complex. See Steven M. Barkan, Roy M. Mersky, and Donald J. Dunn, *Fundamentals of Legal Research* 132–37 (9th ed. 2009).

141. Surrency, *History of American Law Publishing*, 106–9.
142. Abner J. Mikva and Eric Lane, *An Introduction to Statutory Interpretation and the Legislative Process*, 176–78 (1997).
143. 1 U.S.C. § 112.
144. *United States v. Fisher*, 6 U.S. 358, 386 (1805).
145. *Id.*
146. *McCulloch v. Maryland*, 17 U.S. (4 Wheat.) 316, 414 (1819).
147. *Aldridge v. Williams*, 44 U.S. (3 How.) 9, 23–24 (1845).
148. *State v. Duggan*, 6 A. 787, 788 (R.I. 1886).
149. 143 U.S. 457 (1892).
150. *Id.*, 458–9.
151. *Id.*, 465.
152. O. W. Holmes, *The Theory of Legal Interpretation*, 12 Harv. L. Rev. 417, 419 (1899).
153. *Caminetti v. United States*, 242 U.S. 470, 485 (1917).
154. Lawrence Solan, *Law, Language, and Lenity*, 40 Wm. & Mary L. Rev. 57, 100 (1998) (showing increasing reliance by the Supreme Court on legislative history during the period 1890–1939).
155. *Wood v. Duff-Gordon*, 222 N.Y. 88, 91 (1917).
156. *NLRB v. Federbush Co.*, 121 F.2d 954, 957 (2d Cir. 1941).
157. *Cabell v. Markham*, 148 F.2d 737, 739 (2d Cir. 1945).
158. Patricia Wald, *Some Observations on the Use of Legislative History in the 1981 Supreme Court Term*, 68 Iowa L. Rev. 195, 195 (1983).
159. See William N. Eskridge, Jr., *The New Textualism*, 37 UCLA L. Rev. 621, 632–36 (1990).
160. *Conroy v. Askinoff*, 123 L.Ed.2d 229 (1993).
161. *United States v. Granderson*, 511 U.S. 39, 60 (1994).
162. *Chisom v. Roemer*, 501 U.S. 380, 404 (1991) (Scalia, J., dissenting).
163. See William S. Blatt, *The History of Statutory Interpretation: A Study in Form and Substance*, 6 Cardozo L. Rev. 799 (1985).
164. Norman J. Singer, *Statutes and Statutory Construction*, chapter 19 at 71 (1992).
165. Antonin Scalia, *A Matter of Interpretation: Federal Courts and the Law* 31–35 (1997); *Blanchard v. Bergeron*, 489 U.S. 87, 98 (1989).
166. Scalia, *Matter of Interpretation*, 33.
167. Stephen J. Field, *Personal Reminiscences of Early Days in California with Other Sketches* 65 (1893). Thanks to Mark Saatjian for providing this reference.
168. Mikva and Lane, *Introduction to Statutory Interpretation*, 134.
169. The Energy Policy Act of 2005, Pub. L. No. 109–58, 119 Stat. 594 (2005).
170. Scalia, *Matter of Interpretation*, 34–35.
171. See Henry E. Smith, *The Language of Property: Form, Context, and Audience*, 55 Stan. L. Rev. 1105 (2003), who makes this point in a somewhat different context.
172. Peter M. Tiersma, *A Message in a Bottle: Text, Autonomy, and Statutory Interpretation*, 76 Tul. L. Rev. 431 (2001).
173. Douglas Biber and Edward Finegan, *Drift and Evolution of English Style: A History of Three Genres*, 65 Language 487 (1989).
174. Mikva and Lane, *Introduction to Statutory Interpretation*, 138; http://www.archives.gov/legislative/.
175. Bernard S. Jackson, *Making Sense in Law* 57 (1995).

176. See www.wikipedia.org.

177. See, for example, the Legislative Intent Service (http://www.legintent.com) or the Legislative History Clearinghouse (http://www.lhclearinghouse.com/).

178. Scalia, *Matter of Interpretation*, 36.

179. Sometimes statements of legislative purpose or findings are not codified, which means they are part of the statutory law but are not bound with the operative parts of the statute. In that case the preamble or statement will not be quite as accessible, but will still be much easier to locate than a committee report.

180. See Tiersma, *Legal Language*.

Chapter Six

1. *See* I *Blackstone's Commentaries on the Laws of England* 47 (Wayne Morrison ed., 2001).

2. Frederick Craddock Bolland, *The Year Books: Lectures Delivered in the University of London at the Request of the Faculty of Laws* 22 (1921) (quoting Francis Bacon).

3. Matthew Hale, *The History of the Common Law of England* 1–2 (1713; reprinted by Lawbook Exchange, Ltd., Union, New Jersey; 2000).

4. See Richard J. Ross, *The Memorial Culture of Early Modern English Lawyers: Memory as Keyword, Shelter, and Identity, 1560–1640*, 10 Yale J.L. & Human. 229, 313 (1998).

5. Hale mentions that the common law remained uniform because the judges were few in number, sat near each other in Westminster Hall, and commonly discussed cases and judgments. Hale, *History*, 255.

6. J. H. Baker, *An Introduction to English Legal History* 204–7 (3d ed. 1990). See also Paul Brand, *The Beginnings of English Law Reporting* in *Law Reporting in Britain* 1 (Chantal Stebbings ed., 1995).

7. T. F. T. Plucknett, *Early English Legal Literature* 102 (1958).

8. *Id.*, 104.

9. Carlton Kemp Allen, *Law in the Making* 191–95 (7th ed. 1964).

10. Baker, *Introduction*, 211–14.

11. Allen, *Law in the Making*, 199, citing Anon., Y.B. 11 Hen. VII 10 (Mich. pl. 33).

12. Judges and lawyers were already citing cases during the yearbook period but typically relied on their memories, rather than citing to written reports. See John P. Dawson, *The Oracles of the Law* 57 (1968).

13. L. W. Abbott, *Law Reporting In England 1485–1585* 146 (1973).

14. 1 *The Reports of Sir John Spelman* 196 (J. H. Baker ed., 1977), citing *Vernon v. Vernon* and others (C.P. 1531).

15. I *Reports from the Lost Notebooks of Sir James Dyer* 76 (J. H. Baker ed., 1994).

16. Dawson, *Oracles*, 54–55.

17. See *id.*, 55.

18. Allen, *Law in the Making*, 201.

19. Theodore F. T. Plucknett, *Statutes and Their Interpretation in the First Half of the Fourteenth Century* 5 (Harold Dexter Hazeltine ed., 1922).

20. Plucknett, *Early English Legal Literature*, 112.

21. 5 W. S. Holdsworth, *A History of English Law* 371–72 (1927).

22. *Id.*, 371–72.

23. Dawson, *Oracles*, 65–67.

24. Abbott, *Law Reporting*, 249.

25. *Id.*, 251–52.

26. *See* John William Wallace, *The Reporters Arranged and Characterized with Incidental Remarks* 172–75 (4th ed. 1882).

27. Theodore F. T. Plucknett, *A Concise History of the Common Law* 281 (1956).

28. David Ibbetson, *Law Reporting in the 1590s*, in *Law Reporting in Britain* 73, 81 (Chantal Stebbings ed., 1995).

29. *Id.*, 84.

30. Sir Robert Megarry, *A Second Miscellany-at-Law: A Further Diversion for Lawyers and Others* 120 (1973), citing *Slater v. May*, 92 Eng Rep. 210 (K.B. 1704).

31. Glanville Williams, *Learning the Law* 37 (13th ed.; A. T. H. Smith ed., 2006).

32. Wallace, *The Reporters*, 295, citing 1 Shower 252.

33. Wallace, *The Reporters*, 315.

34. Allen, *Law in the Making*, 222.

35. 12 William Holdsworth, *A History of English Law* 154 (1938).

36. Frederick Pollock, *Essays in the Law* 233 (1922).

37. *Rex v. Bembridge*, 99 Eng. Rep. 679, 681 (K.B. 1783).

38. C. G. Moran, *The Heralds of the Law* 88 (1948), quoting *Fisher v. Prince*, 97 Eng. Rep. 876, 876 (K.B. 1762).

39. Suzanne Warren et al., *Legal Research in England and Wales* 14 (1996). Private reports continued to exist, however, even today.

40. Judges have to some extent been reading draft reports of their decisions since the end of the eighteenth century. See Plucknett, *Concise History*, 281.

41. Michael Zander, *The Law-Making Process* 312 (6th ed. 2004).

42. Practice Direction [1963] 1 W.L.R. 1382 (H.L.).

43. See Dawson, *Oracles*, 91–3. The pivotal case was *London Street Tramways Co. v. London County Council* [1898] A.C. 375, 378 (H.L.).

44. Baker, *Introduction*, 229. See also Dawson, *Oracles*, 80, who points out that "[t]heories of precedent could not be strict until reports became reliable, which was around 1800."

45. Steve Hedley, *Words, Words, Words: Making Sense of Legal Judgments, 1875–1940*, in *Law Reporting in Britain* 169, 171–72 (Chantal Stebbings ed., 1995).

46. Dawson, *Oracles*, 94. See also Rupert Cross and J. W. Harris, *Precedent in English Law* 104–8 (4th ed. 1991) for a discussion of the constitutional basis for the change.

47. Alan Paterson, *The Law Lords* 154–69 (1982).

48. Allen, *Law in the Making*, 220.

49. Cited in Moran, *Heralds*, 95.

50. Allen, *Law in the Making*, 260.

51. Glanville Williams, *Learning the Law* 91 (8th ed. 1969). It is not clear that this is still as true as it once was. It seems that nowadays, judges who deliver an extempore judgment may later give a written copy to the reporters for publication. See *Charles v. Hugh James* [2000] 1 All ER 289 (C.A.), which by all indications is an extempore judgment, but which is reported in [2000] 1 W.L.R. 1278 in essentially identical terms.

52. Paterson, *Law Lords*, 10.

53. The example is from *Coventry and Solihull Waste Disposal v. Russell* [2000] 1 All E.R. 97, 99 (H.L.).

54. *S. Cent. Bell Tel. Co. v. Alabama*, 119 S. Ct. 1180, 1185 (1999).

55. Tony Mauro, *Justice's Supreme Use of "I" Sparks a Legal Frenzy*, USA Today, April 2, 1999, at 11A.

56. 526 U.S. 160, 167 (1999).

57. *Scher v. Policyholders Prot. Bd.* [1994] 2 A.C. 54, 101 (H.L.).

58. *In re United Rys. of the Havana & Regla Warehouses Ltd.* [1960] Ch. 52 (C.A.).

59. Paterson, *Law Lords*, at 35–36.

60. *See* Delmar Karlen, *Appellate Courts in the United States and England* 19 (1963) (referring to practice before the New York Appellate Division).

61. *Id.*, 94.

62. *R. v. Preston*, [1994] 2 A.C. 130, 169 (H.L.).

63. 15 William Holdsworth, *A History of English Law* 248 (A. L. Goodhart and H. G. Hanbury eds., 1965).

64. See Karlen, *Appellate Courts*, 89. Karlen concludes from this fact that "the common law of England is far more truly 'unwritten' than the common law of the United States." *Id.*

65. Cross and Harris, *Precedent in English Law*, 72.

66. *Id.*, 52–71.

67. *Id.*, 72.

68. *Nash v. Tamplin & Sons Brewery Brighton Ld.* [1952] A.C. 231, 250 (H.L.).

69. *See* Cross and Harris, *Precedent in English Law*, 48.

70. 159 Eng. Rep. 375, 376.

71. It is incorrectly spelled "consenus ad idem" in the original. For more on this famous case, see A. W. Brian Simpson, *Contracts for Cotton to Arrive: The Case of the Two Ships* Peerless, 11 Cardozo L. Rev. 287 (1989).

72. *Raffles* was not unique in this sense. See *Hills v. Laming* [1853] 9 Ex. 256, 156 Eng. Rep. 109.

73. See Cross and Harris, *Precedent in English Law*, 48.

74. Arthur L. Goodhart, *Determining the* Ratio Decidendi *of a Case* 5 in *Essays in Jurisprudence and the Common Law* 1 (1931).

75. Goodhart's method is to derive the principle of a case by finding (1) the material facts on which the judge based his decision and (2) the decision that the judge made based on those facts. *Id.*, 25. Thus, if the material facts are A and B, and the result is X, then in any future case with facts A and B, the result must be X. *Id.*, 22.

76. Eugene Wambaugh, *The Study of Cases* 6–8 (1891).

77. A. W. B. Simpson, *The Common Law and Legal Theory*, in *Oxford Essays in Jurisprudence* 89 (2d series; A. W. B. Simpson ed., 1973).

78. Blackstone, *Commentaries*, *70–71.

79. Paterson, *Law Lords*, 98; Report of the Interdepartmental Committee on the Court of Criminal Appeal (1965), Cmd 2755, para 250, cited in Cross and Harris, *Precedent in English Law*, 94.

80. See Lon L. Fuller, *The Morality of Law* 39 (1964); John Rawls, *A Theory of Justice* 209 (rev. ed. 1999).

81. *Cassell & Co. v. Broome* [1972] A.C. 1027, 1084–85 (H.L.).

82. Lawrence M. Friedman, *A History of American Law* 323 (2d ed. 1985). A few pre-Revolutionary cases were published after independence. Dallas included some Pennsylvania cases in early volumes of the United States Reports, for instance, as in *Stackhouse's Lessee v. Stackhouse*, 2 U.S. 80 (1766).

83. Edwin C. Surrency, *Law Reports in the United States*, 25 Am. J. Legal Hist. 48, 48–50 (1981).

84. Ephraim Kirby, *Reports of Cases Adjudged in the Superior Court of the State of Connecticut from the Year 1785, to May, 1788* iii (1789).

85. Morris L. Cohen and Robert G. Berring, *How to Find the Law* 53–54 (8th ed. 1983). See also John P. Dawson, *Oracles*, 85–86.

86. 2 U.S. 402 (1792). The case caption misspells the second name as *Braislford*.

87. *Id.*, 405.

88. *Id.*, 405.

89. *Id.*, 406.

90. *Id.*, 407.

91. *Id.*, 407 (italics in original). It seems likely that there would have been some sort of report of this case, but Wilson provides no citation (unless the reporter omitted it).

92. *Id.*, 408.

93. *Id.*

94. James Kent, 1 *Commentaries on American Law* 444 (1st ed. 1826).

95. See Frederick G. Kempin, Jr., *Precedent and Stare Decisis: The Critical Years, 1800 to 1850*, 3 Am. J. Legal Hist. 28, 37–38 (1959).

96. Surrency, *Law Reports*, 55.

97. Dawson, *Oracles*, 86–87.

98. *Cal. Const.* art. VI, § 14.

99. Surrency, *Law Reports*, 56–7.

100. G. Edward White, *History of the Supreme Court of the United States, Volume III: The Marshall Court and Cultural Change, 1815–35* 389 (1988).

101. Dawson, *Oracles*, 86.

102. *See* Surrency, *Law Reports*, 60.

103. In *Wheaton v. Peters*, 33 U.S. 591, 668 (U.S. 1834), the Supreme Court held that a reporter did not have a copyright in the cases he reported. On the issue of whether reporters have a copyrightable interest in their pagination, see *Matthew Bender & Co., Inc. v. West Publ'g Co.*, 158 F.3d 693 (2d Cir. 1998).

104. White, *History of the Supreme Court*, 393–400.

105. *Id.*, 392.

106. *Id.*, 401.

107. Cited in Friedman, *History*, 325.

108. Carl B. Swisher, *History of the Supreme Court of the United States, Volume V: The Taney Period, 1836–64* 310–11 (1974).

109. See, for example, http://www.massreports.com (Massachusetts reporter of decisions); http://courts.state.ar.us/courts/rd_info.html (Arkansas); http://www.kscourts.org/clerk.htm (Kansas); http://www.courts.state.ny.us/reporter (New York) (last visited January 16, 2007).

110. Herbert A. Johnson, *Foundations of Power: John Marshall, 1801–15 (Part Two)* 383 (1981).

111. *Id.*, 382–89.

112. White, *History of the Supreme Court*, 193.

113. *Id.*, 406.

114. *Id.*, 407.

115. *Id.*, 407–8.

116. *Id.*, 408.

117. Swisher, *History of the Supreme Court*, 297–98.

118. Dawson, *Oracles*, 60.

119. Friedman, *History*, 326.

120. See Frederick G. Kempin, *Precedent and Stare Decisis: The Critical Years, 1800 to 1850*, 3 Am. J. Legal Hist. 28 (1959).

121. See generally John Henry Merryman, *The Civil Law Tradition* 19–47 (2d ed. 1985).

122. Merryman, *Civil Law Tradition*, 28.

123. Helmut Coing, *An Intellectual History of European Codification in the Eighteenth and Nineteenth Centures*, in *Problems of Codification* 16 (S. J. Stoljar ed., 1977).

124. *Papers Relative to Codification* 136, cited in Maurice Eugen Lang, *Codification in the British Empire and America* 35 (1927).

125. *Id.*, 33–35.

126. Parliamentary Papers 1854, vol. 53, 391, per Talfourd J., cited in Baker, *Introduction*, 251.

127. See Lang, *Codification*, 40–58; Baker, *Introduction*, 250–52.

128. Thomas Jefferson, *Notes on the State of Virginia* 137 (William Peden ed., 1982).

129. Joseph Story, *Report of the Commissioners Appointed to Consider and Report upon the Practicability and Expediency of Reducing to a Written and Systematic Code the Common Law of Massachusetts, or any Part Thereof* 31 (1837).

130. *Journal of the Convention of the State of New York* 1382 (1846), cited in Lang, *Codification*, 118.

131. *Id.*, 118 n.2.

132. Lang, *Codification*, 122.

133. *Id.*, 128, 131.

134. *Id.*, 135–36. New York did adopt a penal code and a code of criminal procedure. *Id.*, 148.

135. *Id.*, 152.

136. On the *California Civil Code* and its interaction with the common law, see Izhak Englard, Li v. Yellow Cab Co.: *A Belated and Inglorious Centennial of the California Civil Code*, 65 Cal. L. Rev. 4 (1977).

137. See http://www.nccusl.org/nccusl/DesktopDefault.aspx?tabindex=0&tabid=11 (visited March 22, 2004).

138. John Edward Murray, Jr., *Murray on Contracts* 20–22 (3d ed. 1990). Louisiana adopted parts of the *UCC* in 1974. *Id.*, 21.

139. See *UCC* §1–103.

140. http://www.ali.org/index.cfm?fuseaction=about.creationinstitute (visited November 10, 2008).

141. *Id.* For more on the background of the founding of the ALI, see N. E. H. Hull, *Restatement and Reform: A New Perspective on the Origins of the American Law Institute*, 8 Law & Hist. Rev. 55 (1990); Nathan M. Crystal, *Codification and the Rise of the Restatement Movement*, 54 Wash. L. Rev. 239 (1979).

142. See Harvey S. Perlman, *The Restatement Process*, 10 Kan. J. L. & Pub. Pol'y 2 (2000).

143. *In re Marriage of Himes*, 965 P.2d 1087, 1101 (Wash. 1998).

144. *Dexter v. Town of Norway*, 715 A.2d 169, 172 (Me. 1998).

145. *Pilafas v. Ariz. Zoological Soc'y*, 836 P.2d 420, 423 (Ariz. Ct. App. 1992).

146. Sidney W. DeLong, *The New Requirement of Enforcement Reliance in Commercial Promissory Estoppel: Section 90 as Catch-22*, 1997 Wis. L. Rev. 943, 1000.

147. Randy E. Barnett, *The Death of Reliance*, 46 J. Legal Educ. 518, 527 (1996).

148. Roscoe Pound, *What of Stare Decisis?*, 10 Fordham L. Rev. 1, 8 (1941).

149. Edward H. Levi, *An Introduction to Legal Reasoning* 2 (1948).

150. Henry M. Hart and Albert M. Sacks, *The Legal Process: Basic Problems in the Making and Application of Law* 341 (William M. Eskridge, Jr. & Philip P. Frickey eds., 1994).

151. *Id.*, 126.

152. Peter M. Tiersma, *The Textualization of Precedent*, 82 Notre Dame L. Rev. 1187, 1249–1250 (2007).

153. *Villalobos v. United States*, 51 U.S. 541, 555 (1850).

154. Tiersma, *Textualization*, 1250–51.

155. *Id.*, 1252.

156. *Slack v. McDaniel*, 529 U.S. 473, 478 (2000).

157. *Roe v. Flores-Ortega*, 528 U.S. 470, 480 (2000).

158. *Miller v. California*, 413 U.S. 15, 20 (1973) (citation omitted).

159. 413 U.S. at 23–24.

160. Tiersma, *Textualization*, 1254.

161. Robert F. Nagel, *The Formulaic Constitution*, 84 Mich. L. Rev. 165, 165 (1985).

162. *Id.*, 178.

163. *Id.*, 197.

164. Frederick Schauer, *Opinions as Rules*, 62 U. Chi. L. Rev. 1455, 1455 (1995).

165. Frederick Schauer, *Opinions as Rules: The Unpublished Opinions of the Warren Court*, 53 U. Chi. L. Rev. 682, 683 (1986) (book review; emphasis added).

166. *Id.*, 683.

167. Charles W. Collier, *Precedent and Legal Authority: A Critical History*, 1988 Wis. L. Rev. 771, 813–14.

168. *Id.*, 814.

169. An example is *Ord v. Upton* [2000] 1 All E.R. 193, 200–203 (C.A.).

170. 501 U.S. 32, 45–46 (1991) (footnotes and parallel citations omitted).

171. Tiersma, *Textualization*, 1259–60.

172. *Ruffo v. Inmates of Suffolk County Jail*, 502 U.S. 367, 393 (1992).

173. *Guaranty Trust Co. v. York*, 326 U.S. 99, 109 (1945). The test is referred to as such by *Hanna v. Plumer*, 380 U.S. 460, 475 (1965).

174. 249 U.S. 47, 52 (1919).

175. 304 U.S. 144, 152 n.4 (1938). Note that the use of footnotes is itself an indication of a literate mode of thinking. With their more oral tradition, English judges virtually never use them.

176. Tiersma, *Textualization*, 1261–62.

177. Michael B.W. Sinclair, *Anastasoff versus Hart: The Constitutionality and Wisdom of Denying Precedential Authority to Circuit Court Decisions*, 64 U. Pitt. L. Rev. 695, 738–39 (2003).

178. Guy Holborn, *Butterworth's Legal Research Guide* 175 (2d ed. 2001).

179. Thomas J. Young, *A Look at American Law Reporting in the 19th Century*, 68 Law Libr. J. 294, 302 (1975).

180. Friedman, *History*, 621.

181. This means that a court can follow the opinion if persuaded by it but is also free to ignore it.

182. Surrency, *Law Reports*, 65. Surrency traces the rule to a decision made by the Ninth Circuit Court of Appeals in 1973.

183. See generally Salem M. Katsh and Alex V. Chachkes, *Constitutionality of "No-Citation" Rules*, 3 J. App. Prac. & Process 287 (2001); and Robert J. Martineau, *Restrictions on Publication and Citation of Judicial Opinions: A Reassessment*, 28 U. Mich. J.L. Reform 119 (1994) for the history of such rules.

184. See, for example, Mont. Sup. Ct. Internal Op. R. § 1(3)(c); 4th Cir. R. 36(a). For additional examples, see Melissa M. Serfass and and Jessie L. Cranford, *Federal and State Court Rules Governing Publication and Citation of Opinions*, 3 J. App. Prac. & Process 251, 253–85 (2001).

185. Cal. R. Ct. 976(b).

186. See *State v. Gonzales*, 794 P.2d 361, 370–71 (N.M. Ct. App. 1990).

187. Ky. R. Civ. P. 76.28(4)(c); see also Wash. R. App. P. 10.4(h) (stating that unpublished opinions of the court of appeals may not be cited as authority). Most no-citation jurisdictions have an exception, allowing citation to cases "when relevant under the doctrines of law of the case, res judicata, and collateral estoppel." See 9th Cir. R. 36–3(a).

188. See the mission statement of the Committee for the Rule of Law at http://www.nonpublication.com/ (visited June 30, 2004).

189. Richard A. Posner, *The Federal Courts: Crisis and Reform* 123 (1985).

190. See also Joshua R. Mandell, Note, *Trees That Fall in the Forest: The Precedential Effect of Unpublished Opinions*, 34 Loy. L.A. L. Rev. 1255, 1294 (2001).

191. 223 F.3d 898 (8th Cir. 2000), vacated as moot, 235 F.3d 1054 (8th Cir. 2000).

192. 8th Cir. R. 28A(i).

193. 223 F.3d at 905.

194. 223 F.3d at 899–900.

195. On precedent in early America, see also Thomas Healy, *Stare Decisis as a Constitutional Requirement*, 104 W. Va. L. Rev. 43, 73–91 (2001).

196. See also *Hart v. Massanari*, 266 F.3d 1162–69.

197. 235 F.3d 1054 (8th Cir. 2000) (en banc).

198. *See Unpublished Judicial Opinions: Hearing before the Subcommittee on the Courts, the Internet, and Intellectual Property of the Committee on the Judiciary, House of Representatives*, 107th Cong., 2d Sess. (2002).

199. See Stephen R. Barnett, *From* Anastasoff *to* Hart *to West's* Federal Appendix: *The Ground Shifts under No-Citation Rules*, 4 J. App. Prac. & Process 1 (2002).

200. Fed. R. App. P. 32.1.

201. See *Hart v. Massanari*, 266 F.3d 1155 (9th Cir. 2001).

202. See also Robert C. Berring, *Legal Information and the Search for Cognitive Authority*, 88 Cal. L. Rev. 1673 (2000).

203. David I. C. Thomson, *Law School 2.0: Legal Education for a Digital Age* 48 (2008).

204. Frederick Schauer has noted that just as lawyers just read part of a statute, modern online sources make it easy to find and read just part of an opinion. Frederick Schauer, *Opinions as Rules*, 62 U. Chi. L. Rev. 1455, 1471–72 (1995).

Index

Numbers in italics refer to locations where a term is defined or explained.